PIC Microcontrollers

Build Electronics Projects from Scratch

Sarful Hassan

Preface

Welcome to *PIC Microcontrollers Masterclass: Build Electronics Projects from Scratch*. This book is designed to take you on a hands-on journey through the world of PIC microcontrollers, guiding you from fundamental concepts to advanced applications. Whether you're a beginner or an experienced enthusiast, this masterclass will help you unlock the potential of PIC microcontrollers and take your electronics projects to new heights.

Who This Book Is For

This book is for anyone interested in building embedded systems and electronics projects with PIC microcontrollers. Whether you're a student, hobbyist, or professional engineer, you'll find valuable content that will enhance your understanding of PIC programming, sensors, actuators, communication protocols, and more. If you're eager to create real-world projects using PIC microcontrollers, this book is for you.

How This Book Is Organized

The book is organized into easy-to-follow chapters, each dedicated to a specific aspect of working with PIC microcontrollers. It starts with an introduction to the basics of microcontrollers and progresses through more advanced topics, such as sensor integration, motor control, and wireless communication. The chapters build upon each other, offering step-by-step guidance with practical examples and clear explanations.

1. **Introduction to PIC Microcontrollers**

2. **Programming Basics & Embedded C**

3. **Building Real-World Projects**

4. **Communication Protocols**

5. **Advanced Applications in Mechatronics**

6. **Optimizing Power Consumption and Efficiency**

7. **Debugging and Troubleshooting**

Throughout the book, you'll be introduced to both theory and hands-on projects that will help reinforce the concepts you learn.

What Was Left Out

While this book covers a broad range of topics, it's important to note that there are some advanced areas that are beyond the scope of this text. For example, specialized topics such as advanced power electronics, high-speed digital circuits, and proprietary communication protocols are not covered in this book. Instead, the focus is on the foundational knowledge and practical applications to help you get started with PIC microcontrollers.

Code Style (About the Code)

The code examples in this book follow a clean and consistent style to ensure readability and understanding. Code is formatted with clear indentation, appropriate comments, and structured functions to help you follow along easily. The code snippets provided in each chapter are meant to be used directly in your projects, but feel free to modify them to suit your needs. Each example is carefully crafted to demonstrate a specific concept or technique.

Release Notes

This is the first edition of *PIC Microcontrollers Masterclass: Build Electronics Projects from Scratch*. We have tested all the projects and code examples in real-world environments to ensure they are accurate and functional. However, with the rapid development of technology and tools, some software or hardware components may change over time. Please check the accompanying website for the most up-to-date information and resources.

Notes on the First Edition

This edition is the first in a series of planned updates and revisions. We hope to include more advanced topics and new technologies related to PIC microcontrollers in future editions. If you have suggestions or questions, feel free to contact us; we are always looking for ways to improve the book and its content.

MechatronicsLAB Online Learning

MechatronicsLAB offers an extensive range of online courses and resources designed to support your learning journey in mechatronics, electronics, and embedded systems. Our platform provides interactive tools, hands-on simulations, and expert guidance to help you gain practical experience in building real-world projects.

For more information, visit our website: mechatronicslab.net

How to Contact Us

We value your feedback, questions, and suggestions. Feel free to reach out to us via email at:

Email: mechatronicslab.net@gmail.com
Website: mechatronicslab.net

Acknowledgments for the First Edition

We would like to extend our heartfelt thanks to all the contributors who made this book possible. Special thanks to our team of engineers, educators, and technical reviewers for their dedication to providing accurate, comprehensive, and useful content. We'd also like to thank the MechatronicsLAB community for their continued support and engagement in our online courses.

Copyright

Disclaimer

Table of Contents

Chapter 1: Introduction to PIC Microcontrollers

A **microcontroller** is a compact integrated circuit (IC) designed to perform specific control functions in an embedded system. It contains a processor (CPU), memory (RAM and ROM), and input/output (I/O) peripherals on a single chip.

Microcontrollers are used in a wide range of applications, including consumer electronics, automotive systems, medical devices, industrial automation, and household appliances. Their small size, low power consumption, and cost-effectiveness make them ideal for embedded applications.

What is a PIC Microcontroller?

A **PIC (Peripheral Interface Controller) microcontroller** is a family of microcontrollers developed by **Microchip Technology**. PIC microcontrollers are widely used in embedded systems due to their simplicity, affordability, and flexibility.

PIC microcontrollers are based on the **Harvard architecture**, which separates program memory and data memory, allowing for faster processing speeds. They are available in various series, such as the **PIC10, PIC12, PIC16, PIC18, PIC24, and PIC32**, each designed for different levels of complexity and application requirements.

History of PIC Microcontrollers

The PIC microcontroller family was originally developed by **General Instrument** in the late 1970s as a part of their peripheral interface controllers. In 1989, **Microchip Technology** acquired the PIC microcontroller line and further developed it into a widely used architecture in the embedded industry.

History and Evolution of PIC Microcontrollers

Year	Development Milestone
1975	General Instrument introduced the first PIC microcontroller as a peripheral interface controller.
1989	Microchip Technology acquired PIC and started further development.

1993	Introduction of the first flash-programmable PIC microcontroller.
2001	Launch of PIC18 series, offering higher performance and peripherals.
2004	Introduction of dsPIC series for digital signal processing applications.
2008	PIC32 series introduced, featuring a 32-bit architecture.
2013	Enhanced mid-range PIC16F1 series launched with improved performance.
2020	Continued development with advanced connectivity and IoT features.

PIC vs Other Microcontrollers

Feature	PIC Microcontrollers	AVR Microcontrollers	ARM Microcontrollers	8051 Microcontrollers
Architecture	RISC	RISC	RISC	CISC
Bit Width	8-bit, 16-bit, 32-bit	8-bit, 32-bit	32-bit, 64-bit	8-bit
Power Consumption	Low	Low	Medium to High	Medium
Processing Speed	Moderate	Moderate	High	Low
Flash Memory	Yes	Yes	Yes	Limited
Ease of Use	Easy	Moderate	Complex	Simple
Peripheral Support	High	High	Very High	Low
Common Applications	Embedded, IoT, Automation	Consumer Electronics, IoT	High-Performance Systems	Legacy Systems, Education

Features of PIC Microcontrollers

PIC microcontrollers are known for the following key features:

- **RISC Architecture** – Simple instruction set with high-speed processing.
- **Flash Memory** – Reprogrammable memory for easy updates and modifications.
- **Low Power Consumption** – Suitable for battery-powered applications.
- **Wide Operating Voltage** – Supports different voltage levels for various applications.
- **Peripheral Integration** – Includes built-in features like timers, ADC (Analog-to-Digital Converter), PWM (Pulse Width Modulation), UART, SPI, and I²C.
- **In-Circuit Programming (ICSP)** – Allows programming and debugging without removing the chip from the circuit.

Advantages of PIC Microcontrollers

PIC microcontrollers are widely used due to the following advantages:

- **Low cost** compared to other microcontrollers.
- **Easy availability** in different configurations.
- **Efficient power management**, ideal for battery-operated devices.
- **Fast processing speed** due to RISC architecture.
- **Wide range of peripherals** integrated into a single chip.
- **Simple programming** with extensive development support from Microchip.

Applications of PIC Microcontrollers

PIC microcontrollers are used in various industries, including:

- **Consumer Electronics:** Washing machines, microwave ovens, remote controls.
- **Automotive Systems:** Engine control units (ECUs), airbag systems, anti-lock braking systems (ABS).
- **Medical Devices:** Blood pressure monitors, glucose meters, pacemakers.
- **Industrial Automation:** Motor control, robotics, data acquisition systems.
- **Communication Systems:** Wireless modules, RFID readers.

Chapter 2: PIC Architecture

The PIC microcontroller architecture is based on the **Harvard architecture**, where program memory and data memory are separated to enhance processing speed and efficiency. PIC microcontrollers follow a **RISC (Reduced Instruction Set Computing) architecture**, making them optimized for low power consumption and high-speed execution.

Memory Organization

PIC microcontrollers have three primary types of memory:

- **Flash Memory (Program Memory):** Stores program code and is non-volatile.
- **RAM (Data Memory):** Used for temporary data storage during execution.
- **EEPROM (Electrically Erasable Programmable Read-Only Memory):** Stores non-volatile data, such as configuration settings.

CPU and Instruction Set

- PIC microcontrollers use a **RISC-based instruction set**, meaning they execute simple instructions quickly.
- The instruction cycle time is typically **four clock cycles per instruction**.
- Supports **single-cycle instructions** for efficient processing.

I/O Ports

PIC microcontrollers provide multiple **General-Purpose Input/Output (GPIO) ports** to interface with external devices, such as sensors, motors, and LEDs.

- **Digital I/O Pins:** Configurable as input or output.
- **Analog Inputs:** Integrated ADC (Analog-to-Digital Converter) for processing analog signals.
- **PWM Outputs:** Pulse Width Modulation support for motor control and signal generation.

Timers and Counters

- Used for **time delays, event counting, and waveform generation**.
- Configurable as **8-bit or 16-bit timers**.
- Some models include multiple independent timers.

Interrupts
- Supports **external and internal interrupts**.
- Interrupt sources include **timers, ADC conversions, UART communications, and external pins**.
- Prioritized interrupt handling in advanced models.

Analog-to-Digital Converter (ADC)
- Converts analog signals (e.g., temperature, voltage) into digital values.
- Multiple ADC channels for interfacing with sensors.
- Selectable resolution, typically **8-bit or 10-bit**.

Communication Interfaces
PIC microcontrollers support various serial communication protocols:
- **UART (Universal Asynchronous Receiver Transmitter):** Used for serial communication.
- **SPI (Serial Peripheral Interface):** High-speed synchronous communication.
- **I²C (Inter-Integrated Circuit):** Multi-device communication using fewer wires.

Clock System
- Uses an **internal or external oscillator** for clock generation.
- Configurable clock sources include **RC oscillators, quartz crystals, and PLL (Phase-Locked Loop) circuits**.
- Some PIC models support **low-power sleep modes** to optimize energy consumption.

Special Function Registers (SFRs)
- Used for configuring and controlling the microcontroller.
- Include registers for **I/O control, timer settings, ADC configuration, and interrupt management**.

Watchdog Timer (WDT)
- A built-in **safety feature** to reset the microcontroller if it becomes unresponsive.
- Useful for **fault-tolerant applications**.

Power Management
- Supports **low-power modes** to optimize energy efficiency.
- Can enter **sleep mode** to conserve power in battery-operated

applications.

Comparison of PIC Architecture with Other Microcontrollers

Feature	PIC Microcontrollers	AVR Microcontrollers	ARM Microcontrollers
Architecture	Harvard	Harvard	Von Neumann
Instruction Set	RISC	RISC	RISC
Clock Speed	Moderate	Moderate to High	High
Power Consumption	Low	Low	Medium to High
Memory Type	Flash, EEPROM, RAM	Flash, EEPROM, RAM	Flash, SRAM, ROM
Peripheral Support	High	High	Very High
Best Used For	Embedded, IoT, Control	Consumer Electronics, IoT	High-Performance Systems

Pinout and Functionality of PIC Microcontrollers

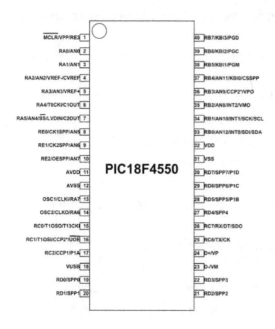

Pin	Function
VDD	Power supply (typically 3.3V or 5V)
VSS	Ground connection
MCLR	Master Clear (Reset) pin
RA0-RA5	General-purpose I/O pins, Analog input
RB0-RB7	Digital I/O pins, Interrupt capability
RC0-RC7	Digital I/O pins, Communication interfaces (SPI, UART, I²C)
XTAL1, XTAL2	External oscillator/crystal input pins
PWM Pins	Pulse Width Modulation output
ADC Channels	Analog inputs for sensors and voltage measurement
TX/RX	UART transmit/receive pins for serial communication
SCL/SDA	I²C Clock and Data lines for communication
SS, SCK, MOSI, MISO	SPI interface pins

Summary

- The **Harvard architecture** in PIC microcontrollers provides **fast and efficient processing**.
- Uses **RISC instruction set** for optimized performance.
- Features a variety of peripherals, including **GPIO, ADC, timers, and communication interfaces**.
- Supports **low-power operation** for battery-based applications.
- PIC microcontrollers are widely used in **embedded systems, industrial automation, and IoT devices**.

This chapter provides a foundational understanding of **PIC microcontroller architecture**, covering its memory structure, processing capabilities, hardware features, and pinout functionality.

Chapter 3: Understanding Registers and Memory Structure

In a PIC microcontroller, **registers and memory structure** play a crucial role in data handling, control execution, and configuration settings. Understanding these elements is essential for optimizing performance and utilizing the microcontroller efficiently.

Types of Memory in PIC Microcontrollers

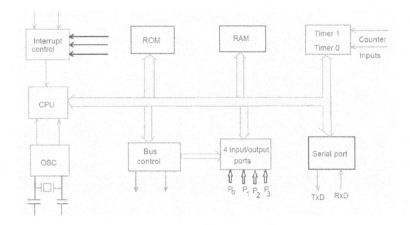

PIC microcontrollers have three primary types of memory:

1. **Program Memory (Flash Memory)**
    a. Stores the compiled program code.
    b. Non-volatile memory, meaning it retains data even after power loss.
    c. Typically ranges from a few kilobytes to several megabytes in high-end PIC models.
    d. Organized into addressable locations where instructions are stored sequentially.
1. **Data Memory (RAM - Random Access Memory)**
    a. Used for temporary storage of variables and program execution data.
    b. Volatile memory, meaning data is lost when power is turned off.
    c. Includes **General Purpose Registers (GPRs)** and **Special Function Registers (SFRs).**

d. The RAM is further divided into different banks to optimize efficiency.

1. **EEPROM (Electrically Erasable Programmable Read-Only Memory)**
   a. Used for storing non-volatile data that can be modified during operation.
   b. Suitable for applications requiring data retention, such as configuration settings.
   c. Requires specific programming sequences to write and erase data.

2. **Registers in PIC Microcontrollers**

Registers are special storage locations that control microcontroller operation. They can be categorized into:

1. **General Purpose Registers (GPRs)**
   a. Used for temporary storage of data and variables.
   b. Can be accessed and modified freely by the program.

2. **Special Function Registers (SFRs)**
   a. Control specific functions of the microcontroller.
   b. Configurable by the programmer to manage peripherals and system settings.
   c. Each SFR is mapped to a specific memory location.

Common Special Function Registers (SFRs)

Register	Function
STATUS	Indicates processor status (Zero flag, Carry flag, etc.)
PORTx	Controls digital I/O pins (PORTA, PORTB, etc.)
TRISx	Sets pin direction (Input or Output) for PORT registers
INTCON	Controls and monitors interrupt sources
TMRx	Timer registers used for delay and timing functions
ADCONx	Configures the Analog-to-Digital Converter (ADC) module
SSPxCON x	Configures SPI/I2C communication protocols

Memory Bank Structure

PIC microcontrollers often have **memory banks** to optimize register accessibility:

- Some microcontrollers have multiple **banks** (e.g., Bank 0, Bank 1, etc.).

- The **BSR (Bank Select Register)** determines which bank is currently accessible.
- Bank switching is necessary when accessing different parts of memory in some models.
- Incorrect bank selection can lead to erroneous data access.

Indirect Addressing and File Registers

- **Indirect Addressing** allows registers to be accessed dynamically through an address pointer.
- The **FSR (File Select Register)** and **INDF (Indirect Register)** are used for indirect addressing.
- This method is useful for working with arrays and dynamic memory allocation.
- Enables more flexible data handling in RAM without direct addressing.

Stack and Program Counter (PC)

- The **Program Counter (PC)** keeps track of the instruction execution sequence.
- The **Stack** is used to store return addresses during function calls and interrupts.
- Most PIC microcontrollers have a limited stack depth (e.g., 8-31 levels).
- The stack operates in a Last In, First Out (LIFO) manner.

Interrupt Handling and Register Usage

- Interrupts use dedicated registers like **INTCON, PIE, and PIR** to enable and handle interrupts.
- When an interrupt occurs, the current execution is paused, and a **context switch** takes place.
- The **RETIE (Return from Interrupt) instruction** restores execution after an interrupt is handled.
- Interrupt latency and priority handling must be considered for real-time applications.

Memory Mapping Example

Memory Type	Address Range	Description
Program Memory	0000h - FFFFh	Stores program instructions
Data Memory	00h - FFh	Stores GPR and SFR data
EEPROM Memory	2100h - 21FFh	Stores non-volatile data

Summary

- PIC microcontrollers feature **Flash Memory, RAM, and EEPROM** for efficient operation.
- Registers are divided into **General Purpose (GPRs)** and **Special Function (SFRs)**.
- The **STATUS, PORT, TRIS, and INTCON** registers are essential for microcontroller control.
- **Memory banks and indirect addressing** help optimize register access.
- The **Program Counter (PC) and Stack** are crucial for execution flow and function calls.
- Proper **interrupt handling and register management** enhance system performance.
- Understanding register operation and memory structure is key to efficient PIC microcontroller programming.

This chapter provides an in-depth look into the **registers and memory structure of PIC microcontrollers**, enabling efficient use of memory resources and control registers.

Chapter 4: PIC Development Tools and Ecosystem

Developing applications with PIC microcontrollers requires a set of **hardware and software tools** that enable programming, debugging, and simulation. Microchip Technology provides a robust development ecosystem, ensuring efficient coding and testing for various PIC microcontroller models. This ecosystem consists of various tools, including IDEs, compilers, programmers, simulators, and development boards, each designed to facilitate different stages of development.

Key Components of the PIC Development Ecosystem

1. **Integrated Development Environments (IDEs)** - Centralized platforms for writing, compiling, debugging, and testing firmware.
2. **Compilers and Assemblers** - Convert high-level code into machine-readable instructions.
3. **Programmers and Debuggers** - Load compiled programs onto microcontrollers and provide real-time debugging capabilities.
4. **Simulation and Emulation Tools** - Virtual environments for testing firmware without physical hardware.
5. **Development Boards and Prototyping Kits** - Pre-configured hardware platforms for rapid prototyping.

Integrated Development Environments (IDEs)

IDE	Description
MPLAB X IDE	Official Microchip IDE for PIC microcontrollers. Supports multiple compilers, debugging, and simulation features.
MPLAB 8 IDE	Legacy IDE, used for older PIC models. Less feature-rich than MPLAB X.

Key Features of MPLAB X IDE:

- Supports Windows, macOS, and Linux.
- Provides an integrated code editor with syntax highlighting and error checking.
- Offers built-in debugging and real-time simulation.
- Plugin support for expanded functionality, including external tools.

- Fully compatible with Microchip's compilers and programmers.

Compilers and Assemblers

Compiler/ Assembler	Description
XC8 Compiler	C compiler for 8-bit PIC microcontrollers. Provides memory-efficient and optimized code generation.
XC16 Compiler	C compiler for 16-bit PIC microcontrollers. Includes support for DSP-enhanced applications.
XC32 Compiler	C compiler for 32-bit PIC microcontrollers. Optimized for high-performance applications.
MPASM Assembler	Legacy assembler for writing low-level assembly code for PIC devices.

Microchip's **XC compilers** offer **free and pro versions**, where the pro version includes advanced optimizations for reduced code size and faster execution.

Programmers and Debuggers

Tool	Function
PICkit 3/4	In-circuit debugging and programming for PIC microcontrollers. Ideal for low-cost development.
MPLAB ICD 4	Advanced debugger with real-time emulation and high-speed programming.
MPLAB Snap	Affordable debugging tool with basic functionalities. Suitable for entry-level development.
MPLAB PM3	Standalone production-grade programmer for high-volume manufacturing.

Key Features of PICkit 4:
- Faster programming speed than PICkit 3.
- Supports a broader range of PIC microcontrollers.
- USB-powered for easy connectivity.
- On-board debugging capability with live variable monitoring.

Simulation and Emulation Tools

Tool	Function
MPLAB SIM	Software-based simulator for debugging PIC firmware in a virtual environment.
Proteus	Third-party simulation tool for virtual PIC circuit design and

VSM	real-world interaction testing.
Real ICE	High-performance in-circuit emulator for real-time debugging and hardware-level testing.

Simulation tools allow developers to test firmware extensively before deployment, reducing errors and debugging time.

Development Boards and Prototyping Kits

Development Board	Description
Curiosity Board	Beginner-friendly development board with built-in programmer/debugger, ideal for learning and prototyping.
Explorer 16/32	Versatile development platform supporting PIC24, dsPIC, and PIC32 series microcontrollers. Suitable for advanced applications.
PICDEM Series	Microchip's demonstration boards designed for evaluating different PIC families with preconfigured test circuits.
Custom PCB Prototyping	Many developers design custom PCBs with PIC microcontrollers tailored to specific applications.

Microchip Libraries and Middleware

Microchip provides software libraries to simplify embedded development:

- **MPLAB Code Configurator (MCC):** Graphical interface that automatically generates peripheral initialization code, reducing manual configuration time.
- **HARMONY Framework:** Middleware framework for PIC32 applications, providing abstraction layers for device drivers and system services.
- **Motor Control Libraries:** Pre-built functions for efficient motor control applications such as BLDC and PMSM drives.
- **TCP/IP Stack:** Pre-configured networking library to support Ethernet, Wi-Fi, and IoT applications with PIC microcontrollers.
- **USB Stack:** Middleware for implementing USB host and device functionality in embedded systems.

Chapter 5: Setting Up MPLAB X IDE

MPLAB X IDE is the official development environment for programming and debugging PIC microcontrollers. It provides a comprehensive suite of tools, including an editor, compiler, debugger, and simulator, making it essential for embedded system development. The IDE is designed to work with various hardware programmers and debuggers, ensuring a seamless development experience for engineers and hobbyists.

System Requirements

Before installing MPLAB X IDE, ensure that your system meets the minimum requirements to avoid compatibility issues:

Requirement	Specification
Operating System	Windows 7/8/10/11, macOS, Linux
Processor	Intel/AMD 64-bit processor
RAM	Minimum 2GB (4GB recommended for smooth operation)
Disk Space	At least 2GB of free storage for IDE and compilers
USB Port	Required for hardware programmers like PICkit 3/4, ICD 4, or Real ICE

Downloading and Installing MPLAB X IDE

To ensure a successful installation, follow these steps:

1. **Visit the Microchip Website:**
   a. Navigate to Microchip's official website and go to the MPLAB X IDE download section.

2. **Select the Appropriate Version:**
   a. Choose the latest stable version compatible with your operating system.
   b. Ensure compatibility with your microcontroller series and debugging tools.

3. **Download and Install:**
   a. Run the installer and follow on-screen instructions.
   b. Accept the license agreement and choose the preferred installation directory.
   c. Install additional drivers if prompted for hardware programmers.

4. **Verify Installation:**
   a. Launch MPLAB X IDE after installation.
   b. Navigate to "Tools" → "Options" → "Embedded" to check if the toolchain and compiler are detected.

Installing XC Compilers

MPLAB X IDE requires XC compilers to compile source code into machine-readable instructions for PIC microcontrollers.

1. **Download XC Compiler:**
   a. Visit Microchip's website and download the required compiler (XC8 for 8-bit, XC16 for 16-bit, or XC32 for 32-bit PIC microcontrollers).
2. **Run the Installer:**
   a. Choose "Free" or "Pro" version (Pro provides enhanced optimizations and performance features).
   b. Follow installation prompts and ensure the compiler is installed in a recognized directory.
3. **Configure the Compiler in MPLAB X:**
   a. Open MPLAB X IDE and navigate to "Tools" → "Options".
   b. Under "Embedded", ensure the installed compiler is detected and set as the default toolchain.

Creating a New Project in MPLAB X

Follow these steps to create a new project:

1. **Open MPLAB X IDE.**
2. **Go to "File" → "New Project".**
3. **Select "Microchip Embedded" → "Standalone Project".**
4. **Choose Your PIC Microcontroller Model** (e.g., PIC16F877A, PIC18F4520, PIC32MX795F512L).
5. **Select a Hardware Debugger/Programmer** (e.g., PICkit 4, ICD 4, or Real ICE).
6. **Choose the XC Compiler** appropriate for your microcontroller.
7. **Set the Project Name and Directory.**
8. **Click "Finish" to generate the project workspace.**

Configuring MPLAB X for First Use

- **Set Compiler Path:** Verify that the XC compiler path is correctly linked in "Tools" → "Options".
- **Customize Editor Settings:** Adjust font size, color themes, and

keybindings for a personalized development experience.

- **Enable Code Completion:** Navigate to "Tools" → "Options" → "Editor" to enable auto-suggestions and syntax highlighting.
- **Set Up Debugging Tools:** Configure debugging settings and add breakpoints to analyze program execution.

Debugging in MPLAB X

- **Using Breakpoints:**
  - Click on the left margin of the editor to set a breakpoint.
  - Run the program in debugging mode to pause execution at the breakpoint.
- **Viewing Registers:**
  - Open "Window" → "Debugging" → "SFRs" (Special Function Registers) to monitor register values in real-time.
- **Step-by-Step Execution:**
  - Use "Step Over" (F6) and "Step Into" (F7) commands for analyzing specific lines of code.
- **Real-Time Variable Monitoring:**
  - Use the "Watch" window to observe variable changes during execution.

Troubleshooting Common Issues

Issue	Possible Solution
Compiler Not Found	Ensure the XC compiler is installed and added to the toolchain. Check "Tools" → "Options" → "Embedded".
Programmer Not Detected	Verify the USB connection, reinstall drivers, or try a different USB port. Ensure the programmer is properly configured in "Project Properties".
Code Not Running on Microcontroller	Verify configuration bits and clock settings. Ensure that the correct microcontroller model is selected.
Debugger Not Working	Check that the correct debugger is selected in "Project Properties". Try restarting MPLAB X or updating firmware for the debugging tool.
Build Fails with Error Messages	Read the error log carefully. Ensure all necessary header files and dependencies are included.

Best Practices for MPLAB X Development

- **Organize Your Project:** Keep source files, header files, and library files in separate folders for better management.
- **Version Control:** Use Git or another version control system to track changes and collaborate with other developers.
- **Regular Backups:** Save copies of your project in different locations to prevent data loss.
- **Optimize Code for Performance:** Use compiler optimizations available in XC compilers to reduce code size and execution time.
- **Read Microcontroller Datasheets:** Always refer to the official Microchip datasheets for accurate information on registers, memory, and peripheral configurations.

Summary

- **MPLAB X IDE** is a powerful tool for developing PIC microcontroller applications.
- The installation process involves setting up the IDE and XC compilers for compiling and debugging C code.
- Creating a new project requires selecting the correct microcontroller, compiler, and debugger.
- Debugging tools such as breakpoints, register monitoring, and variable tracking enhance troubleshooting efficiency.
- Following best practices, such as organizing code, using version control, and reading datasheets, ensures a smooth development experience.

By following this guide, developers can efficiently set up **MPLAB X IDE**, configure the necessary tools, and begin developing embedded applications with PIC microcontrollers.

Chapter 6: First PIC Program

In this chapter, we will write and execute our first PIC microcontroller program using **MPLAB X IDE** and **XC8 Compiler**. We will create a simple LED blinking program to understand basic programming concepts, **port configuration, pin settings, and microcontroller operation**.

Hardware Requirements

To follow this tutorial, you will need:

- **PIC16F877A** (or any compatible PIC microcontroller)
- **MPLAB X IDE** (installed on your computer)
- **XC8 Compiler**
- **PICkit 3/4 or ICD 4** (programmer/debugger)
- **Breadboard**
- **LED**
- **220Ω Resistor**
- **5V Power Supply**
- **Jumper Wires**

Understanding Microcontroller Ports and Pins

PIC microcontrollers contain multiple **I/O ports**, which are groups of pins used for digital and analog input/output operations. Each port is controlled through special registers, which allow configuring the function of each pin.

Registers for Port and Pin Control

- **TRISx (Tri-State Register)**: Controls the direction of each pin in the port (**1 = Input, 0 = Output**).
- **PORTx (Port Register)**: Reads input values from external devices.
- **LATx (Latch Register)**: Writes output values to pins.

Pin Configuration Examples

Setting a Pin as Output

```
TRISBbits.TRISB0 = 0; // Configures RB0 as an output
```

Setting a Pin as Input

```
TRISBbits.TRISB1 = 1; // Configures RB1 as an input
```

Writing High or Low to an Output Pin

```
LATBbits.LATB0 = 1; // Turns RB0 HIGH (ON)
LATBbits.LATB0 = 0; // Turns RB0 LOW (OFF)
```

Reading from an Input Pin

```
int buttonState = PORTBbits.RB1; // Reads the state of
RB1
```

Project Code: LED Blinking Program

```
#include <xc.h>
#define _XTAL_FREQ 4000000   // Define clock frequency

// CONFIG BITS
#pragma config FOSC = HS    // High-Speed Oscillator
#pragma config WDTE = OFF   // Watchdog Timer disabled
#pragma config PWRTE = OFF  // Power-up Timer disabled
#pragma config BOREN = ON   // Brown-out Reset enabled
#pragma config LVP = OFF    // Low Voltage Programming
disabled

void main() {
    TRISBbits.TRISB0 = 0; // Configure RB0 as an output
pin
    while(1) { // Infinite loop
        LATBbits.LATB0 = 1; // Turn ON LED connected to
RB0
        __delay_ms(500); // Wait for 500 milliseconds
        LATBbits.LATB0 = 0; // Turn OFF LED connected
to RB0
        __delay_ms(500); // Wait for another 500
milliseconds
    }
}
```

Line-by-Line Explanation

Line	Code	Explanation
1	#include <xc.h>	Includes the XC8 library required for PIC microcontroller programming.
2	#define _XTAL_FREQ	Defines the oscillator frequency (4MHz)

	4000000	to enable accurate timing with delays.
4-9	`#pragma config` ...	Configures microcontroller settings like oscillator type, watchdog timer, power-up timer, etc.
11	`void main() {`	Entry point of the program where execution starts.
12	`TRISBbits.TRISB0 = 0;`	Configures RB0 as an **output** pin to control an LED.
13	`while(1) {`	Creates an infinite loop to keep the LED blinking continuously.
14	`LATBbits.LATB0 = 1;`	Turns ON the LED connected to **RB0**.
15	`__delay_ms(500);`	Delays execution for **500 milliseconds** to keep the LED ON.
16	`LATBbits.LATB0 = 0;`	Turns OFF the LED connected to **RB0**.
17	`__delay_ms(500);`	Delays execution for **500 milliseconds** to keep the LED OFF before repeating the loop.
18	`}`	Ends the while loop and keeps repeating the blinking sequence.

Compiling and Uploading Code

1. **Build the Project:**
   a. Click **Build (Hammer Icon)** or press **F11**.
   b. Ensure there are no compilation errors.
2. **Program the PIC Microcontroller:**
   a. Click **Make and Program Device (Green Play Icon)**.
   b. The program will be uploaded to the PIC microcontroller.

Debugging Section

Issue	Possible Cause	Solution
LED not blinking	Pin is not set as output	Check TRISB register configuration
No response from input	Incorrect pin mapping	Verify the microcontroller datasheet
UART not working	Baud rate mismatch	Ensure correct baud rate settings

Unstable operation	Power supply fluctuations	Use a stable 5V power source

Best Practices for Using Ports and Pins

Best Practice	Reason
Use LATx for output instead of PORTx	Prevents read-modify-write issues
Enable weak pull-ups when needed	Useful for switch inputs on PORTB
Configure pins properly before using them	Avoids accidental floating inputs
Use header files for pin definitions	Improves code readability and reusability

Summary

- PIC microcontrollers have multiple **ports and pins** that must be configured properly for input and output.
- **TRISx, PORTx, and LATx registers** control pin direction and data manipulation.
- Correct **circuit connections** are necessary to ensure the program functions as expected.
- The **XC8 compiler and MPLAB X IDE** are used to write, compile, and upload programs.
- **Best practices** such as using LATx for outputs, enabling pull-ups, and checking pin configurations improve efficiency.
- **Debugging techniques** help troubleshoot common issues efficiently.

Chapter 7: Introduction to Electrical Components

Understanding the fundamental electrical components used in PIC microcontroller circuits is essential for designing and implementing embedded systems. These components allow the microcontroller to interact with external devices, sensors, and power supplies while ensuring proper circuit functionality.

Basic Electrical Components

1. Resistors

- **Function:** Limit current, divide voltage, pull-up/pull-down resistors.
- **Types:** Fixed, variable (potentiometers), thermistors (temperature-dependent resistors).
- **Common Values:** 220Ω, 1kΩ, 10kΩ.
- **Application in PIC Circuits:**
  - Pull-up resistors for input pins.
  - Current-limiting resistors for LEDs.

2. Capacitors

- **Function:** Store and release electrical charge, filter signals, stabilize voltage.
- **Types:** Electrolytic (high capacitance), Ceramic (low capacitance), Tantalum.
- **Common Values:** 10μF, 100nF, 470μF.
- **Application in PIC Circuits:**
  - Power supply decoupling to smooth voltage.
  - Timing circuits.

3. Diodes

- **Function:** Allow current to flow in one direction, prevent reverse voltage damage.
- **Types:** Standard diodes, Zener diodes (voltage regulation), Schottky diodes (low forward voltage drop).
- **Application in PIC Circuits:**
  - Protection for microcontroller pins.
  - Voltage regulation circuits.

4. Transistors

- **Function:** Act as electronic switches or amplifiers.
- **Types:** Bipolar Junction Transistor (BJT), Field Effect Transistor (FET), MOSFET.
- **Application in PIC Circuits:**
    - Switching high-current loads (e.g., motors, relays).
    - Signal amplification.

5. Inductors

- **Function:** Store energy in a magnetic field, used for filtering and power supply circuits.
- **Application in PIC Circuits:**
    - Noise suppression in power supplies.
    - Boost converters for voltage step-up.

6. Light Emitting Diodes (LEDs)

- **Function:** Emit light when current flows through them.
- **Application in PIC Circuits:**
    - Status indicators.
    - Visual feedback in embedded systems.

7. Switches and Buttons

- **Function:** Allow or block electrical current in a circuit.
- **Types:** Push buttons, toggle switches, rotary encoders.
- **Application in PIC Circuits:**
    - User input buttons.
    - Mode selection switches.

8. Relays

- **Function:** Electromechanical switch controlled by the microcontroller.
- **Types:** Electromagnetic, Solid-state relays.
- **Application in PIC Circuits:**
    - Controlling high-power devices.
    - Isolation between control and load circuits.

9. Potentiometers

- **Function:** Adjustable resistors used for tuning and control.
- **Application in PIC Circuits:**
    - Setting contrast in LCD displays.
    - Variable voltage dividers.

10. Voltage Regulators

- **Function:** Maintain a constant voltage output despite variations in input voltage.
- **Types:** Linear regulators (e.g., 7805), Switching regulators (e.g., LM2575).
- **Application in PIC Circuits:**
  - Providing a stable 5V supply for PIC microcontrollers.

Power Supply Components

Component	Function
Batteries	Provide portable power to microcontroller circuits
Voltage Regulators (e.g., 7805, LM317)	Regulate and stabilize voltage to 5V for PIC microcontrollers
Transformers	Step up or step down AC voltage
Rectifiers	Convert AC to DC using diodes
Capacitors	Used in power supplies for voltage smoothing and filtering

Input Devices for PIC Microcontrollers

Component	Function
Push Buttons	Send digital input signals to the microcontroller
Sensors (Temperature, Light, Motion)	Provide analog or digital signals based on environmental changes
Potentiometers	Used for variable resistance to adjust voltage input
Keypads	Allow multi-button input for user interfaces
Infrared (IR) Sensors	Detect IR signals for remote control applications

Output Devices for PIC Microcontrollers

Component	Function
LEDs	Provide visual indicators for system status
LCD Displays	Display alphanumeric data from the microcontroller
Buzzers	Generate sound signals for alerts and notifications

Relays	Control high-power devices using the microcontroller
Motors (DC, Servo, Stepper)	Provide motion control in robotics and automation

Common Circuit Protection Components

Component	Function
Fuses	Protect circuits by breaking the connection in case of high current
Diodes	Prevent reverse voltage damage to microcontroller pins
Varistors	Absorb voltage spikes to protect sensitive components
Optocouplers	Isolate high-voltage and low-voltage circuits using light signals

Practical Example: LED with a PIC Microcontroller

A simple circuit to control an LED with a PIC microcontroller involves:

- **A 220Ω resistor** to limit current through the LED.
- **An LED** connected to a GPIO pin of the PIC microcontroller.
- **A power supply** (5V) for the microcontroller.

```
#include <xc.h>
#define _XTAL_FREQ 4000000

#pragma config FOSC = HS
#pragma config WDTE = OFF
#pragma config PWRTE = OFF
#pragma config BOREN = ON
#pragma config LVP = OFF

void main() {
    TRISBbits.TRISB0 = 0;
    while(1) {
        LATBbits.LATB0 = 1;
        __delay_ms(500);
        LATBbits.LATB0 = 0;
        __delay_ms(500);
    }
}
```

Summary

- Electrical components such as **resistors, capacitors, transistors, and diodes** are essential in PIC circuits.
- **Power supply components** ensure stable voltage for the microcontroller.
- **Input devices** like switches and sensors provide data to the microcontroller.
- **Output devices** like LEDs, LCDs, and motors allow interaction with the environment.
- **Protection components** safeguard the circuit against voltage spikes and excessive current.
- A practical **LED control circuit** demonstrates how to integrate components with a PIC microcontroller.

This chapter provides a foundational understanding of the essential electrical components used in PIC-based embedded systems.

Chapter 8: Ohm's Law and Circuit Basics

Ohm's Law is fundamental in understanding how electrical circuits operate, especially when working with PIC microcontrollers. This chapter covers Ohm's Law, basic circuit principles, and how they apply to microcontroller-based systems.

Ohm's Law

Ohm's Law states that the voltage (V) across a resistor is directly proportional to the current (I) flowing through it, with resistance (R) being the constant of proportionality:

$V = I \times R$

Where:

- **V** = Voltage (Volts, V)
- **I** = Current (Amperes, A)
- **R** = Resistance (Ohms, Ω)

Key Concepts of Ohm's Law

- If **voltage increases**, current increases (if resistance remains constant).
- If **resistance increases**, current decreases (if voltage remains constant).
- If **current increases**, voltage increases (if resistance remains constant).

Applications of Ohm's Law in PIC Circuits

- Determining the appropriate resistor values for LEDs.
- Calculating current draw of microcontroller circuits.
- Ensuring power supply designs provide safe and sufficient voltage and current.
- Protecting microcontroller pins from excessive current.

Basic Circuit Components in PIC Circuits

Component	Symbol	Function
Resistor	R	Limits current, divides voltage
Capacitor	C	Stores charge, filters noise
Diode	D	Allows current to flow in one direction
Transistor	Q	Acts as a switch or amplifier
LED	LED	Emits light when current flows

Switch	SW	Controls electrical connections
Power Supply	V	Provides voltage and current

Power and Energy in Microcontroller Circuits

Power (P) in an electrical circuit is given by: $P = V \times I$

Where:

- **P** = Power (Watts, W)
- **V** = Voltage (Volts, V)
- **I** = Current (Amperes, A)

Power dissipation considerations:

- Ensure resistors can handle the power they dissipate.
- Use heat sinks for power transistors when necessary.
- Avoid overloading power supplies.

Practical Example: LED Circuit with Ohm's Law

Given:

- **LED Forward Voltage:** 2V
- **Microcontroller Output Voltage:** 5V
- **Desired LED Current:** 10mA

Using Ohm's Law: $R = (V_{supply} - V_{LED}) / I_{led}$

Thus, a **300Ω resistor** is used to limit the current.

Circuit Diagram Explanation:

- The anode of the LED is connected to **RB0 (PIC output pin).**
- The cathode is connected to one end of the **300Ω resistor.**
- The other end of the resistor is connected to **GND.**

Code to Blink LED using PIC Microcontroller

```
#include <xc.h>
#define _XTAL_FREQ 4000000
void main() {
    TRISBbits.TRISB0 = 0; // Set RB0 as an output
    while(1) {
        LATBbits.LATB0 = 1; // Turn LED ON
        __delay_ms(500);
        LATBbits.LATB0 = 0; // Turn LED OFF
        __delay_ms(500);
    }
}
```

Safety Considerations in Circuit Design

- **Avoid excessive current draw**: Exceeding microcontroller pin current ratings can cause damage.
- **Proper resistor selection**: Always calculate correct resistance values to protect LEDs and other components.
- **Stable power supply**: Ensure that your power supply provides a consistent voltage without fluctuations.
- **Use decoupling capacitors**: These stabilize power supply voltages and reduce noise.

Common Mistakes and Troubleshooting Tips

Issue	Possible Cause	Solution
LED not turning on	Resistor value too high	Use a lower-value resistor
LED too dim	Current too low	Check resistor calculation
Overheating components	Excess current flow	Verify Ohm's Law calculations
Microcontroller reset unexpectedly	Power supply instability	Use decoupling capacitors

Summary

- Ohm's Law defines the relationship between voltage, current, and resistance.
- Series circuits share the same current, while parallel circuits share voltage.
- Voltage dividers are useful in microcontroller circuits.
- Power calculations ensure safe operation of electronic components.
- A resistor is required to limit current in an LED circuit.
- Stable power supplies and proper resistor values prevent circuit damage.

Understanding these principles helps in designing **stable, safe, and efficient** PIC microcontroller-based systems.

Chapter 9: Resistors, Capacitors, and Inductors

Resistors, capacitors, and inductors are essential passive components in electronic circuits, including those built around PIC microcontrollers. Each component has a specific role in circuit design, affecting voltage, current, and signal processing.

Resistors in PIC Microcontroller Circuits

A resistor opposes the flow of electric current, which helps in controlling voltage levels, limiting current, and dividing voltage in circuits.

Common Uses in PIC Circuits:

- **Current Limiting for LEDs:** Protects LEDs from excessive current using Ohm's Law.
- **Pull-up and Pull-down Resistors:** Ensures a defined logic level at microcontroller input pins.
- **Voltage Dividers:** Scales down voltage for analog sensors and ADC inputs.
- **Timing Circuits:** Used in RC (Resistor-Capacitor) networks for oscillators and delays.

Different Types of Resistors:

- **Fixed Resistors:** Provide a constant resistance value.
- **Variable Resistors (Potentiometers):** Adjustable resistance used for tuning circuits.
- **Thermistors:** Resistance changes with temperature, used in temperature sensing.
- **LDR (Light Dependent Resistors):** Resistance varies with light intensity, used in automatic lighting.

Formula: $V = I \times R$

Power Dissipation in Resistors: Power dissipation in a resistor is calculated as: $P = V \times IP$ Excessive power dissipation leads to heating, which can degrade performance and cause failure.

Real-Life Example Using a Resistor:

- **Scenario:** An LED circuit powered by a **5V supply** with an LED requiring **2V forward voltage** and **10mA current**.

- **Calculation:** $R = \frac{5V - 2V}{10mA} = 300\Omega \, R$
- **Power Dissipation:** $P = V \times I = (5V - 2V) \times 10mA = 30mW \, P =$
- **Real-Life Loss:** Heat generation reduces efficiency, requiring a properly rated resistor.

Capacitors in PIC Microcontroller Circuits

A capacitor stores and releases electrical energy, playing a crucial role in stabilizing voltage and filtering noise.

Common Uses in PIC Circuits:

- **Decoupling and Bypassing:** Removes power supply fluctuations and stabilizes voltage.
- **Oscillator Circuits:** Works with quartz crystals to provide clock signals for the microcontroller.
- **Timing Circuits:** Used with resistors in RC networks for accurate time delays.
- **Filter Circuits:** Reduces noise in power supply and signal lines.

Different Types of Capacitors:

- **Electrolytic Capacitors:** High capacitance, used for power supply filtering.
- **Ceramic Capacitors:** Low capacitance, used for high-frequency filtering.
- **Tantalum Capacitors:** Stable and high-performance, used in compact circuits.
- **Film Capacitors:** High reliability, used in AC signal filtering.

Formula: $Q = C \times V \, Q$

Power Dissipation in Capacitors: While capacitors do not dissipate power like resistors, losses occur due to:

- **Leakage Current:** Small current flow through the dielectric material.
- **Equivalent Series Resistance (ESR):** Causes heating and efficiency loss.
- **Dielectric Absorption:** Some stored charge remains, causing signal distortion.

Real-Life Example Using a Capacitor:

- **Scenario:** Power supply filtering in a **5V microcontroller circuit** using a **100µF capacitor**.
- **Calculation:** $Q=C\times V=100\,\mu F\times 5V=0.5mCQ$
- **Real-Life Loss:** ESR and leakage current cause power loss, affecting long-term reliability.

Inductors in PIC Microcontroller Circuits

An inductor stores energy in a magnetic field and resists changes in current, making it useful in power management and noise filtering.

Common Uses in PIC Circuits:

- **Power Supply Filtering:** Used in combination with capacitors to smooth voltage fluctuations.
- **Switching Regulators:** Forms part of DC-DC converters for efficient power management.
- **Noise Suppression:** Reduces high-frequency noise in signal lines.

Different Types of Inductors:

- **Air-Core Inductors:** Used in high-frequency applications.
- **Iron-Core Inductors:** Used in power supplies for energy storage.
- **Ferrite Beads:** Suppress high-frequency noise in circuits.
- **Toroidal Inductors:** Compact and efficient for power regulation.

Power Dissipation in Inductors:

- **Copper Losses:** Resistance of the wire causes power dissipation.
- **Core Losses:** Energy loss due to hysteresis and eddy currents in the core material.
- **Parasitic Capacitance:** Causes unwanted oscillations and losses.

Real-Life Example Using an Inductor:

- **Scenario:** A **100µH inductor** in a DC-DC converter with **2A ripple current**.
- **Real-Life Loss:** Core heating and wire resistance reduce efficiency in power converters.

Practical Example: Power Supply Decoupling

A stable power supply is essential for PIC microcontroller operation.

A decoupling capacitor is used to reduce voltage spikes.

Circuit Components:

- **Microcontroller Power Supply (5V)**
- **10μF Electrolytic Capacitor (Bulk filtering)**
- **0.1μF Ceramic Capacitor (High-frequency noise filtering)**

Connection:

- **10μF capacitor** is connected **between VCC and GND** to stabilize voltage.
- **0.1μF capacitor** is placed **as close as possible to the microcontroller's power pins** for noise filtering.

Summary

- **Resistors** control current and voltage, used for LED protection, pull-up/down resistors, and voltage dividers.
- **Capacitors** stabilize voltage, remove noise, and assist in timing circuits.
- **Inductors** store energy, filter noise, and are used in power circuits.
- **Different types of resistors, capacitors, and inductors** are used based on circuit requirements.
- **Power dissipation and real-life losses** impact the efficiency and longevity of electronic components.
- **Real-life examples with calculations** demonstrate practical applications of these components.
- Proper selection of these components ensures stable and reliable microcontroller operation.

Understanding these passive components is crucial for designing efficient circuits that work seamlessly with PIC microcontrollers.

Chapter 10: Understanding Diodes and LEDs

Diodes and Light Emitting Diodes (LEDs) are critical components in PIC microcontroller circuits. Diodes allow current to flow in only one direction, while LEDs emit light when forward biased. Understanding their characteristics, types, and applications helps in designing reliable embedded systems.

Diodes in PIC Microcontroller Circuits

A diode is a semiconductor device that permits current to flow in one direction while blocking it in the reverse direction.

Common Uses in PIC Circuits:

- **Reverse Polarity Protection:** Prevents damage due to incorrect power supply connections.
- **Flyback Protection in Inductive Loads:** Protects microcontrollers from voltage spikes when turning off inductors (e.g., motors, relays).
- **Rectification:** Converts AC to DC in power supplies.
- **Voltage Clamping:** Limits voltage spikes in sensitive circuits.

Different Types of Diodes:

- **Standard Rectifier Diodes (1N4007):** Used in power supplies for rectification.
- **Schottky Diodes (1N5819):** Fast switching, low voltage drop diodes.
- **Zener Diodes:** Used for voltage regulation and protection.
- **Light Emitting Diodes (LEDs):** Emit visible or infrared light.
- **Photodiodes:** Convert light into electrical current for sensing applications.

Formula for Forward Voltage Drop:

$V_f = I \times R_{internal} + V_{junction}$

Where:

- **V_f** = Forward voltage drop (typically 0.7V for silicon diodes).
- **I** = Current flowing through the diode.
- **R_{internal}** = Internal resistance of the diode.
- **V_{junction}** = Diode junction voltage.

Example: Reverse Polarity Protection for PIC Circuit A 1N4007

diode is placed in series with the **5V power supply** to prevent damage if the power is connected incorrectly.

- **Diode Forward Voltage Drop: 0.7V**
- **Effective Voltage to PIC: 5V - 0.7V = 4.3V** (Acceptable for many PIC microcontrollers).

LEDs in PIC Microcontroller Circuits

An LED is a diode that emits light when a current flows through it in the forward direction. It requires a current-limiting resistor to prevent excessive current flow.

Common Uses in PIC Circuits:

- **Status Indicators:** Showing microcontroller activity.
- **Display Systems:** Used in 7-segment displays and LCD backlights.
- **Optocouplers:** Used for electrical isolation in circuits.
- **IR Transmitters:** Used in remote controls and object detection.

Different Types of LEDs:

- **Standard LEDs:** Used for visual indicators (red, green, blue, etc.).
- **High Brightness LEDs:** Used for illumination.
- **RGB LEDs:** Can emit multiple colors by controlling separate red, green, and blue elements.
- **Infrared LEDs (IR LEDs):** Used in remote controls and sensors.

Formula for Current Limiting Resistor Selection:

$R = (V_{supply} - V_{LED}) / I_{led}$

Where:

- **V_{supply}** = Supply voltage.
- **V_{LED}** = LED forward voltage (typically 2V for red LEDs, 3V for blue/white LEDs).
- **I_{LED}** = Desired LED current (typically 10mA - 20mA).

Example: LED Blinking Circuit with PIC Microcontroller

- **Supply Voltage:** 5V
- **LED Forward Voltage:** 2V
- **Desired Current:** 10mA
- **Resistor Calculation:** $R = 5V - 2V 10mA = 300\Omega R = \frac{5V - 2V}{10mA} = 300\Omega$

Code to Blink an LED using PIC Microcontroller

```c
#include <xc.h>
#define _XTAL_FREQ 4000000

void main() {
    TRISBbits.TRISB0 = 0; // Set RB0 as output
    while(1) {
        LATBbits.LATB0 = 1; // Turn LED ON
        __delay_ms(500);
        LATBbits.LATB0 = 0; // Turn LED OFF
        __delay_ms(500);
    }
}
```

Power Dissipation in LEDs and Diodes Power dissipated in a diode or LED is given by: $P = Vf \times IP = V\_f \mid times\ I$

- **For a red LED (V_f = 2V, I = 10mA):** $P = 2V \times 10mA = 20mWP = 2V \mid times\ 10mA = 20mW$
- **For a Schottky diode (V_f = 0.3V, I = 1A):** $P = 0.3V \times 1A = 0.3WP = 0.3V \mid times\ 1A = 0.3W$

Real-Life Losses in Diodes and LEDs

- **Heat Dissipation:** High current LEDs require heat sinks to prevent overheating.
- **Efficiency Losses:** Some energy is lost as heat instead of light.
- **Aging Effects:** LEDs lose brightness over time due to degradation of the semiconductor material.

Practical Example: Protecting a Microcontroller Pin with a Diode If an external switch is connected to a microcontroller pin, a diode (e.g., **1N4148**) can be used to clamp overvoltage and protect the microcontroller.

- **Supply Voltage:** 5V
- **Overvoltage Clamping Voltage:** 5.6V (Using a Zener diode)
- **Resistor Value:** 1kΩ to limit excess current.

Chapter 11: Transistors and MOSFETs in PIC Circuits

Transistors and MOSFETs are crucial components in PIC microcontroller circuits. They function as electronic switches, amplifiers, and signal processors. Understanding their working principles, types, and practical applications helps in designing efficient embedded systems.

Transistors in PIC Microcontroller Circuits

A transistor is a semiconductor device that can amplify or switch electronic signals. The two main types are Bipolar Junction Transistors (BJTs) and Field Effect Transistors (FETs).

Common Uses in PIC Circuits:

- **Switching Loads:** Controls motors, relays, and LEDs with a small signal from the microcontroller.
- **Signal Amplification:** Boosts weak signals for sensors and communication modules.
- **Current Regulation:** Used in voltage regulators and power management circuits.

Types of Transistors:

- **Bipolar Junction Transistors (BJTs):** Current-controlled devices, further classified into NPN and PNP.
- **Field Effect Transistors (FETs):** Voltage-controlled devices with high input impedance.
- **Darlington Transistors:** Two BJTs combined for high current gain.

Formula for Transistor Switching: For a BJT in saturation mode:
$IC = \beta \times IBI\_C$

- I_C = Collector current
- I_B = Base current
- β (hFE) = Current gain of the transistor

Example: Switching an LED with a BJT

- **Supply Voltage:** 5V
- **LED Current:** 20mA
- **BJT Gain (β):** 100

MOSFETs in PIC Microcontroller Circuits

A MOSFET (Metal-Oxide-Semiconductor Field-Effect Transistor) is a type of transistor that offers efficient high-speed switching.

Common Uses in PIC Circuits:

- **Power Switching:** Drives high-power loads with minimal control current.
- **Pulse Width Modulation (PWM):** Used in motor speed and LED brightness control.
- **Voltage Level Shifting:** Converts signals between different voltage levels.

Types of MOSFETs:

- **N-Channel MOSFET:** Most commonly used for low-side switching.
- **P-Channel MOSFET:** Used in high-side switching applications.
- **Enhancement Mode MOSFET:** Requires a positive gate voltage to turn on.
- **Depletion Mode MOSFET:** Conducts even without a gate voltage.

Formula for MOSFET Operation: For an N-channel MOSFET in saturation mode: $ID=K(VGS-Vth)2I\_D$

Where:

- I_D = Drain current
- **K** = Device constant
- V_{GS} = Gate-to-source voltage
- V_{th} = Threshold voltage

Example: Controlling a Motor with an N-Channel MOSFET

- **MOSFET:** IRF540 (R_DS(on) = 0.044Ω)
- **Motor Current:** 2A
- **Gate Drive Voltage:** 5V

Power Dissipation and Efficiency Considerations

- **BJT Switching Losses:** Slow switching speed results in heat dissipation.
- **MOSFET Efficiency:** Low R_DS(on) minimizes power loss.
- **Heat Management:** Use heat sinks for high-current applications.

Real-Life Applications of Transistors and MOSFETs in PIC Circuits

- **Relay Driving:** A BJT or MOSFET is used to control a relay for high-power applications.

- **PWM Control for Motors:** MOSFETs efficiently modulate speed using PWM signals.
- **Current Protection Circuits:** Transistors limit excessive current draw in circuits.

Summary

- **Transistors** and **MOSFETs** are essential for power switching and signal control in PIC microcontroller circuits.
- **BJTs** require base current for operation, while **MOSFETs** are voltage-controlled devices with high efficiency.
- **Switching calculations** ensure the right selection of base/gate resistors for optimal performance.
- **Power dissipation management** is crucial to avoid excessive heat in high-power applications.
- **Practical applications** include LED switching, motor control, and relay driving.

Understanding transistors and MOSFETs enhances the design and efficiency of PIC-based embedded systems.

Chapter 12: Power Supply and Voltage Regulators

A stable and efficient power supply is essential for the proper functioning of PIC microcontrollers. Voltage regulators ensure that the microcontroller receives a constant voltage despite variations in input power. Understanding power supply components and regulator types helps in designing reliable circuits.

Power Supply Requirements for PIC Microcontrollers

PIC microcontrollers typically operate at **3.3V** or **5V**, requiring a regulated power source for stable operation.

Basic Power Supply Components:

- **Transformers:** Convert AC voltage to a different level.
- **Rectifiers (Diodes):** Convert AC to DC.
- **Capacitors:** Smooth out voltage fluctuations.
- **Voltage Regulators:** Provide a stable output voltage.
- **Batteries:** Portable power sources for microcontroller applications.

Types of Power Supplies

1. **Linear Power Supply:**
   a. Uses a transformer, rectifier, and a linear voltage regulator.
   b. Provides clean and stable voltage but is inefficient due to heat dissipation.
2. **Switching Power Supply (SMPS):**
   a. Converts DC voltage using high-frequency switching.
   b. More efficient than linear regulators, suitable for battery-powered applications.
3. **Battery Power Supply:**
   a. Direct DC source from batteries.
   b. Requires voltage regulation for microcontroller stability.

Voltage Regulators in PIC Circuits

A voltage regulator maintains a constant voltage level regardless of changes in input voltage or load.

Common Types of Voltage Regulators:

- **Linear Regulators (e.g., 7805, 7812, LM317):** Simple but

inefficient due to heat dissipation.
- **Low Dropout (LDO) Regulators (e.g., AMS1117, MCP1700):** Require minimal voltage difference between input and output.
- **Switching Regulators (e.g., Buck, Boost Converters):** Highly efficient for converting power.
- **Zener Diode Regulators:** Used for low-current voltage stabilization.

Voltage Regulator Selection Guide:

Regulator Type	Efficiency	Use Case
7805 (5V Linear)	Low (~40%)	Simple circuits, low power applications
LM317 (Adjustable)	Low (~50%)	Custom voltage outputs, low power
AMS1117 (3.3V LDO)	Moderate (~70%)	3.3V circuits, battery-powered devices
Buck Converter	High (~90%)	Efficient step-down voltage conversion
Boost Converter	High (~85%)	Step-up voltage conversion from lower battery voltage

Example: 5V Power Supply Using a 7805 Regulator
- **Input Voltage:** 7V - 12V DC
- **Output Voltage:** 5V DC
- **Components:**
  - 7805 Voltage Regulator
  - 10µF and 0.1µF Capacitors
  - Bridge Rectifier (if AC input is used)

Circuit Connection:
1. Connect **input voltage (7-12V)** to the **VIN** pin of the 7805.
2. Ground **GND** pin.
3. Connect **VOUT (5V)** to the PIC microcontroller and other components.
4. Place **capacitors (10µF and 0.1µF)** near the regulator for stability.

Power Dissipation Calculation in Linear Regulators

$P=(V_{IN}-V_{OUT}) \times I$

- **Example:** If **VIN = 9V, VOUT = 5V**, and **I = 100mA**:

$P=(9V-5V)\times0.1A=0.4W$

- Heat sink may be required to dissipate excess heat.

Real-Life Applications of Voltage Regulators in PIC Circuits

- **Microcontroller Boards:** Providing stable 5V or 3.3V power.
- **Battery-Powered Systems:** Using buck/boost converters to extend battery life.
- **Industrial Automation:** Regulated power supply ensures consistent performance.

Troubleshooting Power Supply Issues

Issue	Possible Cause	Solution
PIC not powering up	Insufficient voltage	Check voltage at microcontroller pins
Overheating regulator	Excessive input voltage	Use a heat sink or switch to an SMPS
Voltage fluctuations	Poor capacitor placement	Place decoupling capacitors close to regulator
High power loss	Inefficient linear regulator	Use a switching regulator for better efficiency

Summary

- **Power supply stability** is critical for PIC microcontrollers to function reliably.
- **Voltage regulators** provide a stable voltage despite input fluctuations.
- **Linear regulators** are simple but inefficient, while **switching regulators** offer high efficiency.
- **Power dissipation calculations** help in selecting appropriate regulators.
- **Efficiency comparisons show that switching regulators are significantly better for power conservation.**
- **Troubleshooting guides help diagnose and fix power supply issues.**
- **Real-life applications** range from embedded systems to industrial automation.

Understanding power supplies and voltage regulators enables designing **stable, efficient, and reliable** PIC microcontroller-based circuits.

Chapter 13: Basics of Embedded C Programming

Embedded C is the programming language used for writing firmware that controls PIC (Peripheral Interface Controller) microcontrollers. Embedded C allows direct interaction with the hardware, enabling the programming of real-time embedded systems, including device control, sensor interaction, and data processing. The ability to control hardware directly through registers and I/O operations makes it critical for applications such as robotics, automotive systems, consumer electronics, and industrial controls.

In this chapter, we will cover the essential elements needed to write embedded software for PIC microcontrollers, including setting up the development environment, understanding the structure of an embedded C program, and interfacing with hardware components.

Setting Up the Development Environment

To program a PIC microcontroller using Embedded C, you need the appropriate tools to write, compile, and upload the code to the microcontroller. The following tools are commonly used:

1. **MPLAB X IDE (Integrated Development Environment)**
2. MPLAB X IDE is Microchip's official development platform for programming PIC microcontrollers. It provides an intuitive graphical interface to write, compile, and debug your Embedded C programs.
3. **XC8 Compiler**

The XC8 is the C compiler used for 8-bit PIC microcontrollers. It converts your Embedded C code into machine-readable instructions that the microcontroller can execute.

4. **PICkit Programmer**

The PICkit is a hardware tool used to flash (program) the compiled firmware onto the microcontroller. It interfaces with your computer via USB and connects to the target microcontroller through its ICSP (In-Circuit Serial Programming) port.

Setting Up the Environment:

- Install MPLAB X IDE from the Microchip website.
- Install the XC8 compiler to ensure your code can be compiled for PIC microcontrollers.

- Connect the PICkit Programmer to your computer and the microcontroller to upload the program.

Basic Structure of an Embedded C Program

An Embedded C program written for PIC microcontrollers generally follows a standard structure that includes essential components like header files, configuration settings, initialization of peripherals, and the main function.

1. Header Files

Header files contain definitions of constants, function prototypes, and libraries required for specific functions. These files are included at the beginning of the program to make the necessary functions available.

Example:

```
#include <xc.h>  // This is the primary header for PIC
microcontrollers.
```

2. Configuration Bits

Configuration bits set up essential features of the microcontroller, such as the oscillator type, watchdog timer, and brown-out reset. These settings are applied during the compilation.

Example:

```
#pragma config FOSC = HS    // High-Speed Oscillator
```

3. Main Function

The `main()` function contains the primary execution code of the program. It often includes an infinite loop (`while(1)`) to ensure continuous execution on the microcontroller.

4. Peripheral Initialization

This section configures I/O ports, timers, and other peripherals (such as ADC, PWM, etc.) before they are used in the program.

5. Infinite Loop

Microcontrollers run indefinitely, so the `main()` function typically contains an infinite loop to keep the program active. This loop is where the main operations of the program are executed repeatedly.

Example Program: LED Blinking with PIC16F877A

Here's a simple example where an LED connected to pin RB0 of a PIC16F877A microcontroller will blink on and off every 500ms.

```
#include <xc.h>
#define _XTAL_FREQ 4000000  // Define the crystal
frequency (4 MHz)

// CONFIG BITS
#pragma config FOSC = HS     // High-Speed Oscillator
#pragma config WDTE = OFF    // Disable Watchdog Timer
#pragma config PWRTE = OFF   // Disable Power-up Timer
#pragma config BOREN = ON    // Enable Brown-out Reset
#pragma config LVP = OFF     // Disable Low Voltage
Programming

void main() {
    TRISBbits.TRISB0 = 0; // Set RB0 as output (LED
control pin)

    while(1) {
        LATBbits.LATB0 = 1; // Turn the LED ON
        __delay_ms(500);    // Wait for 500ms
        LATBbits.LATB0 = 0; // Turn the LED OFF
        __delay_ms(500);    // Wait for 500ms
    }
}
```

Explanation of the Code:
- **`#include <xc.h>`**: This line includes the header file for XC8, which contains essential definitions for working with PIC microcontrollers.
- **`#define _XTAL_FREQ 4000000`**: Defines the crystal oscillator frequency (4 MHz in this case). This is used for accurate timing in delay functions.
- **`TRISBbits.TRISB0 = 0;`**: Configures pin RB0 (on port B)

as an output (0 for output, 1 for input). The LED will be connected to this pin.

- **LATBbits.LATB0 = 1;**: Sets the output on RB0 to HIGH, turning the LED ON.
- **__delay_ms(500);**: This built-in function creates a delay of 500 milliseconds (half a second). This is commonly used to create a simple delay between actions like turning the LED on and off.
- **while(1)**: This infinite loop keeps the program running forever. The LED will continuously blink on and off.

Working with Input and Output (I/O) Ports

PIC microcontrollers have several I/O ports (like PORTA, PORTB, etc.) for interacting with external devices (LEDs, sensors, switches). Each I/O port has two main registers:

- **TRISx**: The TRIS register configures the direction of the pins on a port (1 for input, 0 for output).
- **PORTx**: The PORT register reads values from input pins (e.g., button states).
- **LATx**: The LAT register is used to write values to output pins (e.g., to turn an LED on or off).

Example: Reading a Button Press on RB1

```
TRISBbits.TRISB1 = 1; // Set RB1 as input (button pin)
if (PORTBbits.RB1 == 1) {  // Check if button is
pressed
    LATBbits.LATB0 = 1;    // Turn LED ON if button is
pressed
} else {
    LATBbits.LATB0 = 0;    // Turn LED OFF if button is
not pressed
}
```

Using Timers for Delay Management

PIC microcontrollers have built-in timers that allow for precise time delays without relying on the CPU for processing. Timers are especially useful for generating time delays, generating PWM signals, or creating time-based events.

Example: Configuring Timer0

```
T0CON = 0b10000111; // Configure Timer0 with a 256
prescaler
while (INTCONbits.TMR0IF == 0); // Wait for the Timer0
overflow
INTCONbits.TMR0IF = 0; // Clear the Timer0 overflow
flag
```

- **T0CON**: A register used to configure Timer0's control settings, such as the prescaler and enable bit.
- **INTCONbits.TMR0IF**: A flag that gets set when the timer overflows.

Interfacing with Peripherals

1. **Interfacing an LCD with PIC** LCDs can be interfaced with microcontrollers to display information.

Example:

```
Lcd_Init();            // Initialize the LCD
Lcd_Set_Cursor(1, 1);  // Move cursor to row 1,
column 1
Lcd_Write_String("Hello!"); // Display message on the
LCD
```

2. **Generating PWM Signal for Motor Control** Pulse Width Modulation (PWM) is commonly used for controlling the speed of motors.

Example:

```
CCP1CON = 0b00001100; // Configure CCP1 module for PWM
mode
PR2 = 255;            // Set PWM frequency
CCPR1L = 128;         // Set the duty cycle to 50%
```

Interrupts in Embedded C

Interrupts allow the microcontroller to respond to external events without polling or constantly checking for conditions. This makes embedded systems more efficient.

Example: Enabling External Interrupt on RB0

```
INTCONbits.INT0IE = 1;    // Enable external interrupt
on RB0
INTCONbits.INT0IF = 0;    // Clear the interrupt flag
GIE = 1;                  // Enable global interrupts
```

Troubleshooting Embedded C Programs

Issue	Possible Cause	Solution
Code does not compile	Missing #include <xc.h>	Include the correct header files.
LED does not turn on	Incorrect TRIS configuration	Ensure TRISx is set correctly.
Microcontroller resets	Watchdog Timer enabled	Disable the Watchdog Timer (WDT).

Summary

- **Embedded C** provides direct control over hardware, making it essential for PIC microcontrollers.
- The key components of an Embedded C program include **header files**, **configuration bits**, **peripheral initialization**, and an **infinite loop**.
- **Timers** and **interrupts** allow for precise event handling and efficient resource management.
- **I/O ports** enable interaction with external devices like LEDs, buttons, and sensors.

This chapter covered the basics of Embedded C programming for PIC microcontrollers, providing a foundation for building embedded systems.

Chapter 14: Understanding Data Types and Variables

Data types and variables are fundamental concepts in programming. When writing code for PIC microcontrollers using Embedded C, understanding how to use data types efficiently is crucial for controlling hardware and optimizing memory usage. This chapter covers the types of data used in PIC microcontroller programming, how to define variables, and how to choose the appropriate data types for different applications.

Key Concepts of Data Types and Variables

In Embedded C programming, variables are used to store values that the microcontroller uses during program execution. These variables are defined with specific data types that determine the size and type of value they can hold. Understanding these data types is essential for efficient memory management and program execution.

Data Type	Size	Description	Example Use Case
char	8-bit	Stores a single character or small integer value (-128 to 127)	Storing user input, small counters
unsigned char	8-bit	Stores only positive values (0 to 255)	Storing positive values like sensor readings
int	16-bit	Stores integers (-32,768 to 32,767)	General-purpose integer variables
unsigned int	16-bit	Stores positive integers (0 to 65,535)	Counting operations, timers
float	32-bit	Stores floating-point numbers with decimal precision	Storing sensor measurements with decimals

Basic Rules for Using Data Types and Variables

Rule	Correct Example	Incorrect Example
Choose the correct data type based on the range of values you need to store.	`int count = 100;`	`char count = 10000;` (overflow)
Use unsigned data types when only positive values are needed.	`unsigned int value = 500;`	`int value = 500;` (incorrect for large positive values)
For floating-point values, use float.	`float temperatur e = 25.5;`	`int temperature = 25.5;` (loss of precision)
Always initialize variables before use.	`int x = 0;`	`int x;` (undefined behavior)

Syntax Table for Declaring Variables

SL	Function	Syntax/Example	Description
1	Declare an integer	`int variable_name = value;`	Declares an integer variable and initializes it.
2	Declare an unsigned integer	`unsigned int variable_name = value;`	Declares an unsigned integer variable.
3	Declare a floating-point variable	`float variable_name = value;`	Declares a floating-point variable.
4	Declare a character variable	`char variable_name = value;`	Declares a character variable.
5	Declare an unsigned character variable	`unsigned char variable_name = value;`	Declares an unsigned character variable.

Syntax Explanation

1. Declaring an Integer

What does declaring an integer do?
In Embedded C, integers are used to store whole numbers.
Declaring an integer initializes a memory space that can hold values
within a defined range. An integer can store values that are positive,
negative, or zero. In PIC microcontrollers, the size of an integer is
typically 16 bits, which allows for a range of -32,768 to 32,767.
Syntax:
```
int variable_name = value;
```

Example:
```
int counter = 100; // Declare an integer and initialize
it to 100
```

Explanation:
This code declares an integer variable counter and initializes it to
the value of 100. The variable counter can now store any integer
within the range of -32,768 to 32,767. Using int is appropriate when
you need to store numbers like loop counters, general-purpose
calculations, or negative values, such as when calculating
differences in sensor readings.
If you mistakenly use a char data type for a value like 10000 (which
exceeds the range of -128 to 127), you could cause an overflow or
unexpected behavior in the program.

2. Declaring an Unsigned Integer

What does declaring an unsigned integer do?
Unsigned integers are used when you only need to store positive
numbers. Since they don't need to account for negative values, they
can represent a larger range of positive values than a signed
integer. For example, an unsigned 16-bit integer can hold values
from 0 to 65,535, while a signed integer only holds values from -
32,768 to 32,767.
Syntax:
```
unsigned int variable_name = value;
```

Example:
```
unsigned int sensorData = 5000; // Declare an unsigned
integer for sensor data
```

Explanation:
Here, the variable `sensorData` is declared as an unsigned integer. It can hold only positive values, ranging from 0 to 65,535. This is ideal for cases where you are sure that the variable will never need to store negative numbers, such as counting sensor readings or representing data like time in milliseconds.
Using an unsigned integer is important when dealing with positive-only values, as using a signed integer for the same purpose could waste memory or cause unexpected behavior due to the inclusion of negative ranges.

3. Declaring a Floating-Point Variable

What does declaring a floating-point variable do?
Floating-point variables store numbers with decimal points. They are ideal for applications that require precision, such as when working with real-world measurements like temperature, humidity, or pressure. The `float` data type in Embedded C typically occupies 32 bits of memory, which allows for storage of numbers with decimal points and a large range of values.
Syntax:
```
float variable_name = value;
```

Example:
```
float temperature = 23.5; // Declare a floating-point
variable for temperature
```

Explanation:
This code declares a variable `temperature` as a `float` and initializes it with the value `23.5`. Floating-point numbers allow you to represent continuous values like 23.5°C or 98.6°F, which would be impossible with integers that can only store whole numbers. The `float` data type is crucial when high precision is needed, such as

for analog sensor readings (e.g., temperature sensors) where decimals are significant.
If you used an integer for `temperature = 23.5`, the fractional part (".5") would be lost, leading to imprecise readings and errors.

4. Declaring a Character Variable

What does declaring a character variable do?
Character variables are used to store a single character, such as a letter or symbol. The `char` data type stores values from -128 to 127, and each character is represented using its ASCII (American Standard Code for Information Interchange) value. For example, the character `'A'` has an ASCII value of 65, and `'B'` has a value of 66.

Syntax:
```
char variable_name = value;
```

Example:
```
char status = 'A'; // Declare a character variable for status
```

Explanation:
The variable `status` is a `char`, which can store a single character. In this case, it holds the character `'A'`. This is useful in cases where you need to store a small amount of data such as user input or status codes, like `'A'` for "active" or `'I'` for "inactive."
In embedded systems, `char` variables are often used to store data for communication protocols, such as sending ASCII characters over UART to communicate with other devices.

Working with I/O Ports and Variables

In PIC microcontroller programming, variables are often used to control I/O ports, which interface with external devices. For example, setting a variable to control the state of a pin on a port can turn an LED on or off.

Example:
```
TRISBbits.TRISB0 = 0;  // Set RB0 as output
LATBbits.LATB0 = 1;    // Turn LED ON on RB0
```

Explanation:

Here, `TRISBbits.TRISB0` configures the RB0 pin as an output. The `LATBbits.LATB0` line is used to control the logic level of the RB0 pin, turning the LED on by setting it high (1). Using variables like `TRISBbits` and `LATBbits` provides an easy way to manage pin configurations and control external devices like LEDs or motors.

Real-life Applications Project: Controlling a Motor with Variables

In this project, we'll use variables to control a motor's speed through PWM (Pulse Width Modulation) using a PIC microcontroller.

Required Components:

- PIC Microcontroller (e.g., PIC16F877A)
- Motor (DC or Stepper)
- PWM-capable pin (e.g., CCP1 pin)
- Power Supply

Circuit Connection Table:

Component	Pin Connection
Motor	PWM-capable pin (e.g., CCP1)
PIC Microcontroller	CCP1 Pin

Project Code

```
void main() {
    TRISCbits.TRISC2 = 0;   // Set CCP1 pin as output
    PR2 = 255;              // Set PWM frequency
    CCP1CON = 0x0C;         // Configure CCP1 in PWM
mode
    while(1) {
        CCPR1L = 128;       // Set duty cycle to 50%
(half speed)
        __delay_ms(1000);   // Delay for 1 second

        CCPR1L = 255;       // Set duty cycle to 100%
(full speed)
        __delay_ms(1000);   // Delay for 1 second
    }
}
```

Chapter 15: Control Structures in C

Control structures are the backbone of any program, allowing you to dictate the flow of execution based on conditions or repeating actions. For PIC microcontrollers, control structures in Embedded C help manage tasks such as sensor reading, decision making, and periodic tasks. This chapter will explore common control structures like loops, conditional statements, and more advanced constructs like switch-case and interrupt handling, specifically tailored for PIC microcontroller programming.

Key Concepts of Control Structures

Control structures in Embedded C help in directing the program's flow. These structures ensure that actions are performed in specific scenarios or repeatedly over time. They are essential for real-time tasks where the PIC microcontroller needs to respond dynamically to external inputs or time-dependent actions.

Control Structure	Description	Example Use Case
`if` and `else`	Conditional branching based on boolean expressions.	Deciding whether a sensor reading exceeds a threshold.
`while`	Repeats a block of code while a condition is true.	Continuous reading of sensor data.
`for`	Iterative loop with a defined number of iterations.	Performing a task a fixed number of times.
`switch`	Selects one of many code blocks to execute based on an expression.	Handling different user inputs or sensor states.
`interrupt`	Allows the program to respond to external or internal interrupts.	Responding to hardware interrupts from sensors.

Basic Rules for Using Control Structures

Rule	Correct Example	Incorrect Example
Use if and else to check conditions.	`if (temperature > 30) { // Turn on fan }`	`if (temperature > 30) { // Turn on fan } else if (temperature < 10) { // Turn on heater }` (Unnecessary else if for fan control)
Use while for indefinite loops.	`while (sensor_value < 100) { // Wait for sensor to reach 100 }`	`while (1) { // Infinite loop without condition }`
Use for loops for fixed iteration.	`for (int i = 0; i < 10; i++) { // Loop 10 times }`	`for (int i = 0; i < ; i++) { }` (Missing stop condition)
Break from loops when conditions are met.	`while (1) { if (button_pressed) break; }`	`while (true) { continue; }` (Unnecessary continue in infinite loop)

Syntax Table for Control Structures

SL	Function	Syntax/Example	Description
1	if Condition	`if (condition) { // Code block }`	Executes code block if the condition is true.
2	else	`else { // Code block }`	Executes code block if the if condition is false.
3	while Loop	`while (condition) { // Code block }`	Repeats the code block while the condition is true.

4	for Loop	`for (initialization; condition; increment) { // Code block }`	Executes code block a fixed number of times.
5	switch Case	`switch (expression) { case value: // Code break; default: // Code }`	Selects code block based on expression match.

Syntax Explanation

1. Using the `if` and `else` Statements

What does an `if` statement do?
The `if` statement allows you to execute a block of code only when a certain condition is true. It's a fundamental structure for decision-making. If the condition evaluates to true, the code inside the `if` block is executed. If not, the program skips the block. You can add an `else` block for situations where you want to run code if the condition is false.

Syntax:
```
if (condition) {
    // Code block to execute if condition is true
} else {
    // Code block to execute if condition is false
}
```

Example:
```
if (temperature > 30) {
    PORTBbits.RB0 = 1;   // Turn on cooling system
} else {
    PORTBbits.RB0 = 0;   // Turn off cooling system
}
```

Explanation:

In this example, the `if` statement checks if the variable `temperature` is greater than 30. If true, the cooling system (connected to pin RB0) is turned on by setting the pin high (1). If the temperature is not greater than 30, the `else` block executes, and the cooling system is turned off by setting the pin low (0).
This structure is useful for making real-time decisions based on sensor readings, like controlling devices depending on environmental conditions.

2. Using the `while` Loop

What does a `while` loop do?
The `while` loop repeats a block of code as long as a specific condition is true. It is ideal for situations where you want the code to keep executing until a certain condition changes, like waiting for a sensor to exceed a threshold.
Syntax:

```
while (condition) {
    // Code block to execute while the condition is
true
}
```

Example:

```
while (sensor_value < 100) {
    sensor_value = read_sensor();   // Continuously read
sensor value
}
```

Explanation:
This loop continuously reads the sensor value until it is greater than or equal to 100. The loop will only stop when the condition `sensor_value < 100` becomes false. This kind of loop is useful for monitoring real-time data until a desired state is reached.

3. Using the `for` Loop

What does a `for` loop do?
A `for` loop is used when you know in advance how many times you want to execute a block of code. It is ideal for situations like repeating a task a fixed number of times, such as cycling through an array or controlling a PWM signal for a specific duration.
Syntax:

```
for (initialization; condition; increment) {
    // Code block to execute
}
```

Example:

```
for (int i = 0; i < 10; i++) {
    PORTBbits.RB0 = 1;   // Toggle an LED 10 times
    __delay_ms(500);     // Wait for 500ms
    PORTBbits.RB0 = 0;   // Turn off LED
    __delay_ms(500);     // Wait for 500ms
}
```

Explanation:
The `for` loop in this example will toggle an LED connected to RB0 on and off 10 times. The loop initializes the variable i to 0, runs as long as i is less than 10, and increments i after each iteration. This type of loop is ideal for fixed iterations and is highly efficient for time-based control or iterative tasks.

4. Using the `switch` Statement

What does a `switch` statement do?
The `switch` statement is used to perform different actions based on different conditions. Unlike multiple `if-else` statements, a `switch` can be more efficient and cleaner when you need to check multiple conditions based on the value of a single variable or expression.

Syntax:
```
switch (expression) {
    case value1:
        // Code block to execute if expression equals
value1
        break;
    case value2:
        // Code block to execute if expression equals
value2
        break;
    default:
        // Code block to execute if expression doesn't
match any case
}
```

Example:
```
switch (user_input) {
    case 'A':
        PORTBbits.RB0 = 1;  // Turn on LED
        break;
    case 'B':
        PORTBbits.RB0 = 0;  // Turn off LED
        break;
    default:
        PORTBbits.RB1 = 1;  // Error indication
}
```

Explanation:
In this example, the switch statement checks the value of user_input. If it is 'A', the LED on RB0 is turned on. If it is 'B', the LED is turned off. If user_input is neither 'A' nor 'B', the default case is executed, turning on an error indicator on RB1. This structure is efficient when dealing with multiple possible cases.

Real-life Applications Project: LED Control Using Control Structures
In this project, we will use control structures to manage an LED based on different user inputs.

Required Components:
- PIC Microcontroller (e.g., PIC16F877A)
- LED
- Button (for user input)
- Power Supply

Circuit Connection Table:

Component	Pin Connection
Button	RB0
LED	RB1
PIC Microcontroller	RB0, RB1

Project Code:

```c
void main() {
    TRISBbits.TRISB0

= 1;  // Set RB0 as input for button
    TRISBbits.TRISB1 = 0;   // Set RB1 as output for LED

    while(1) {
        if (PORTBbits.RB0 == 1) {
            PORTBbits.RB1 = 1;   // Turn on LED
        } else {
            PORTBbits.RB1 = 0;   // Turn off LED
        }
    }
}
```

Expected Results: The LED will turn on when the button is pressed, and it will turn off when the button is released. The program continuously checks the button's state using an `if` statement and controls the LED accordingly.

Chapter 16: Functions and Macros in Embedded C

Functions and macros are two essential concepts in C programming that help structure code efficiently and make it more reusable. They allow developers to avoid redundancy, improve code readability, and manage complex logic in a more organized manner. This chapter focuses on the usage of functions and macros in Embedded C, specifically in the context of programming PIC microcontrollers. We'll cover defining functions, using macros, and best practices for both to optimize microcontroller applications.

Key Concepts of Functions and Macros

Functions and macros help manage repetitive tasks, making code more modular and efficient. Functions allow you to encapsulate a set of instructions under a single name, while macros provide a way to define reusable code snippets that are expanded during preprocessing.

Concept	Description	Example Use Case
Function	A block of code that can be executed when called, with optional parameters.	Performing sensor reading or controlling outputs.
Macro	A preprocessor directive that defines a code snippet to be substituted.	Defining constants, simple functions for optimization.
Function Return	Functions may return values, allowing for dynamic behavior in applications.	Returning calculated data from a function.
Function Arguments	Functions can take arguments to make them more flexible and reusable.	Passing sensor data to a function for processing.

Basic Rules for Using Functions and Macros

Rule	Correct Example	Incorrect Example
Use functions for complex tasks.	`int readTemperatu re() { // Return temp`	`int readTemperature() { // Hardcoded logic inside main }`

		data }
Avoid defining complex logic in macros.	`#define SQUARE(x) ((x)*(x))`	`#define SQUARE(x) { x = x*x; }` (Complex logic in macros)
Functions should have meaningful names.	`void turnOnLED() { PORTBbits.RB0 = 1; }`	`void f1() { PORTBbits.RB0 = 1; }`
Use macros for simple, frequently used expressions.	`#define MAX_TEMP 100`	`#define MAX_TEMP if(temp > 100) { // Logic }` (Macro with complex conditions)

Syntax Table for Functions and Macros

SL	Function/Macro	Syntax/Example	Description
1	Defining a Function	`return_type function_name(parameters) { // Code }`	Defines a function with specific parameters and a return type.
2	Calling a Function	`function_name(arguments);`	Calls a defined function with appropriate arguments.
3	Defining a Macro	`#define MACRO_NAME(parameters) code`	Defines a macro to replace code snippets in the program.
4	Calling a Macro	`MACRO_NAME(arguments);`	Invokes a macro to replace the code during preprocessing.
5	Function Return Value	`return value;`	Used within a function to return a value.

Syntax Explanation

1. Defining a Function

What does a function do?
A function in C allows you to define a block of code that can be
executed repeatedly with different inputs. Functions help break
down complex tasks into smaller, manageable pieces, improving
code clarity and reuse.

Syntax:
```c
return_type function_name(parameters) {
    // Code block
    return value;  // Return a value (optional)
}
```

Example:
```c
int readTemperature() {
    int temperature = ADC_Read();  // Read ADC value
    return temperature;            // Return
temperature
}
```

Explanation:
In this example, the `readTemperature()` function is defined to read
the temperature from an ADC (Analog-to-Digital Converter) and
return the value. The function is then reusable anywhere in the
program by calling `readTemperature()`, and it simplifies the main
code structure.

2. Calling a Function

What does calling a function do?
Calling a function executes the code within it. This allows you to use
the function's return values or have side effects, like modifying
hardware registers or performing calculations, every time the
function is invoked.

Syntax:
```c
function_name(arguments);
```

Example:
```
int temperature = readTemperature();   // Call the
function
```

Explanation:
In this example, readTemperature() is called, and its return value is stored in the temperature variable. Functions can be called multiple times with different arguments or in different parts of the program, improving modularity.

3. Defining a Macro

What does a macro do?
A macro is a code snippet defined using the #define preprocessor directive. The code inside the macro is inserted at the point where it is called, reducing the need for repetitive code. Macros are typically used for simple expressions like constants or small code replacements.
Syntax:
```
#define MACRO_NAME(parameters) code
```

Example:
```
#define SQUARE(x) ((x) * (x))   // Macro to calculate
square of a number
```

Explanation:
The SQUARE(x) macro takes an argument x and returns its square. This is done by replacing SQUARE(x) with ((x) * (x)) during preprocessing, making it more efficient than writing a function for such a simple operation.

4. Calling a Macro

What does calling a macro do?
When a macro is called, the preprocessor replaces it with the code that was defined for it. This happens before the code is compiled, making macros a powerful tool for optimizing frequently used expressions or constants.
Syntax:

```
MACRO_NAME(arguments);
```

Example:
```
int result = SQUARE(5);   // Calls the macro to
calculate the square of 5
```

Explanation:
When SQUARE(5) is called, the preprocessor replaces it with ((5) * (5)), which results in result = 25;. Macros are faster than functions because they avoid the overhead of function calls.

Real-life Applications Project: PWM Control Using Functions and Macros

In this project, we will create a function to control PWM (Pulse Width Modulation) for a motor and a macro to define PWM pin assignments. This will demonstrate the power of both functions and macros in managing complex tasks and optimizing code.

Required Components:
- PIC Microcontroller (e.g., PIC16F877A)
- Motor (DC)
- PWM Pin (e.g., RB1)
- Power Supply

Circuit Connection Table:

Component	Pin Connection
PWM Pin (e.g., RB1)	Output Pin for Motor
Motor	Connected to PWM Pin
PIC Microcontroller	RB1

Project Code:

```
// Macro to define PWM Pin
#define PWM_PIN RB1

// Function to start PWM on the motor
void startPWM(int dutyCycle) {
    // Set PWM frequency and duty cycle
    PWM1_LoadDutyValue(dutyCycle);   // Assuming PWM1
module is used
}
```

```
// Main function
void main() {
    TRISBbits.TRISB1 = 0;   // Set RB1 as output for PWM
signal

    while(1) {
        startPWM(128);   // Start PWM with 50% duty
cycle
        __delay_ms(1000);   // Wait for 1 second
        startPWM(255);   // Full duty cycle (100%)
        __delay_ms(1000);   // Wait for 1 second
    }
}
```

Explanation:
- The macro PWM_PIN is defined to make it easier to change the pin used for PWM. This can be modified in one place if needed, making the code more adaptable.
- The function startPWM(int dutyCycle) is used to encapsulate the logic for setting the PWM duty cycle. This makes the code modular and reusable.
- In the main() function, the PWM is controlled by calling startPWM() with different duty cycle values to control the motor's speed.

Expected Results:
The motor will switch between a 50% duty cycle (moderate speed) and a 100% duty cycle (full speed) every second. The use of functions and macros makes the code more organized and easy to modify if changes to the pin assignments or PWM behavior are required.

Chapter 17: Writing and Compiling Programs in MPLAB X

MPLAB X is a powerful Integrated Development Environment (IDE) designed for programming PIC microcontrollers. It allows for the development, debugging, and compilation of code, offering a smooth workflow for embedded systems development. This chapter will guide you through the steps to write, compile, and debug programs using MPLAB X for PIC microcontrollers.

Key Concepts of MPLAB X

MPLAB X IDE is widely used in embedded system development for its ease of use, flexibility, and comprehensive set of tools. Understanding its basic features is crucial for efficiently programming PIC microcontrollers.

Concept	Description	Example Use Case
Project Setup	Organizing the files and configuration settings to begin development.	Creating a new project for a temperature sensor.
Editor	Writing code in C or assembly language within the IDE.	Writing the main program loop for a microcontroller.
Compiler	Converting the written code into machine-readable instructions.	Compiling a program to be loaded onto the PIC.
Debugger	Testing the program, setting breakpoints, and checking for errors.	Stepping through code to find bugs in a motor control system.
Simulator	Simulating PIC microcontroller operations without hardware.	Testing the logic of the program before hardware deployment.

Basic Rules for Using MPLAB X

Rule	Correct Example	Incorrect Example
Start by creating a new project.	`File -> New Project -> Select PIC family`	Editing files directly without creating a project.

Write code in C or assembly.	`int main() { // Start writing code }`	Writing code without defining a main function.
Include necessary header files.	`#include <xc.h>`	Forgetting to include PIC-specific header files.
Use appropriate compiler and debugger.	`Select PIC16F877A compiler in project properties`	Using an unsupported PIC model in the project settings.

Syntax Table for Writing and Compiling Programs

SL	Step	Action/Syntax	Description
1	Create a New Project	`File -> New Project -> Choose PIC Microcontroller`	Start a new project and select the microcontroller.
2	Write Code	`#include <xc.h> int main() { // Code }`	Write your embedded C code inside the main function.
3	Configure Project Settings	`Right-click project -> Properties -> Select Compiler`	Choose the correct PIC model and compiler settings.
4	Compile the Code	`Click Build`	Converts your source code into machine code.
5	Debug the Program	`Click Debug`	Start debugging the program and set breakpoints if necessary.

Syntax Explanation

1. Creating a New Project

What does creating a new project do?
Creating a new project in MPLAB X allows you to organize your code, configure the correct microcontroller settings, and ensure that the necessary files are included. It sets up the environment for writing and compiling the program.

Syntax:
- Open MPLAB X.
- Go to `File -> New Project`.
- Select the type of project (e.g., Standalone Project) and the PIC microcontroller family you are working with.
- Choose a name and location for the project, and click `Finish`.

Example:
```
File -> New Project -> Standalone Project -> PIC16F877A
```

Explanation:
This step creates a new project in MPLAB X, targeting the PIC16F877A microcontroller. The IDE will set up all the necessary configurations for this microcontroller, such as the correct header files and settings for the selected compiler.

2. Writing Code

What does writing code do?
Writing code in MPLAB X IDE involves specifying the logic for your program. This code can be in C, and the MPLAB X editor helps with syntax highlighting, error checking, and code completion.

Syntax:
```c
#include <xc.h>  // Include necessary header file for PIC
int main() {
    TRISB = 0x00;  // Set PORTB as output
    while(1) {
        LATB = 0xFF;  // Set PORTB to high (turn on LEDs)
    }
}
```

Explanation:
Here, the program sets PORTB as an output and continuously writes a high value to PORTB. The #include <xc.h> includes the PIC-specific header file for configuring the microcontroller. The code is simple, but as you add more logic, MPLAB X will help ensure it is syntactically correct.

3. Configuring Project Settings

What does configuring project settings do?

Before compiling, it's important to ensure that the settings for the target PIC microcontroller and compiler are correct. Configuring these settings ensures that the compiler generates machine code that is compatible with the selected PIC model.

Syntax:

- Right-click on the project in the Project Explorer.
- Select Properties.
- Under Project Properties, choose the correct PIC model and set the appropriate options for the compiler.

Example:

```
Project -> Properties -> PIC16F877A -> XC8 Compiler
```

Explanation:

In this step, you specify the PIC16F877A microcontroller and select the XC8 compiler, ensuring that MPLAB X knows which compiler to use for compiling your code. This ensures that the code is optimized for the selected microcontroller.

4. Compiling the Code

What does compiling the code do?

Compiling transforms your written code into machine code that the PIC microcontroller can execute. The compiler checks the syntax, converts the code into an executable file, and reports any errors or warnings.

Syntax:

- Click the Build button in MPLAB X.

Example:

```
Click the Build icon (hammer icon)
```

Explanation:

After you've written the code and set the project properties, clicking Build compiles your program. If there are any errors in your code (e.g., syntax errors), they will be displayed in the output window, and you can fix them before proceeding to the next step.

5. Debugging the Program

What does debugging the program do?
Debugging allows you to test your code in real-time, set breakpoints, and step through the program line by line. It helps identify bugs, watch variables, and observe program flow, making it a vital step in development.

Syntax:
- Click the Debug button to start debugging the program.

Example:
```
Click the Debug icon (bug icon)
```

Explanation:
When you click the Debug button, MPLAB X connects to the debugger and loads the program onto the target hardware. You can set breakpoints and use step-by-step execution to analyze how your code behaves. If a bug is encountered, you can modify the code and recompile to fix it.

Real-life Application Project: LED Blinking with PIC Microcontroller
In this project, we will create a simple program that blinks an LED connected to PORTB of a PIC16F877A microcontroller. We will write the code in MPLAB X, compile it, and debug the program.

Required Components:
- PIC16F877A Microcontroller
- LED
- Resistor (for LED current-limiting)
- Breadboard and Jumper wires
- MPLAB X IDE and PICkit programmer

Circuit Connection Table:

Component	Pin Connection
LED	Connected to PORTB, Pin 0
Resistor	220 ohms between LED and ground
PIC Microcontroller	PORTB Pin 0 connected to LED

Project Code:

```c
#include <xc.h> // Include the necessary PIC header
file

#define _XTAL_FREQ 4000000  // Define the oscillator
frequency (4 MHz)

void main() {
    TRISB = 0x00;    // Set PORTB as output
    while(1) {
        LATB = 0x01;  // Set PORTB Pin 0 high (turn on
LED)
        __delay_ms(500); // Wait for 500ms
        LATB = 0x00;  // Set PORTB Pin 0 low (turn off
LED)
        __delay_ms(500); // Wait for 500ms
    }
}
```

Explanation:

- The TRISB = 0x00; statement sets PORTB as output.
- The LATB = 0x01; statement turns on the LED connected to PORTB Pin 0.
- The __delay_ms(500); introduces a 500ms delay between turning the LED on and off, making it blink.
- The process repeats indefinitely in the while(1) loop.

Expected Results:

Once you compile and debug the program, the LED will blink every 500 milliseconds. This simple project demonstrates how to write and compile a program using MPLAB X, and test it on actual hardware.

Chapter 18: A to Z PWM for PIC Microcontrollers

Pulse Width Modulation (PWM) is a powerful technique used to control the power delivered to electrical devices, such as motors, LEDs, and heating elements. In the context of PIC microcontrollers, PWM is commonly used to control the brightness of LEDs, the speed of motors, and other applications that require variable control over a digital output signal. In this chapter, we will explore PWM in detail, how it works, and how to use it with PIC microcontrollers.

Key Concepts of PWM

PWM involves modulating the width of a digital pulse to control the power delivered to a load. The basic idea is that by adjusting the duty cycle of the signal (the proportion of time the signal is high versus low), we can control the effective power delivered to a device.

Concept	Description	Example Use Case
Duty Cycle	The percentage of time the PWM signal is high (ON).	Adjusting the brightness of an LED.
Frequency	The number of times the PWM signal oscillates per second.	Controlling the speed of a DC motor.
Resolution	The precision of PWM control (i.e., how finely the duty cycle can be adjusted).	Fine control of an LED's brightness.
Carrier Frequency	The base frequency at which PWM operates.	Controlling a motor's speed without audible noise.

Basic Rules for Using PWM with PIC Microcontrollers

Rule	Correct Example	Incorrect Example
Set the correct PWM frequency.	T2CON = 0x05; (Set Timer2 for PWM)	Forgetting to set the correct frequency for PWM control.
Use the appropriate PWM pins.	PWM1CON = 0xC0; (Configure PWM on a specific pin)	Using pins that do not support PWM functionality.
Ensure proper	TMR2 = 0; (Set up the	Not configuring the timer

configuration of Timer.	timer for PWM output)	correctly for PWM.
Adjust the duty cycle with registers.	CCPR1L = dutyCycle; (Set duty cycle for PWM)	Using an incorrect register for controlling the duty cycle.

Syntax Table for PWM Control

SL	Function	Syntax/Example	Description
1	Set Timer2 for PWM	`T2CON = 0x05;`	Configure Timer2 to operate in PWM mode.
2	Set the PWM Duty Cycle	`CCPR1L = dutyCycle;`	Set the PWM duty cycle by loading the value into CCPR1L.
3	Set PWM Frequency	`PR2 = 255;`	Configure the PWM period using the PR2 register.
4	Enable PWM Output	`T2CONbits.TMR2ON = 1;`	Start Timer2 for PWM operation.
5	Turn Off PWM	`T2CONbits.TMR2ON = 0;`	Stop Timer2 and turn off the PWM output.

Syntax Explanation

1. Set Timer2 for PWM

What does setting Timer2 for PWM do?
Timer2 is often used to generate PWM signals in PIC microcontrollers. By setting the correct configuration for Timer2, the microcontroller can generate a PWM signal with the desired frequency.

Syntax:
```
T2CON = 0x05;
```
Example:
```
T2CON = 0x05; // Configure Timer2 for PWM with prescaler
```

Explanation:
In this example, `T2CON = 0x05;` sets the control register for Timer2. The `0x05` value sets the prescaler and enables the timer. The frequency of the PWM signal is derived from this configuration.

2. Set the PWM Duty Cycle

What does setting the PWM duty cycle do?
The duty cycle controls how long the PWM signal stays "on" during each cycle. By adjusting the duty cycle, you can control how much power is delivered to the connected load.
Syntax:
```
CCPR1L = dutyCycle;
```

Example:
```
CCPR1L = 128; // Set duty cycle to 50% (out of 255)
```

Explanation:
The `CCPR1L` register stores the duty cycle value for the PWM signal. In this case, setting the duty cycle to 128 will result in a 50% duty cycle if the PWM period is set to 255.

3. Set PWM Frequency

What does setting the PWM frequency do?
The frequency of the PWM signal determines how quickly it switches on and off. A higher frequency results in smoother control for most applications, such as motor speed control.
Syntax:
```
PR2 = 255;
```

Example:
```
PR2 = 255; // Set PWM period to the maximum value (255)
```
Explanation:
The `PR2` register defines the period of the PWM signal. By setting it to 255, the PWM signal will have the highest possible frequency within the timer's range.

4. Enable PWM Output

What does enabling the PWM output do?
After configuring the timer and the duty cycle, you need to enable
the timer to generate the PWM output. This step starts the PWM
signal generation.
Syntax:
```
T2CONbits.TMR2ON = 1;
```

Example:
```
T2CONbits.TMR2ON = 1; // Enable PWM by starting Timer2
```

Explanation:
This line of code sets the TMR2ON bit in the T2CON register to 1,
which starts the timer and activates PWM generation.

5. Turn Off PWM

What does turning off the PWM output do?
If you want to stop generating the PWM signal, you can disable
Timer2. This effectively turns off the PWM output.
Syntax:
```
T2CONbits.TMR2ON = 0;
```

Example:
```
T2CONbits.TMR2ON = 0; // Stop PWM by disabling Timer2
```

Explanation:
Setting TMR2ON = 0 will stop the timer and turn off the PWM signal.
This is useful when you want to halt the PWM control or switch to
another mode of operation.
**Real-life Application Project: LED Brightness Control Using
PWM**
In this project, we will use PWM to control the brightness of an LED
connected to a PIC microcontroller. By varying the duty cycle, we
can change the LED's brightness from fully off to fully on.
Required Components:
- PIC16F877A Microcontroller

- LED
- Resistor (for current limiting)
- Breadboard and jumper wires
- MPLAB X IDE and PICkit programmer

Circuit Connection Table:

Component	Pin Connection
LED	Connected to PORTC, Pin 0
Resistor	220 ohms between LED and ground
PIC Microcontroller	PORTC Pin 0 connected to LED

Project Code:

```c
#include <xc.h> // Include the necessary PIC header file
#define _XTAL_FREQ 4000000  // Define the oscillator frequency (4 MHz)
void main() {
    TRISC = 0x00;    // Set PORTC as output
    T2CON = 0x05;    // Configure Timer2 for PWM operation
    PR2 = 255;       // Set the PWM period
    CCP1CON = 0x0C;  // Set CCP1 module to PWM mode
    T2CONbits.TMR2ON = 1; // Start Timer2 for PWM generation
    while(1) {
        CCPR1L = 128;   // Set duty cycle to 50% (LED brightness)
        __delay_ms(1000); // Wait for 1 second

        CCPR1L = 255;   // Set duty cycle to 100% (LED full brightness)
        __delay_ms(1000); // Wait for 1 second
        CCPR1L = 0;     // Set duty cycle to 0% (LED off)
        __delay_ms(1000); // Wait for 1 second
    }
}
```

Explanation:

- The `TRISC = 0x00;` line sets PORTC as an output port.
- The `T2CON = 0x05;` configures Timer2 for PWM operation.
- The `CCP1CON = 0x0C;` sets the CCP1 module to PWM mode.
- The `CCPR1L = 128;` sets the duty cycle to 50%, which will make the LED glow with medium brightness.
- The `__delay_ms(1000);` introduces a delay of 1 second between brightness changes.

Expected Results:

The LED will blink with varying brightness levels: first at 50%, then at 100%, and finally off. This will repeat in a loop, demonstrating how PWM can be used

for controlling brightness.

Conclusion:

In this chapter, we covered the basics of PWM and its usage with PIC microcontrollers. We explored the fundamental concepts, syntax, and practical examples to help you get started with PWM in your own projects.

Chapter 19: Memory Management in PIC Microcontrollers

Memory management is a crucial aspect of embedded systems development. In PIC microcontrollers, memory management involves understanding how different types of memory (such as program memory, data memory, and special function registers) are utilized for efficient operation. Efficient use of memory ensures that programs run smoothly within the constraints of the microcontroller, leading to better performance and reliability.

This chapter will dive into the different memory types in PIC microcontrollers, their functions, and how to manage them effectively.

Key Concepts of Memory in PIC Microcontrollers

PIC microcontrollers typically have several types of memory, each serving a distinct purpose. Proper memory management involves understanding the size, location, and usage of each type.

Concept	Description	Example Use Case
Program Memory (Flash)	Stores the firmware (code) of the microcontroller. It is non-volatile.	Holding the main application code for a temperature sensor.
Data Memory (RAM)	Temporary memory for data storage during execution. It is volatile.	Storing variables used during real-time operations.
EEPROM Memory	Non-volatile memory for storing small amounts of data, such as settings.	Storing configuration parameters that persist after reset.
Special Function Registers (SFRs)	Control the operation of the microcontroller (e.g., port directions, timers).	Configuring I/O ports and controlling timers.
Stack Memory	Stores return addresses during function calls and interrupt handling.	Managing function calls and interrupt return addresses.

Basic Rules for Managing Memory in PIC Microcontrollers

Rule	Correct Example	Incorrect Example
Optimize program memory usage.	Use efficient algorithms to reduce program size.	Using inefficient code that occupies large amounts of flash.
Use RAM efficiently.	Use variables only when needed, and free memory when done.	Allocating unnecessary memory that wastes available RAM.
Store persistent data in EEPROM.	Save configuration settings in EEPROM for persistence.	Storing frequently updated data in EEPROM (which is slower).
Take care when using SFRs.	Set SFR bits in the appropriate registers.	Modifying SFRs without understanding their functions.
Use the stack for function calls.	Let the microcontroller automatically manage the stack.	Overwriting the stack, causing function return errors.

Memory Organization in PIC Microcontrollers

In PIC microcontrollers, memory is divided into various segments. Each segment has a specific function and access method:

Memory Type	Size	Purpose	Access Method
Program Memory	Typically 2K to 32K bytes	Stores the executable code. It is non-volatile and read-only.	Flash memory, accessed via program counter.
Data Memory (RAM)	256 bytes to 4K bytes	Stores data during runtime. Volatile memory that clears on reset.	Direct memory access (DMA) or variable storage.
EEPROM	Typically 64 to 512 bytes	Stores small amounts of non-volatile data (e.g., settings).	Byte-level access through memory-mapped registers.

SFRs	Fixed size (e.g., 256 bytes)	Special function registers control specific hardware features.	Direct access by CPU.
Stack	Fixed size (varies)	Stores return addresses for function calls and interrupts.	Managed by the hardware stack pointer.

Types of Memory in Detail

1. Program Memory (Flash Memory)

Program memory in PIC microcontrollers stores the firmware, which is the core set of instructions that the microcontroller executes. This memory is non-volatile, meaning it retains data even when power is lost. Flash memory is read-only during normal operation, though it can be reprogrammed when needed.

Key Considerations:

- Program memory is limited in size, and large applications may require optimization of code.
- PIC microcontrollers support techniques like compression to save space.

2. Data Memory (RAM)

Data memory, also called RAM (Random Access Memory), is used for temporary storage during the execution of a program. It is volatile, which means all data stored in RAM is lost when the power is turned off or the device is reset.

Key Considerations:

- Use as little RAM as possible to leave space for variables, buffers, and the stack.
- Variables that do not need to persist beyond power cycles should be stored in RAM.

3. EEPROM (Electrically Erasable Programmable Read-Only Memory)

EEPROM is non-volatile memory that can store small amounts of data, even when power is turned off. It is commonly used for storing settings, configuration parameters, or user data that need to persist after a reset.

Key Considerations:
- EEPROM has a limited number of write cycles (usually around 1 million), so it should not be used for frequently updated data.
- Use EEPROM for persistent storage of settings and calibration data.

4. Special Function Registers (SFRs)

SFRs control the operation of the microcontroller, such as enabling or disabling peripherals, controlling timers, and configuring I/O pins. These registers are usually mapped to specific memory addresses and provide a way to control hardware features directly.

Key Considerations:
- Modifying SFRs directly impacts the functionality of the microcontroller.
- Incorrect modification of SFRs can lead to undesired behavior or malfunction of peripherals.

5. Stack Memory

The stack is used to store return addresses during function calls and interrupt handling. The microcontroller automatically manages the stack during normal operation. Overwriting the stack (e.g., by using too much RAM for local variables) can lead to stack overflows or incorrect program execution.

Key Considerations:
- Stack memory is limited, and recursive function calls may exhaust stack space if not carefully managed.
- Ensure that the stack is not overflowed, especially in deep function call chains.

Managing Memory in PIC Microcontrollers

1. Optimizing Program Memory

In embedded systems, efficient use of program memory is crucial. This can be achieved by:
- Using efficient algorithms and data structures.
- Compressing data when possible.
- Minimizing the number of instructions and using shorter instruction sets.

Example:

```
// Efficient code for controlling an LED
LATAbits.LATA0 = 1;   // Turn on LED connected to Port
```

```
A pin 0
__delay_ms(500);        // Wait for 500ms
LATAbits.LATA0 = 0;     // Turn off LED
```

This code uses minimal instructions to achieve the goal, which saves space in program memory.

2. Efficient Use of Data Memory

Proper management of data memory (RAM) involves:

- Storing temporary data in RAM.
- Avoiding the use of large arrays or buffers unless necessary.
- Using memory optimization techniques like variable sharing or dynamic memory allocation (if supported).

3. Using EEPROM Efficiently

EEPROM should be used sparingly because it has a limited number of write cycles. Write to EEPROM only when necessary (e.g., when settings change or user input is saved).

4. Special Function Register Management

Special Function Registers (SFRs) should be configured at the start of a program. Once configured, avoid unnecessary changes to these registers during runtime, as this could result in unexpected behavior.

5. Stack Memory and Function Calls

The stack is automatically managed by the PIC microcontroller, but it is important to be aware of its limits:

- Avoid deep recursion, which can overflow the stack.
- Be cautious about using large local variables within functions.

Real-life Application Project: Temperature Sensor with EEPROM Storage

In this project, we will create a temperature sensor system using a PIC microcontroller. The system will read the temperature from a sensor, display it on an LCD, and store the current temperature in EEPROM for later retrieval.

Required Components:

- PIC16F877A Microcontroller
- Temperature Sensor (e.g., LM35)
- LCD Display
- EEPROM memory
- MPLAB X IDE and PICkit programmer

Circuit Connection Table:

Component	Pin Connection
Temperature Sensor	Analog input to PORTA, Pin 0
LCD Display	Connected to PORTB
EEPROM	Connected to I2C pins (if external)

Project Code:

```c
#include <xc.h> // Include the necessary PIC header
file
#include <stdio.h>
#include "lcd.h"  // Assume LCD functions are
implemented

#define _XTAL_FREQ 4000000  // Define the oscillator
frequency (4 MHz)

void main() {
    TRISAbits.TRISA0 = 1;   // Set PORTA pin 0 as input
for the temperature sensor
    TRISB = 0x00;           // Set PORTB as output for
LCD
    LCD_Init();             // Initialize the LCD

    while(1) {
        int temperature = Read_ADC(0);   // Read
temperature from sensor
        char tempStr[10];
        sprintf(tempStr, "Temp: %dC", temperature); //
Convert to string

        LCD_Clear();   // Clear LCD display
        LCD_Print(tempStr); // Display temperature

        // Store temperature in EEPROM if changed
        if (temperature != EEPROM_Read(0x00)) {
            EEPROM_Write(
```

0x00, temperature); }

```
    __delay_ms(1000); // Delay for 1 second
}
```

```
}
```

// Function to read ADC value from a given channel int Read_ADC(int channel) { ADCON0 = (channel << 2); // Set the channel ADCON0bits.GO = 1; // Start the conversion while (ADCON0bits.GO); // Wait until conversion is complete return (ADRES); // Return the ADC result }

Expected Results:

- The temperature sensor will read the temperature, and it will display the value on the LCD.
- The temperature value will be stored in EEPROM and updated when a change is detected.

Chapter 20: Configuring GPIO Pins

General Purpose Input/Output (GPIO) pins are essential components of any microcontroller, including PIC microcontrollers. These pins can be used to either read inputs from external devices (like sensors) or send output signals to devices such as LEDs or motors. In this chapter, we will explore how to configure GPIO pins on a PIC microcontroller, allowing you to interface with various peripherals.

Key Concepts of GPIO Pins

GPIO pins are versatile pins on the microcontroller that can serve multiple purposes, such as digital input or output, analog input, or other specialized functions (e.g., PWM, I2C, SPI). Properly configuring GPIO pins is crucial for ensuring correct behavior in embedded systems.

Concept	Description	Example Use Case
Input Pin	Used to read signals from external devices.	Reading a button press.
Output Pin	Used to send signals to external devices.	Controlling an LED.
Pull-up/Pull-down	Used to set a default state for input pins.	Ensuring a button input reads a stable value.
Analog Pin	Used to read analog signals, converting them to digital values.	Reading a temperature sensor.
Digital Pin	Used to read or send digital signals (high/low).	Turning on/off an LED.

Basic Rules for Configuring GPIO Pins

Rule	Correct Example	Incorrect Example
Configure the direction of the pin (input or output).	TRISB = 0x00; (set PORTB as output)	Not setting the direction register for input/output.
Use the correct register for input/output operations.	LATB = 0x01; (output to PORTB)	Using the wrong register to control the pin state.

Configure internal pull-ups for inputs.	WPUB = 0x01; (enable pull-up on PORTB Pin 0)	Forgetting to enable pull-ups for input pins.
Set the appropriate ADC configuration for analog pins.	ADCON1 = 0x06; (set all pins to digital)	Using analog pins without proper configuration.

Syntax Table for Configuring GPIO Pins

S.L	Function	Syntax/Example	Description
1	Set Pin Direction	TRISB = 0x00;	Configure PORTB as output (TRISB is the direction register).
2	Set Pin High (Output)	LATB = 0x01;	Set the output state of PORTB Pin 0 to high.
3	Set Pin Low (Output)	LATB = 0x00;	Set the output state of PORTB Pin 0 to low.
4	Read Pin Value (Input)	if (PORTBbits.RB0 == 1)	Check the input value of PORTB Pin 0.
5	Enable Pull-up Resistor	WPUB = 0x01;	Enable internal pull-up resistor on PORTB Pin 0.
6	Set Pin to Analog Mode (ADC)	ADCON1 = 0x06;	Configure all pins as digital.

Syntax Explanation

1. Set Pin Direction

What does setting the pin direction do?

The TRIS (Tri-state) register is used to define whether a GPIO pin is set as an input or output. A value of 0 makes the pin an output, while 1 makes it an input. Setting the direction of the pin ensures that the microcontroller knows how to interact with that pin.

Syntax:

```
TRISB = 0x00;  // Set PORTB as output
```

Example:
```
TRISB = 0x00;   // Set all pins of PORTB to output
```

Explanation:
This command sets all the pins of PORTB as output pins. If you want to configure specific pins, you can modify individual bits within the TRIS register (e.g., `TRISBbits.TRISB0 = 0`; to set Pin 0 of PORTB as an output).

2. Set Pin High (Output)

What does setting the pin high do?

When you want to output a high signal (logic 1) to a pin, you write a 1 to the corresponding bit in the LAT (latch) register. This turns on the voltage at that pin (usually 5V or 3.3V, depending on the microcontroller).

Syntax:
```
LATB = 0x01;   // Set PORTB Pin 0 high
```

Example:
```
LATBbits.LATB0 = 1;   // Set PORTB Pin 0 high
```

Explanation:
The LATB register holds the output values for PORTB. Setting the bit corresponding to Pin 0 (i.e., `LATBbits.LATB0`) to 1 will turn that pin high.

3. Set Pin Low (Output)

What does setting the pin low do?
When you want to output a low signal (logic 0) to a pin, you write a 0 to the corresponding bit in the LAT register. This turns off the voltage at that pin (usually 0V or ground).

Syntax:
```
LATB = 0x00;   // Set PORTB Pin 0 low
```

Example:
```
LATBbits.LATB0 = 0;   // Set PORTB Pin 0 low
```

Explanation:
By writing 0 to the corresponding bit in LATB, you set the pin to low, effectively turning off any output on that pin.

4. Read Pin Value (Input)

What does reading the pin value do?
To read the state of a GPIO pin configured as an input, you access the PORT register. This will give you the current value of the pin (either 0 or 1).
Syntax:

```
if (PORTBbits.RB0 == 1) {  // Check if Pin 0 of PORTB
is high
    // Do something
}
```

Example:

```
if (PORTBbits.RB0 == 0) {  // Check if Pin 0 is low
    LATBbits.LATB0 = 1;     // Set Pin 0 high
}
```

Explanation:
The PORTB register gives the input state of PORTB. Here, we check if the state of Pin 0 is high or low. If the pin is low, the program sets it high.

5. Enable Pull-up Resistor

What does enabling the pull-up resistor do?
Internal pull-up resistors are often used in input configurations to ensure that the input pin is in a defined state (either high or low) when no external signal is present. Enabling the pull-up keeps the input pin high by default.
Syntax:

```
WPUB = 0x01;  // Enable pull-up on PORTB Pin 0
```

Example:

```
WPUBbits.WPUB0 = 1;  // Enable pull-up on PORTB Pin 0
```

Explanation:
By writing 1 to the corresponding bit in the WPUB register, we enable the pull-up resistor for Pin 0 on PORTB. This ensures that the pin reads high when not actively driven low.

6. Set Pin to Analog Mode (ADC)

What does setting a pin to analog mode do?
To configure a pin as an analog input, you need to modify the ADCON1 register (or the equivalent register, depending on the PIC model). This is necessary when reading sensors that output analog signals.

Syntax:
```
ADCON1 = 0x06;  // Set all pins to digital mode
```

Example:
```
ADCON1 = 0x00;  // Set all pins to analog mode
```

Explanation:
This configures all the pins as either analog or digital, depending on the value in the ADCON1 register. Setting it to 0x06 configures all pins as digital, while setting it to 0x00 configures the pins for analog input.

Real-life Application Project: Reading a Button Press
In this project, we will use a GPIO pin to read the state of a button and turn on an LED when the button is pressed.

Required Components:
- PIC16F877A Microcontroller
- Button
- LED
- Resistor (for LED and button)
- Breadboard and Jumper wires

Circuit Connection Table:

Component	Pin Connection
Button	Connected to PORTB Pin 0 (input)
LED	Connected to PORTB Pin 1 (output)

Steps:

1. Configure PORTB Pin 0 as input to read the button state.
2. Configure PORTB Pin 1 as output to control the LED.
3. Enable pull-up resistor on Pin 0 to ensure stable high when the button is not pressed.
4. In the main program loop, check the state of the button.
5. If the button is pressed (Pin 0 reads low), set Pin 1 high to turn on the LED.

Code Example:

```
void main() {
    TRISB = 0x01;   // Set PORTB Pin 0 as input and Pin
1 as output
    WPUB = 0x01;    // Enable pull-up on Pin 0

    while (1) {
        if (PORTBbits.RB0 == 0) {  // Button pressed
            LATBbits.LATB1 = 1;      // Turn on LED
        } else {
            LATBbits.LATB1 = 0;       // Turn off LED
        }
    }
}
```

Expected Results:

When the button is pressed, the LED connected to Pin 1 will turn on. When the button is released, the LED will turn off. This simple application demonstrates how to configure GPIO pins for input and output.

Real-life Applications of GPIO Pins

- **Home Automation:** Control lights, fans, and other devices using GPIO pins.
- **Security Systems:** Interface with sensors, like motion detectors, to trigger alarms.
- **Robotics:** Control motors and sensors using GPIO pins for robot navigation.
- **Embedded Systems:** Used for communication between different parts of a system, such as buttons and displays.

Chapter 21: Using Internal and External Pull-up Resistors

In embedded systems, particularly in microcontrollers like the PIC series, it is common to use pull-up or pull-down resistors to ensure stable and predictable input behavior. These resistors are essential for defining the state of a digital input pin when no active signal is driving it. This chapter explores the use of both internal and external pull-up resistors to improve input signal reliability and stability.

Key Concepts of Pull-up Resistors

A **pull-up resistor** connects a digital input pin to a high voltage level (typically Vcc), ensuring the pin reads a "high" state (logic 1) when the external signal is disconnected or not actively driven. The alternative is a **pull-down resistor**, which connects the pin to ground, ensuring a "low" state (logic 0) in the absence of an active signal.

Concept	Description	Example Use Case
Internal Pull-up	Resistor integrated into the microcontroller for convenience.	Used in simple circuits to avoid external components.
External Pull-up	An external resistor added to the input pin for stability.	Used when the internal pull-up is insufficient or not available.
Pull-down Resistor	Ensures the input pin is held low by connecting it to ground.	Used for logic level stabilization when no active signal is provided.

Basic Rules for Using Pull-up Resistors

Rule	Correct Example	Incorrect Example
Use internal pull-ups when available and appropriate.	WPUB = 0x01; (enable pull-up on PORTB Pin 0)	Not enabling pull-ups on input pins.
Ensure proper resistor value for external pull-ups.	Use a 10kΩ resistor for pull-up (typical value)	Using too low or too high a resistor value.

Configure pin direction to input before using pull-ups.	`TRISBbits.TRISB0 = 1;` (set Pin 0 as input)	Forgetting to set the pin as input before enabling pull-ups.
Use pull-down resistors in noisy environments to ensure stable low states.	Connect a 10kΩ resistor between the pin and ground.	Not using pull-down in noisy circuits.

Syntax Table for Using Pull-up Resistors

SL	Function	Syntax/Example	Description
1	Enable Internal Pull-up (on Input Pin)	`WPUBbits.WPUB0 = 1;`	Enable internal pull-up resistor for Pin 0 on PORTB.
2	Set Pin Direction as Input	`TRISBbits.TRISB0 = 1;`	Set PORTB Pin 0 as input to use pull-up resistor.
3	Enable Internal Pull-up for Multiple Pins	`WPUB = 0xFF;`	Enable pull-ups for all pins in PORTB.
4	External Pull-up Setup	Connect a 10kΩ resistor between pin and Vcc.	Physical connection, no direct syntax.
5	Disable Internal Pull-up	`WPUBbits.WPUB0 = 0;`	Disable the pull-up resistor on Pin 0 of PORTB.
6	Read Pin with Pull-up Resistor	`if (PORTBbits.RB0 == 1)`	Read the state of Pin 0 to check if the pull-up is active.

Syntax Explanation
1. Enable Internal Pull-up (on Input Pin)
What does enabling the internal pull-up do?
The PIC microcontroller allows you to enable internal pull-up resistors on input pins to ensure a stable logic level when the pin is not actively driven by an external signal. By configuring the corresponding **WPUB** register, you can enable the pull-up resistor for a specific pin.

Syntax:
```
WPUBbits.WPUB0 = 1;   // Enable internal pull-up on
PORTB Pin 0
```

Example:
```
WPUBbits.WPUB0 = 1;   // Enable the internal pull-up
resistor for PORTB Pin 0
```

Explanation:
This command enables the internal pull-up resistor for Pin 0 of
PORTB. It ensures that if no external signal is driving the pin, it will
default to a high state (logic 1).

2. Set Pin Direction as Input

What does setting the pin direction do?
Before enabling a pull-up resistor, the pin must be set to input mode.
This is done by configuring the corresponding **TRIS** (Tri-state)
register. If the pin is not set as an input, the pull-up resistor will have
no effect.

Syntax:
```
TRISBbits.TRISB0 = 1;   // Set PORTB Pin 0 as input
```

Example:
```
TRISBbits.TRISB0 = 1;   // Configure Pin 0 of PORTB as
input
```

Explanation:
By setting the TRIS register bit for Pin 0 to 1, we configure the pin as
an input. This is necessary for using the pull-up resistor, as it
ensures the microcontroller will read the pin state.

3. Enable Internal Pull-up for Multiple Pins

What if you want to enable pull-ups for multiple pins?
If you want to enable the pull-up resistors on multiple pins at once,
you can write a value to the **WPUB** register where each bit
represents a pin. Setting a bit to 1 enables the pull-up for that pin.

Syntax:
```
WPUB = 0xFF;  // Enable pull-ups for all PORTB pins
```

Example:
```
WPUB = 0xFF;  // Enable internal pull-up resistors for
all pins on PORTB
```

Explanation:
This command enables the internal pull-up resistors for all pins of PORTB (PORTB Pin 0 to Pin 7). It's a convenient way to enable pull-ups for multiple input pins at once.

4. External Pull-up Setup

What is an external pull-up resistor?
An external pull-up resistor is a resistor physically connected between the input pin and the positive voltage supply (Vcc). This is typically used when the internal pull-up resistors are not sufficient, or when the microcontroller does not have internal pull-up capability for a specific pin.

How to Set Up:
- Connect a 10kΩ resistor between the input pin and Vcc (positive voltage supply).
- Ensure the input pin is configured as an input.

Example:
```
// Physical setup: Connect 10kΩ resistor between the
input pin and Vcc.
TRISBbits.TRISB0 = 1;  // Set the input pin direction
for PORTB Pin 0
```

Explanation:
You must physically add an external pull-up resistor between the pin and Vcc. The microcontroller does not require additional code to enable an external pull-up, but you must configure the pin as an input to properly read its value.

5. Disable Internal Pull-up

What does disabling the pull-up do?
If you no longer need the internal pull-up resistor, you can disable it by clearing the corresponding bit in the **WPUB** register. This can be useful if the pin will be used in a different configuration or when you no longer need to maintain the high state.
Syntax:
```
WPUBbits.WPUB0 = 0;  // Disable internal pull-up on
PORTB Pin 0
```

Example:
```
WPUBbits.WPUB0 = 0;  // Disable pull-up on PORTB Pin 0
```

Explanation:
This command disables the internal pull-up resistor for Pin 0 of PORTB, so the pin will no longer default to a high state when it is not driven by an external signal.

6. Read Pin with Pull-up Resistor

What does reading the pin value do?
After enabling a pull-up resistor, you can read the value of the pin using the **PORT** register. The pull-up ensures that the pin will read as high when it is not actively driven low.
Syntax:
```
if (PORTBbits.RB0 == 1) {
    // Do something if Pin 0 is high
}
```
Example:
```
if (PORTBbits.RB0 == 0) {
    LATBbits.LATB1 = 1;  // Turn on LED if Pin 0 is low
}
```
Explanation:
This code checks if Pin 0 of PORTB reads low, which would indicate that the button connected to it has been pressed. The internal pull-up resistor ensures that the pin reads high when the button is not pressed.

Real-life Application Project: Button Press with Pull-up Resistor
In this project, we use a pull-up resistor to read a button press, turning on an LED when the button is pressed. The internal pull-up resistor is used for simplicity.

Required Components:
- PIC16F877A Microcontroller
- Pushbutton
- LED
- Resistors
- Breadboard and Jumper wires

Circuit Connection Table:

Component	Connection
Pushbutton	Between PORTB Pin 0 and ground
LED	Between PORTB Pin 1 and ground
Internal Pull-up	Enabled on PORTB Pin 0

Steps:
1. Set PORTB Pin 0 as input and enable the pull-up resistor.
2. Set PORTB Pin 1 as output to control the LED.
3. Continuously check the state of PORTB Pin 0 in the main loop.
4. If the button is pressed, turn on the LED by setting PORTB Pin 1 high.

Code Example:

```
void main() {
    TRISB = 0x01;   // Set PORTB Pin 0 as input and Pin
1 as output
    WPUB = 0x01;    // Enable pull-up on Pin 0

    while (1) {
        if (PORTBbits.RB0 == 0) {  // Button pressed
            LATBbits.LATB1 = 1;      // Turn on LED
        } else {
            LATBbits.LATB1 = 0;      // Turn off LED
        }
    }
}
```

Expected Results:

When the button is pressed, the LED connected to Pin 1 will turn on. When the button is released, the LED will turn off. This demonstrates the functionality of both internal pull-up resistors and basic input-output operations with GPIO pins.

Real-life Applications of Pull-up Resistors

- **Button Inputs:** Ensuring reliable high state when buttons are not pressed.
- **Sensors:** Stable readings for open/closed contacts in switches or sensors.
- **Communication:** Interfacing with other devices that require stable input signals.
- **Low-power Systems:** Using internal pull-ups for minimal external component usage.

Chapter 22: Understanding Timers and Counters

Timers and counters are essential components in embedded systems, particularly in microcontrollers like the PIC series. They are used for various applications such as time delays, frequency measurements, pulse width modulation (PWM), and event counting. This chapter explores how to effectively use timers and counters in PIC microcontrollers to create time-dependent operations and event-based systems.

Key Concepts of Timers and Counters

A **timer** is a hardware peripheral that generates a time delay or triggers an event at regular intervals. Timers in PIC microcontrollers can be used to generate precise time delays, measure elapsed time, and control the timing of other peripheral devices. A **counter** is similar to a timer, but it counts external events, such as pulses or edges of a signal. Timers and counters are usually driven by an internal clock (like the system clock or an external clock source).

Concept	Description	Example Use Case
Timer	A hardware register that increments at regular intervals.	Used for generating time delays in software.
Counter	A hardware register that counts external events or pulses.	Used for measuring the frequency of an input signal.
Prescaler	A division factor for the timer clock, slowing down the timer.	Used to extend the timer range or create slower intervals.
Overflow	When the timer or counter reaches its maximum value and resets.	Used to trigger an interrupt or action at regular intervals.

Basic Rules for Using Timers and Counters

Rule	Correct Example	Incorrect Example
Use the prescaler to adjust the timer frequency.	`T0CONbits.T0CS = 0; T0CONbits.T0PS = 0x07;` (Use prescaler)	Not adjusting prescaler for long delays.
Configure the correct timer for your needs.	Use Timer0 for small delays and Timer1 for long delays.	Using Timer1 for a small delay or Timer0 for long delays.
Set the timer direction (up or down) based on the application.	Use TMR0 for up-counting and TMR1 for down-counting.	Not setting up the timer correctly for counting direction.
Enable interrupts if you want time-based actions.	`INTCONbits.TMR0IE = 1;` (Enable Timer0 interrupt)	Forgetting to enable interrupts for time-based actions.
Use the TMRx register to read the timer value.	`unsigned int time = TMR0;` (Read Timer0 value)	Not reading the timer value to track elapsed time.

Syntax Table for Timers and Counters

SL	Function	Syntax/Example	Description
1	Configure Timer0	`T0CONbits.T0CS = 0; T0CONbits.T0PS = 0x07;`	Configure Timer0 for internal clock with prescaler.
2	Start Timer0	`T0CONbits.TMR0ON = 1;`	Start Timer0 by setting the TMR0ON bit.
3	Read Timer0 Value	`unsigned int time = TMR0;`	Read the current value of Timer0.
4	Configure Timer1	`T1CONbits.TMR1CS = 0;`	Configure Timer1 for internal clock source.
5	Start Timer1	`T1CONbits.TMR1ON = 1;`	Start Timer1 by setting the TMR1ON bit.
6	Read Timer1 Value	`unsigned int time1 = TMR1;`	Read the current value of Timer1.

7	Set Timer2 Prescaler	`T2CONbits.T2CKPS = 0x04;`	Set Timer2 prescaler for time adjustment.
8	Start Timer2	`T2CONbits.TMR2ON = 1;`	Start Timer2 by setting the TMR2ON bit.
9	Stop Timer2	`T2CONbits.TMR2ON = 0;`	Stop Timer2 by clearing the TMR2ON bit.

Syntax Explanation

1. Configure Timer0

What does configuring Timer0 do?
To use Timer0, you must configure the prescaler, clock source, and other settings using the **T0CON** register. The prescaler allows you to adjust the frequency of the timer, and the clock source specifies whether the timer will use the internal system clock or an external clock.

Syntax:
```
T0CONbits.T0CS = 0;  // Select internal clock source
for Timer0
T0CONbits.T0PS = 0x07;  // Set prescaler to 256 for
Timer0
```

Example:
```
T0CONbits.T0CS = 0;  // Use internal clock source for
Timer0
T0CONbits.T0PS = 0x07;  // Set prescaler to 256 (slow
timer)
```

Explanation:
This code configures Timer0 to use the internal clock source and sets the prescaler to 256. The prescaler slows down the timer, making it useful for longer time intervals or slower events.

2. Start Timer0

What does starting Timer0 do?

To start Timer0, you need to set the **TMR0ON** bit in the **T0CON** register. This initiates the timer, and it will start incrementing or counting based on the configured settings.

Syntax:
```
T0CONbits.TMR0ON = 1;   // Start Timer0
```

Example:
```
T0CONbits.TMR0ON = 1;   // Start Timer0 to begin
counting
```

Explanation:

This command sets the TMR0ON bit to 1, enabling the timer to start running. It will continue to increment until the timer overflows or a preset condition is met.

3. Read Timer0 Value

What does reading Timer0's value do?

You can read the current value of Timer0 using the **TMR0** register. This value represents the number of ticks or increments the timer has gone through since it was last reset.

Syntax:
```
unsigned int time = TMR0;   // Read the current value of
Timer0
```

Example:
```
unsigned int time = TMR0;   // Store Timer0 value to
check elapsed time
```

Explanation:

This command reads the value of Timer0 and stores it in the variable `time`. This value can then be used to calculate elapsed time or trigger actions after a set time period.

4. Configure Timer1

What does configuring Timer1 do?
To use Timer1, configure the **T1CON** register. You can set the clock source, prescaler, and enable/disable the timer. Timer1 is often used for longer delays or precise timing operations due to its higher resolution.
Syntax:
```
T1CONbits.TMR1CS = 0;  // Select internal clock source
for Timer1
```

Example:
```
T1CONbits.TMR1CS = 0;  // Use internal clock for Timer1
```

Explanation:
This code configures Timer1 to use the internal clock source. This is a common setting for most applications requiring a precise timing reference.

5. Start Timer1

What does starting Timer1 do?
Similar to Timer0, Timer1 can be started by setting the **TMR1ON** bit in the **T1CON** register.
Syntax:
```
T1CONbits.TMR1ON = 1;  // Start Timer1
```

Example:
```
T1CONbits.TMR1ON = 1;  // Start Timer1 to begin
counting
```

Explanation:
This code starts Timer1 by setting the TMR1ON bit, allowing it to count until it reaches its overflow point or is otherwise stopped.

6. Read Timer1 Value

What does reading Timer1's value do?
To check how long Timer1 has been running, you can read the **TMR1** register. This value gives you an idea of the number of clock cycles or ticks Timer1 has counted since it was last reset.

Syntax:
```
unsigned int time1 = TMR1;  // Read the current value
of Timer1
```

Example:
```
unsigned int time1 = TMR1;  // Store Timer1 value to
track elapsed time
```

Explanation:
This code reads the value of Timer1 and stores it in the variable time1. You can use this value to measure elapsed time or trigger time-based actions.

Real-life Application Project: Stopwatch Using Timer
In this project, we will use Timer0 to create a basic stopwatch that counts seconds and displays the time on an LED display.

Required Components:
- PIC microcontroller
- Timer0 for time counting
- 7-segment LED display
- Pushbutton for starting and stopping the stopwatch

Steps:
1. Configure Timer0 with a 1-second delay using the prescaler.
2. Set up the 7-segment display to show the elapsed time in seconds.
3. Use a pushbutton to start and stop the stopwatch.
4. Use Timer0 to increment a counter every second.
5. Display the elapsed time on the LED display.

Code Example:

```c
void main() {
    TRISB = 0x00;  // Set PORTB as output for LED
display
    TRISD = 0x01;  // Set PORTD Pin 0 as input for
pushbutton
    T0CON = 0x07;   // Configure Timer0 with prescaler
256
    T0CONbits.TMR0ON = 1;  // Start Timer0

    unsigned int seconds = 0;

    while (1) {
        if (PORTDbits.RD0 == 0) {  // Button pressed
            seconds++;  // Increment second counter
            LATB = seconds;  // Update LED display with
seconds
            __delay_ms(1000);  // 1-second delay
        }
    }
}
```

Expected Results:

The stopwatch should increment the displayed time every second when the pushbutton is pressed. The time will be displayed on the 7-segment LED display, and the stopwatch will stop when the button is released.

Real-life Applications of Timers and Counters

- **Time-based events:** Creating time delays and periodic actions in embedded systems.
- **Event counting:** Counting pulses from sensors or external events.
- **PWM signals:** Generating pulse-width modulation signals for motor control or lighting.
- **Frequency measurement:** Measuring the frequency of external signals by counting pulses.

Chapter 23: Working with Interrupts

Interrupts are a powerful feature in embedded systems, allowing the microcontroller to respond quickly to events in real time. By using interrupts, the system can handle multiple tasks concurrently, without needing to constantly check or poll for events. In this chapter, we will explore how to configure and use interrupts in PIC microcontrollers, focusing on their setup, handling, and practical applications.

Key Concepts of Interrupts

An **interrupt** is a signal that temporarily halts the current execution of the program, allowing the microcontroller to execute a special piece of code, known as an **interrupt service routine (ISR)**. After the ISR is executed, the microcontroller resumes the original program where it left off. Interrupts are typically used for tasks like handling external signals, timers, or communication events.

Concept	Description	Example Use Case
Interrupt Service Routine (ISR)	A function that handles the interrupt when triggered.	Used to process an external button press or timer overflow.
Interrupt Enable (IE)	Enables interrupts globally or for specific peripherals.	Used to enable a specific interrupt, like Timer0 interrupt.
Global Interrupt Enable	A global bit that allows or disables interrupts in the system.	Controls whether any interrupts can be processed.
Interrupt Flag (IF)	A flag that indicates if an interrupt has occurred.	A flag set when a timer overflow occurs, signaling an interrupt.
Interrupt Priority	Defines the priority of an interrupt.	Used when multiple interrupts are triggered simultaneously.

Basic Rules for Using Interrupts

Rule	Correct Example	Incorrect Example
Enable global interrupts before handling any interrupt.	`INTCONbits.GIE = 1;` (Enable global interrupt flag)	Forgetting to enable global interrupts.
Set up interrupt flags before enabling the interrupt.	`INTCONbits.TMR0IF = 0;` (Clear interrupt flag before enabling)	Not clearing interrupt flags before enabling interrupts.
Write an interrupt service routine (ISR) to handle the interrupt.	`void __interrupt() ISR() { ... }` (Define ISR for interrupt handling)	Forgetting to implement an ISR to handle the interrupt.
Ensure that you handle the interrupt flag within the ISR.	`INTCONbits.TMR0IF = 0;` (Clear flag within ISR)	Not clearing the interrupt flag inside ISR.
Disable interrupts when they are no longer needed to avoid unwanted ISR executions.	`INTCONbits.GIE = 0;` (Disable interrupts)	Leaving interrupts enabled when no longer needed.

Syntax Table for Interrupts

SL	Function	Syntax/Example	Description
1	Enable global interrupts	`INTCONbits.GIE = 1;`	Enable global interrupt flag to allow interrupts.
2	Disable global interrupts	`INTCONbits.GIE = 0;`	Disable global interrupt flag to prevent interrupts.
3	Enable Timer0 interrupt	`INTCONbits.TMR0IE = 1;`	Enable interrupt for Timer0 overflow.
4	Clear Timer0 interrupt flag	`INTCONbits.TMR0IF = 0;`	Clear the interrupt flag after ISR execution.

5	Enable Peripheral Interrupts	`INTCONbits.PEIE = 1;`	Enable peripheral interrupt enable bit.
6	Configure interrupt priority (if available)	`INTCON2bits.TMR0I P = 1;`	Set priority for Timer0 interrupt.
7	Interrupt service routine (ISR) definition	`void __interrupt() ISR() { ... }`	Define the ISR to handle interrupts.

Syntax Explanation

1. Enable Global Interrupts

What does enabling global interrupts do?
Global interrupts enable the microcontroller to respond to interrupts from any source, whether they are peripheral or external. The `GIE` bit in the `INTCON` register must be set to 1 to allow interrupts to be processed.
Syntax:
```
INTCONbits.GIE = 1;  // Enable global interrupt flag
```

Example:
```
INTCONbits.GIE = 1;  // Global interrupts enabled
```
Explanation:
This line of code sets the global interrupt enable bit (`GIE`) to 1, allowing interrupts to be processed by the microcontroller. Without this setting, interrupts will not be recognized, even if the interrupt flags are set.

2. Enable Peripheral Interrupts

What does enabling peripheral interrupts do?
Peripheral interrupts are specific to certain microcontroller peripherals like timers, ADCs, UARTs, etc. Enabling peripheral interrupts allows these specific interrupt sources to trigger an interrupt when their conditions are met.

Syntax:
```
INTCONbits.PEIE = 1;   // Enable peripheral interrupts
```

Example:
```
INTCONbits.PEIE = 1;   // Peripheral interrupt enable
```

Explanation:
Setting PEIE (Peripheral Interrupt Enable) to 1 enables the microcontroller to process interrupts from peripherals like Timer0, UART, etc. This is necessary to allow the handling of interrupts from peripherals even when the global interrupt flag is set.

3. Enable Timer0 Interrupt

What does enabling the Timer0 interrupt do?
To enable an interrupt triggered by the Timer0 overflow, you need to set the TMR0IE bit in the INTCON register. This tells the microcontroller to trigger an interrupt whenever Timer0 reaches its maximum value and overflows.
Syntax:
```
INTCONbits.TMR0IE = 1;   // Enable Timer0 interrupt
```

Example:
```
INTCONbits.TMR0IE = 1;   // Enable interrupt for Timer0
overflow
```

Explanation:
By setting TMR0IE to 1, the Timer0 interrupt is enabled. This interrupt will occur when Timer0 overflows, meaning it exceeds its maximum count (255 for an 8-bit timer). An interrupt will be generated and passed to the interrupt service routine (ISR) to handle the overflow.

4. Clear Timer0 Interrupt Flag

What does clearing the Timer0 interrupt flag do?
After the ISR has been executed, the interrupt flag (TMR0IF) must be cleared in order to reset the interrupt condition and prevent the ISR from being called repeatedly.

Syntax:
```
INTCONbits.TMR0IF = 0;   // Clear Timer0 interrupt flag
```
Example:
```
INTCONbits.TMR0IF = 0;   // Clear the interrupt flag
after ISR
```
Explanation:
This command clears the interrupt flag associated with Timer0. After processing the interrupt, you need to clear the flag to avoid triggering the ISR again for the same event. This ensures that the microcontroller can handle new interrupts without mistakenly responding to the same event multiple times.

5. Interrupt Service Routine (ISR)

What is an ISR and how is it written?
An ISR is a special function designed to handle interrupts. When an interrupt occurs, the microcontroller temporarily halts the execution of the main program and jumps to the ISR. After executing the ISR, the microcontroller returns to the main program. Writing an ISR requires using the __interrupt() keyword in MPLAB X.

Syntax:
```
void __interrupt() ISR() {
    // Interrupt handling code
}
```
Example:
```
void __interrupt() ISR() {
    if (INTCONbits.TMR0IF) {  // Check if Timer0 caused
the interrupt
        // Handle Timer0 overflow event
        INTCONbits.TMR0IF = 0;   // Clear interrupt flag
    }
}
```
Explanation:
This is a basic ISR structure. When an interrupt occurs, the microcontroller jumps to this function. Inside the ISR, we check if the interrupt flag TMR0IF is set, which indicates that the interrupt was caused by Timer0. After handling the interrupt, we clear the flag to prevent the interrupt from being triggered again.

Real-life Application Project: Button Press Interrupt
In this project, we will use a button press to trigger an interrupt.
When the button is pressed, the microcontroller will stop the
execution of the main program and run the ISR to toggle an LED.
Required Components:
- PIC microcontroller
- Pushbutton
- LED
- Resistors for button and LED

Steps:
1. Configure the button as an input and the LED as an output.
2. Enable the interrupt for the button press (change of state).
3. Implement an ISR to handle the button press and toggle the
   LED.

Code Example:
```
void __interrupt() ISR() {
    if (INTCONbits.INTF) {  // Check if external
interrupt occurred
        LATBbits.LATB0 = !LATBbits.LATB0;  // Toggle
LED
        INTCONbits.INTF = 0;  // Clear interrupt flag
    }
}
void main() {
    TRISBbits.TRISB0 = 0;  // Set RB0 as output (LED)
    TRISDbits.TRISD0 = 1;  // Set RD0 as input (button)
    INTCONbits.GIE = 1;  // Enable global interrupt
    INTCONbits.PEIE = 1;  // Enable peripheral
interrupt
    INTCONbits.INTF = 0;  // Clear interrupt flag
    INTCONbits.INTE = 1;  // Enable external interrupt
on RD0
    while (1) {
        // Main loop continues while waiting for
interrupt
    }
}
```

Expected Results:

- The LED will toggle every time the button is pressed.
- The interrupt ensures that the microcontroller responds immediately to the button press, regardless of what the main program is doing.

Real-life Applications of Interrupts

- **Real-time communication:** Handling UART communication where data needs to be processed as soon as it's received.
- **Sensor data acquisition:** Reading data from sensors at precise intervals.
- **Control systems:** Implementing feedback loops where the system responds to external conditions.
- **Human-machine interaction:** Button presses or other user inputs requiring immediate action, like in devices with UI feedback.

Chapter 24: Serial Communication (UART, USART)

Serial communication is one of the most commonly used methods of data transfer between microcontrollers and external devices such as computers, sensors, or other microcontrollers. For PIC microcontrollers, UART (Universal Asynchronous Receiver/Transmitter) and USART (Universal Synchronous/Asynchronous Receiver/Transmitter) modules are used for serial communication. This chapter explores how to configure and use these modules for communication in PIC-based applications.

Key Concepts of UART/USART Communication

- **UART (Universal Asynchronous Receiver/Transmitter):** UART is used for asynchronous serial communication, where data is sent one bit at a time without the need for a clock signal. It only requires two wires: TX (Transmit) and RX (Receive).
- **USART (Universal Synchronous/Asynchronous Receiver/Transmitter):** USART can work in both asynchronous and synchronous modes. In asynchronous mode, it works the same as UART, but in synchronous mode, it uses an additional clock line for more synchronized data transfer.
- **Baud Rate:** The baud rate determines the speed of data transmission. Both transmitting and receiving devices must operate at the same baud rate for proper communication.
- **Parity, Stop Bits, and Data Bits:** These settings define how the data will be formatted. Common settings are 8 data bits, no parity, and 1 stop bit.

Basic Rules for Using UART/USART

Rule	Correct Example	Incorrect Example
Set the baud rate	`SPBRG = 25;` (for 9600 baud at 4 MHz clock)	`SPBRG = 100;` (incorrect baud rate for the clock speed)
Enable serial communication	`RCSTAbits.SPEN = 1;`	Missing the SPEN bit to enable serial port.
Configure TX and RX pins correctly	`TRISCbits.TRISC6 = 0;`	Incorrect pin direction configuration.
Enable continuous receive interrupts	`RCIE = 1;`	Missing enable interrupt for UART receive.

Syntax Table

SL	Function	Syntax/Example	Description
1	Set the baud rate	`SPBRG = value;`	Sets the baud rate for serial communication.
2	Initialize the UART module	`TXSTAbits.TXEN = 1;` `RCSTAbits.CREN = 1;`	Enables the transmitter (TX) and receiver (RX).
3	Send data through UART	`TXREG = data;`	Transmits data via the UART transmitter register.
4	Receive data through UART	`data = RCREG;`	Reads received data from the UART receiver register.
5	Check if data is received	`RCIF = 1;`	Checks the UART receive interrupt flag.

Syntax Explanation

1. Set the Baud Rate
What does setting the baud rate do?
Setting the baud rate is essential for configuring the communication speed between the microcontroller and the external device. The baud rate must be the same on both ends for successful data transmission.
Syntax:
```
SPBRG = value;
```

Example:
```
SPBRG = 25;  // For 9600 baud at 4 MHz system clock
```

Example Explanation:
This sets the baud rate to 9600 based on a system clock of 4 MHz. The SPBRG register (Serial Port Baud Rate Generator) is used to set the appropriate value for the desired baud rate.

2. Initialize the UART Module
What does initializing the UART module do?
Initialization of the UART module involves enabling the transmitter and receiver, which allows the microcontroller to send and receive serial data.
Syntax:
```
TXSTAbits.TXEN = 1;  // Enable transmitter
RCSTAbits.CREN = 1;  // Enable receiver
```

Example:
```
TXSTAbits.TXEN = 1;  // Enable the transmitter (TX)
RCSTAbits.CREN = 1;  // Enable the receiver (RX)
```

Example Explanation:
This code enables both the transmitter and receiver in the UART module. Without enabling these, the microcontroller cannot send or receive data.

3. Send Data Through UART

What does sending data through UART do?

Sending data involves placing the byte to be transmitted into the TXREG register, which then serializes the data and sends it over the TX pin.

Syntax:

```
TXREG = data;  // Place data to be sent in TXREG
register
```

Example:

```
TXREG = 'A';  // Transmit character 'A'
```

Example Explanation:

This places the ASCII value of 'A' into the TXREG register, which then transmits the character over the TX line.

4. Receive Data Through UART

What does receiving data through UART do?

The received data is stored in the RCREG register. This data can be read and processed as it arrives.

Syntax:

```
data = RCREG;  // Read received data from RCREG
```

Example:

```
data = RCREG;  // Read received data
```

Example Explanation:

This code reads the received data from the RCREG register and stores it in the variable data.

5. Check if Data is Received

What does checking if data is received do?

Before reading data from RCREG, it's important to check if the UART module has received any data. The RCIF interrupt flag will be set when data is received.

Syntax:

```
if (RCIF) {
    // Data received
}
```

Example:

```
if (RCIF) {
    data = RCREG;  // Read the received byte
}
```

Example Explanation:

This checks the RCIF (Receive Interrupt Flag) bit. If it is set, the code reads the received byte from the RCREG register.

Real-life Applications Project: Serial Communication with a PC

In this project, we will use UART to communicate with a PC through the serial port. The microcontroller will send a string of characters, and the PC will display the received string.

Required Components

Component	Description
PIC Microcontroller	The microcontroller that will send data.
PC with Serial Port	The PC for receiving and displaying data.
USB to Serial Converter	Converts USB to serial for communication.

Circuit Connection Table

Component	Pin Connection
PIC Microcontroller	TX -> USB to Serial Converter RX
USB to Serial Converter	TX -> PC Serial Port RX

Project Code

```
void main() {
    SPBRG = 25;  // Set baud rate to 9600 for 4 MHz
clock
    TXSTAbits.TXEN = 1;  // Enable transmitter
    RCSTAbits.CREN = 1;  // Enable receiver

    while (1) {
        if (RCIF) {
            char receivedData = RCREG;  // Read
received data
            TXREG = receivedData;  // Send received
data back to PC
        }
    }
}
```

Expected Results:
- The microcontroller continuously reads data from the serial port.
- Any character sent from the PC is immediately echoed back to the PC via the serial communication.

Real-life Applications of Serial Communication
- **Data logging systems:** Sending data from embedded devices to a PC or server for storage and analysis.
- **Embedded device configuration:** Configuring microcontroller parameters from a PC via a terminal program.
- **Wireless communication:** Serial communication is commonly used in wireless modules like Bluetooth, Zigbee, and Wi-Fi.

Understanding UART/USART communication is crucial for interfacing embedded systems with other devices. It forms the foundation for many communication protocols used in real-time embedded systems.

Chapter 25: I2C Communication with PIC

I2C (Inter-Integrated Circuit) is a popular communication protocol used to connect multiple devices with a microcontroller. It allows for two-way communication between the master (microcontroller) and one or more slave devices using just two lines: data (SDA) and clock (SCL). This chapter will guide you on how to implement I2C communication with PIC microcontrollers, including configuration, sending and receiving data, and real-life applications.

Key Concepts of I2C Communication

- **Master and Slave Devices:** In an I2C communication setup, the microcontroller typically acts as the master, and peripheral devices like sensors or other microcontrollers act as slaves.
- **SDA and SCL Lines:** The I2C protocol uses two main lines: SDA (Serial Data) for data transmission and SCL (Serial Clock) for synchronization of data transfers.
- **Addressing:** Each slave device on the I2C bus has a unique address. This address is used by the master to communicate with a specific slave.
- **Start and Stop Conditions:** Communication is initiated with a start condition and terminated with a stop condition. These conditions are signaled by changes in the SDA and SCL lines.
- **Acknowledge (ACK):** After each byte of data is transmitted, the receiver sends an ACK bit to confirm successful receipt.

Basic Rules for Using I2C

Rule	Correct Example	Incorrect Example
Set up the I2C master and slave address	I2C1ADD = 0x30;	I2C1ADD = 0x60; (incorrect slave address)
Enable the I2C module	I2C1CONbits. I2CEN = 1;	Missing I2CEN bit to enable I2C communication
Initiate a communication with a slave	I2C1CONbits. SEN = 1;	Not setting the start condition properly

	Wait for the transfer to complete	`while (I2C1STATbits.TRSTAT);`	Not waiting for the transfer to complete

Syntax Table

SL	Function	Syntax/Example	Description
1	Set the I2C Slave Address	`I2C1ADD = address;`	Sets the slave address for communication.
2	Enable the I2C Module	`I2C1CONbits.I2CEN = 1;`	Enables the I2C module for communication.
3	Start I2C Communication	`I2C1CONbits.SEN = 1;`	Initiates a start condition for I2C communication.
4	Send Data Through I2C	`I2C1TRN = data;`	Loads data to be transmitted through I2C.
5	Wait for Data Transmission to Finish	`while (I2C1STATbits.TRSTAT);`	Waits for the transmission to complete.
6	Receive Data Through I2C	`data = I2C1RCV;`	Reads received data from the I2C bus.

Syntax Explanation

1. Set the I2C Slave Address
What does setting the I2C slave address do?
Setting the slave address allows the microcontroller to know which device it will communicate with. This address is used in the communication process to identify the slave device.
Syntax:
`I2C1ADD = address;`

Example:
`I2C1ADD = 0x50;   // Set slave address to 0x50`

Example Explanation:
This sets the slave device address to 0x50, which is the address of the target I2C device. The master will use this address to initiate communication with the slave.

2. Enable the I2C Module
What does enabling the I2C module do?
Enabling the I2C module allows the microcontroller to communicate via the I2C protocol. Without enabling the I2C module, the communication will not be possible.
Syntax:
```
I2C1CONbits.I2CEN = 1;
```

Example:
```
I2C1CONbits.I2CEN = 1;   // Enable I2C module
```

Example Explanation:

This code enables the I2C communication module, allowing data transfer to occur between the master and slave devices.

3. Start I2C Communication
What does initiating a start condition do?
A start condition tells the slave that the master is about to initiate communication. It is the first step in any I2C communication exchange.
Syntax:
```
I2C1CONbits.SEN = 1;
```

Example:
```
I2C1CONbits.SEN = 1;   // Initiate Start Condition
```

Example Explanation:
This starts the I2C communication by sending a start condition. Once the slave device detects the start condition, it is ready to receive data from the master.

4. Send Data Through I2C
What does sending data through I2C do?
This places the byte of data to be transmitted in the I2C transmit register. The data is then sent to the slave device over the I2C bus.
Syntax:
```
I2C1TRN = data;
```

Example:
```
I2C1TRN = 0xA5;   // Send byte 0xA5 to slave device
```

Example Explanation:
This loads the value 0xA5 into the transmit register I2C1TRN and begins transmitting the byte to the slave device.

5. **Wait for Data Transmission to Finish**

What does waiting for data transmission to finish do?
The TRSTAT bit indicates the status of the transmission. The code waits for this bit to clear, signaling that the transmission is complete.
Syntax:
```
while (I2C1STATbits.TRSTAT);
```

Example:
```
while (I2C1STATbits.TRSTAT);   // Wait for transmission
to complete
```

Example Explanation:
This code ensures that the master waits for the data to be successfully transmitted before proceeding further in the program. It ensures that the next transmission doesn't begin before the previous one is complete.

6. **Receive Data Through I2C**

What does receiving data through I2C do?
When the master receives data from the slave, it is placed in the I2C1RCV register, which can then be read by the master.
Syntax:
```
data = I2C1RCV;
```

Example:
```
data = I2C1RCV;   // Read the received byte from slave
```
Example Explanation:
This code reads the data received from the slave into the variable data.

Real-life Applications Project: I2C Temperature Sensor
In this project, we will use I2C communication to read data from a temperature sensor (such as the LM75 or TMP102) and display the temperature on a serial monitor.

Required Components

Component	Description
PIC Microcontroller	The master device that will communicate with the sensor.
I2C Temperature Sensor	The slave device that provides temperature data.
Pull-up Resistors	Required on SDA and SCL lines for proper communication.

Circuit Connection Table

Component	Pin Connection
PIC Microcontroller	SDA -> Pin 5, SCL -> Pin 6
I2C Temperature Sensor	SDA -> Pin 5, SCL -> Pin 6, VCC -> 3.3V, GND -> Ground

Project Code

```
void main() {
    unsigned char tempData;

    I2C1ADD = 0x48;  // Slave address of the
temperature sensor
    I2C1CONbits.I2CEN = 1;  // Enable I2C communication

    while (1) {
        I2C1CONbits.SEN = 1;  // Send start condition
        while (I2C1STATbits.TRSTAT);  // Wait for
transmission to complete

        I2C1TRN = 0x00;  // Send register address to
read from
        while (I2C1STATbits.TRSTAT);  // Wait for
transmission to complete

        I2C1CONbits.RSEN = 1;  // Restart condition
        while (I2C1STATbits.TRSTAT);  // Wait for
restart to complete

        I2C1TRN = 0x01;  // Read data from register
```

```
    while (I2C1STATbits.TRSTAT);  // Wait for
transmission to complete

        tempData = I2C1RCV;  // Read the received data
        UART_Write(tempData);  // Display temperature
on UART
    }
}
```

Expected Results:

- The master PIC microcontroller successfully reads the temperature data from the I2C sensor.
- The temperature data is sent to the UART and displayed on the serial monitor.

Real-life Applications of I2C Communication

1. **Sensor Networks:** I2C is used in various sensor applications, such as temperature, pressure, and humidity sensors.
2. **Display Modules:** LCD and OLED displays use I2C to communicate with microcontrollers.
3. **EEPROMs and RTCs:** I2C is commonly used to communicate with external EEPROM and real-time clock (RTC) modules for non-volatile memory storage and timekeeping.
4. **Motor Controllers:** I2C communication is often used to control motor drivers, enabling precise control in robotics and automation systems.

This chapter provides a detailed overview of how to implement I2C communication with PIC microcontrollers, from setting up the hardware to programming the software, and concludes with a practical project on interfacing a temperature sensor.

Chapter 26: SPI Protocol in PIC

The Serial Peripheral Interface (SPI) is a synchronous data transfer protocol used to communicate between microcontrollers and peripheral devices. It is widely used for applications requiring fast data transmission, such as sensors, memory cards, and displays. In this chapter, we will explore how to use SPI communication with PIC microcontrollers, focusing on configuring the hardware, understanding the communication protocol, and implementing real-life applications.

Key Concepts of SPI

SPI is a full-duplex communication protocol that allows two devices to exchange data simultaneously. The protocol consists of four main signals:

- **MOSI (Master Out Slave In)**: Carries data from the master to the slave.
- **MISO (Master In Slave Out)**: Carries data from the slave to the master.
- **SCK (Serial Clock)**: A clock signal generated by the master to synchronize data transmission.
- **SS (Slave Select)**: A signal that selects the slave device for communication.

Concept	Description	Example
SPI	Full-duplex serial communication protocol	Communication between PIC and sensors.
MOSI	Data line for master to slave communication	Sending data to peripheral devices.
MISO	Data line for slave to master communication	Receiving data from sensors.
SCK	Clock signal for data synchronization	Controls timing of data transfer.
SS	Signal to select slave device	Identifies which slave device the master is communicating with.

Basic Rules for Using SPI

Rule	Correct Example	Incorrect Example
Use SPI in master or slave mode as required.	SSPSTAT = 0x40; SSPCON = 0x20;	SSPSTAT = 0x80; (Incorrect configuration)
Ensure that the clock polarity and phase match between master and slave.	Set CKP and CKE in SSPCON.	Mismatch in clock polarity between devices.
Use the appropriate pins for SPI communication.	SCK -> pin 5, MOSI -> pin 6, MISO -> pin 7.	Incorrect pin connections.
Use the SS pin to select the slave device.	SS connected to the CS pin of the slave.	Not using the SS pin for selecting slave.

Syntax Table

S L	Function	Syntax/Example	Description
1	Initialize SPI	SSPCON = 0x20;	Configures the SPI in master mode.
2	Send data via SPI	SSPBUF = data;	Sends data to the slave device.
3	Receive data via SPI	receivedData = SSPBUF;	Reads the received data from the SPI buffer.
4	Set clock polarity	CKP = 0;	Sets the clock polarity for SPI communication.

Syntax Explanation

1. Initialize SPI

To initialize the SPI module, configure the relevant registers such as SSPCON and SSPSTAT. For example, setting SSPCON = 0x20 configures the PIC as a master device with an SPI clock source and enables SPI.

Syntax:
```
SSPCON = 0x20;  // Master mode with clock source and
enable SPI
```

Example:
```
SSPCON = 0x20;   // Set SPI to master mode
```

Explanation:
This sets the PIC microcontroller as the SPI master device. The SPI communication will be enabled, and the correct clock source will be chosen for synchronization.

2. Send Data via SPI

The SSPBUF register holds the data to be transmitted. Writing data to this register initiates the transfer over SPI. After sending the data, the master waits until the transfer is complete.

Syntax:
```
SSPBUF = data;   // Load data into the SPI buffer
```

Example:
```
SSPBUF = 0x55;   // Send the data 0x55
```

Explanation:
This loads the SSPBUF register with the data 0x55 and starts the transmission. The data will be transmitted on the MOSI line to the slave.

3. Receive Data via SPI

The received data can be read from the SSPBUF register after the transmission is complete. To ensure the data is valid, check the SSPIF flag, which indicates that the data is ready to be read.

Syntax:
```
receivedData = SSPBUF;   // Read the received data from
the SPI buffer
```

Example:
```
receivedData = SSPBUF;   // Store the received data
```

Explanation:
This reads the data received from the slave device into the receivedData variable. Ensure that the data is valid by checking the SSPIF flag before reading.

4. Set Clock Polarity

The clock polarity (CKP) and clock phase (CKE) control the timing of data sampling and clock edge. The CKP bit controls the idle state of the clock, while CKE determines when data is sampled.

Syntax:
```
CKP = 0;  // Set clock polarity to idle-low
```

Example:
```
CKP = 0;  // Set clock polarity to idle-low
```

Explanation:
 This ensures that the clock signal will be low when idle. Proper synchronization of clock polarity is essential for successful SPI communication between master and slave.

Real-life Applications Project: SPI Communication with a Temperature Sensor

In this project, we will use SPI communication to interface a PIC microcontroller with a temperature sensor, such as the MCP3008, which communicates with the microcontroller via SPI. The temperature sensor will output analog data, which we can convert to a digital signal and then read via SPI. The microcontroller will display the temperature readings.

Required Components

Component	Description
PIC Microcontroller	The main controller for the SPI communication.
MCP3008 ADC	An 8-channel ADC that communicates via SPI.
Temperature Sensor	A sensor like LM35 or similar, connected to one of the ADC channels.
LCD Display	To display the temperature readings.
Jumper Wires	For making the necessary connections.

Circuit Connection Table

Component	Pin Connection
MCP3008	VCC to 5V, GND to GND, SCLK to SCK, MOSI to MOSI, MISO to MISO, SS to CS pin of PIC
PIC Microcontroll er	SCK to SCK pin, MOSI to MOSI pin, MISO to MISO pin, SS to CS pin of MCP3008
LCD Display	Connect the LCD to the appropriate pins for communication (using 4-bit mode).

Project Code

```
#include <xc.h>
#include <stdio.h>
#include "lcd.h"

// Function prototypes
void SPI_Init(void);
unsigned char SPI_Read(void);
void SPI_Write(unsigned char data);
unsigned int Read_ADC(unsigned char channel);

void main(void) {
    unsigned int tempReading = 0;
    char buffer[16];

    // Initialize LCD
    LCD_Init();
    // Initialize SPI
    SPI_Init();

    // Main loop
    while(1) {
        // Read the temperature from the sensor
(channel 0)
        tempReading = Read_ADC(0);

        // Convert ADC reading to temperature
        float temperature = (tempReading * 5.0 /
```

```c
1023.0) * 100.0; // Example conversion for LM35

        // Display temperature on LCD
        sprintf(buffer, "Temp: %.2f C", temperature);
        LCD_Clear();
        LCD_WriteString(buffer);

        __delay_ms(1000);  // Wait for 1 second
    }
}

void SPI_Init(void) {
    // Set up the SPI module for communication
    TRISC5 = 0;  // SCK as output
    TRISC3 = 0;  // MOSI as output
    TRISC4 = 1;  // MISO as input
    TRISAbits.TRISA5 = 0; // CS as output

    SSPSTAT = 0x40; // Sample data at middle of clock
cycle
    SSPCON = 0x20;  // Enable SPI in master mode
}

unsigned char SPI_Read(void) {
    while (!SSPIF);  // Wait for data to be received
    SSPIF = 0;       // Clear interrupt flag
    return SSPBUF;   // Return received data
}

void SPI_Write(unsigned char data) {
    SSPBUF = data;  // Load data into buffer to
transmit
    while (!SSPIF); // Wait for transmission to
complete
    SSPIF = 0;      // Clear interrupt flag
}
```

```
unsigned int Read_ADC(unsigned char channel) {
    unsigned int ADC_value;

    // Select the ADC channel
    SPI_Write(0x
```

06 | (channel << 3));

 ADC_value = SPI_Read() << 8; // Read high byte

 ADC_value |= SPI_Read(); // Read low byte

return ADC_value;

```
}
```

Explanation:

1. SPI Initialization: The `SPI_Init()` function sets up the SPI communication for the PIC microcontroller in master mode.

2. Reading ADC Data: The `Read_ADC()` function sends a command to the MCP3008 to select the channel, reads the high byte, and then the low byte to get the 10-bit ADC result.

3. Converting ADC to Temperature: The ADC value is converted to a temperature using the appropriate formula. For example, with the LM35 temperature sensor, each ADC step corresponds to a 10mV change in voltage, which can be converted to degrees Celsius.

4. Displaying Temperature: The temperature value is displayed on the LCD using `LCD_WriteString()`. The LCD updates every second.

Chapter 27: External Interrupts and Pin Change Interrupts

External interrupts and pin change interrupts are essential features for handling asynchronous events in embedded systems. These interrupts allow microcontrollers to respond immediately to specific external events, such as button presses, sensor triggers, or signal changes, without continuously polling the state of the input. In this chapter, we will discuss how to configure and use external interrupts and pin change interrupts in PIC microcontrollers for efficient event handling.

Key Concepts of External Interrupts and Pin Change Interrupts

- **External Interrupts (INTx)**: These interrupts are triggered by external signals on specific pins of the microcontroller (e.g., INT0, INT1, etc.). They allow the microcontroller to respond to changes in input signals, such as the rising or falling edge of a pulse.
- **Pin Change Interrupts**: These interrupts are triggered by a change in the state of a pin, whether the input signal is high or low. Unlike external interrupts, pin change interrupts can be configured for multiple pins, allowing a wider range of events to be detected.

Concept	Description	Example
External Interrupts	Interrupts triggered by an external signal on specific pins (e.g., INT0, INT1).	Detecting a button press.
Pin Change Interrupts	Interrupts triggered by a change in the state of a pin (either high or low).	Detecting signal changes from sensors.

Basic Rules for Using External and Pin Change Interrupts

Rule	Correct Example	Incorrect Example
Enable global and peripheral interrupts.	GIE = 1; PEIE = 1;	Missing interrupt enable.
Configure the interrupt pin and trigger condition.	Set INT0, INT1 for edge detection.	Forgetting to configure the interrupt pin.

Use the appropriate interrupt flag for handling.	Check INTF flag to see if interrupt occurred.	Ignoring interrupt flags.
Clear the interrupt flag after handling.	`INTF = 0;`	Not clearing interrupt flag.

Syntax Table

SL	Function	Syntax/Example	Description
1	Enable Global Interrupts	`GIE = 1; PEIE = 1;`	Enables global and peripheral interrupts.
2	Configure INT0 Pin	`TRISB0 = 1;`	Set INT0 pin as input.
3	Enable INT0 Interrupt	`INTCONbits.INT0IE = 1;`	Enable INT0 interrupt.
4	Set INT0 Edge Detection	`INTCON2bits.INTEDG0 = 1;`	Set rising edge trigger for INT0.
5	Clear Interrupt Flag	`INTCONbits.INT0IF = 0;`	Clear interrupt flag after handling.

Syntax Explanation

1. Enable Global and Peripheral Interrupts

To enable interrupts globally, you need to set both the global interrupt enable (GIE) bit and the peripheral interrupt enable (PEIE) bit. This allows the microcontroller to respond to interrupts from both peripheral devices and external signals.

Syntax:

```
GIE = 1;  // Enable global interrupt enable
PEIE = 1; // Enable peripheral interrupt enable
```

Example:

```
GIE = 1;  // Enable global interrupts
PEIE = 1; // Enable peripheral interrupts
```

Explanation:

This code snippet enables the global interrupts (GIE) and peripheral interrupts (PEIE), which are necessary to handle any interrupt events properly.

2. Configure INT0 Pin

The INT0 pin (external interrupt 0) should be configured as an input pin to allow it to detect external signals. This is typically done by setting the appropriate TRIS register bit to 1 (input).
Syntax:
```
TRISB0 = 1;  // Set RB0 pin as input for INT0
```

Example:
```
TRISB0 = 1;  // Set RB0 as input pin for external
interrupt
```

Explanation:
 This code configures pin RB0 as an input, which is connected to the INT0 interrupt source. The input state of this pin will trigger an interrupt based on the edge detection configured.

3. Enable INT0 Interrupt

The INT0 interrupt needs to be enabled by setting the corresponding interrupt enable bit in the interrupt control register. This is done by setting INT0IE in the INTCON register.
Syntax:
```
INTCONbits.INT0IE = 1;  // Enable INT0 interrupt
```

Example:
```
INTCONbits.INT0IE = 1;  // Enable interrupt on INT0
```
Explanation:
 This line of code enables the interrupt for the INT0 pin. Once this is set, any valid external event on the INT0 pin will trigger an interrupt.

4. Set INT0 Edge Detection

For external interrupts, you can configure the edge that triggers the interrupt (rising or falling edge). This can be controlled by setting the INTEDG0 bit in the INTCON2 register.
Syntax:
```
INTCON2bits.INTEDG0 = 1;  // Interrupt on rising edge
for INT0
```

Example:
```
INTCON2bits.INTEDG0 = 1;  // Interrupt on rising edge
```

Explanation:
This configures INT0 to trigger an interrupt on the rising edge of the signal, meaning the interrupt will occur when the voltage goes from low to high.

5. Clear Interrupt Flag

After the interrupt has been handled, the interrupt flag needs to be cleared to prevent the interrupt from being triggered again. This can be done by clearing the interrupt flag bit (INT0IF) in the INTCON register.

Syntax:
```
INTCONbits.INT0IF = 0;  // Clear the INT0 interrupt
flag
```

Example:
```
INTCONbits.INT0IF = 0;  // Clear the interrupt flag for
INT0
```

Explanation:
This code clears the interrupt flag (INT0IF) to prevent the interrupt from being re-triggered until the next valid external event occurs. It's a crucial step in managing interrupts properly.

Real-life Applications Project: Button Press Interrupt

In this project, we will configure an external interrupt to detect a button press. When the button is pressed, it will trigger an interrupt, and the microcontroller will perform a specific task, such as toggling an LED.

Required Components

Component	Description
PIC Microcontroller	The main controller for the interrupt handling.
Push Button	Used to trigger the interrupt.
LED	To visually indicate the interrupt action.

Resistor	Used to pull-up the button input.
Jumper Wires	For making the necessary connections.

Circuit Connection Table

Component	Pin Connection
Push Button	One side to the INT0 pin (RB0), other side to ground with a pull-up resistor.
LED	Connected to any output pin (e.g., RB1), with current-limiting resistor.

Project Code

```
#include <xc.h>
#define _XTAL_FREQ 4000000  // Define system clock
frequency
// Interrupt Service Routine (ISR)
void __interrupt() ISR() {
    if (INTCONbits.INT0IF) {  // Check if INT0
interrupt occurred
        LATBbits.LATB1 = !LATBbits.LATB1;  // Toggle
LED on RB1
        INTCONbits.INT0IF = 0;  // Clear interrupt flag
    }
}
void main(void) {
    TRISBbits.TRISB0 = 1;  // Set RB0 as input for INT0
    TRISBbits.TRISB1 = 0;  // Set RB1 as output for LED
    LATBbits.LATB1 = 0;    // Initial state of LED
(OFF)
    INTCONbits.INT0IE = 1;  // Enable INT0 interrupt
    INTCONbits.INT0IF = 0;  // Clear INT0 interrupt
flag
    INTCONbits.GIE = 1;     // Enable global interrupts
    INTCONbits.PEIE = 1;    // Enable peripheral
interrupts
    while(1) {
        // Main loop can perform other tasks while
waiting for interrupts
    }
}
```

Explanation:
  1. **Interrupt Service Routine (ISR):**
  The ISR() function is executed when an interrupt occurs. It checks if the INT0 interrupt flag is set, indicating that the button was pressed, and toggles the LED state.
  2. **Main Function:**
  In the main loop, the microcontroller continually waits for the button press interrupt to occur. The interrupt handling is done in the background.

Expected Results:
When the button connected to the INT0 pin is pressed, the interrupt will be triggered, and the microcontroller will toggle the LED state. This
will demonstrate how to use external interrupts for event-driven actions.

Real-life Application:
  • **Home Automation:** This button press interrupt can be used in home automation systems where a simple button press can turn on/off devices or trigger other actions.
  • **Alarm Systems:** External interrupts can be used in alarm systems to trigger responses like turning on lights or sending alerts when a door is opened or a sensor is activated.

Chapter 28: Interfacing Temperature Sensors

Interfacing temperature sensors with PIC microcontrollers is a common task in embedded systems. Temperature sensors can provide valuable data for monitoring environments, controlling heating and cooling systems, or triggering alarms. In this chapter, we will explore how to interface temperature sensors with a PIC microcontroller, focusing on common types of sensors like thermistors, LM35, and digital sensors like the DS18B20.

Key Concepts of Temperature Sensors

- **Thermistors**: A thermistor is a type of resistor whose resistance varies significantly with temperature. Thermistors can be used to measure temperature by measuring changes in their resistance and converting it into a voltage using a voltage divider circuit.
- **LM35**: The LM35 is an analog temperature sensor that provides an output voltage that is linearly proportional to the Celsius temperature. It has a simple analog output, which makes it easy to interface with the analog-to-digital converter (ADC) of a PIC microcontroller.
- **DS18B20**: The DS18B20 is a digital temperature sensor that communicates over the 1-Wire protocol. It requires only one data pin for communication and can be daisy-chained with multiple sensors.

Sensor Type	Output	Interface	Applications
Thermistor	Analog	Voltage Divider	Home Automation, Weather Stations
LM35	Analog	ADC	Temperature Monitoring, Environmental Systems
DS18B20	Digital	1-Wire Protocol	Industrial, IoT Devices, Home Automation

Basic Rules for Interfacing Temperature Sensors

Rule	Correct Example	Incorrect Example
Use the correct voltage range for the sensor.	LM35 operates at 5V, DS18B20 at	Exceeding the voltage rating of the sensor.

		3.3V or 5V.	
Ensure ADC resolution is sufficient for precise readings.	Use a 10-bit ADC for better precision.	Using low-resolution ADCs may result in poor accuracy.	
For digital sensors, use proper communication protocol.	DS18B20 requires a single-wire interface.	Improper wiring or communication errors.	
Use appropriate pull-up resistors for digital sensors.	DS18B20 requires a 4.7kΩ pull-up resistor.	Missing pull-up resistor for digital sensors.	

Syntax Table

SL	Function	Syntax/Example	Description
1	Set LM35 Analog Pin	`TRISA0 = 1;`	Set the analog pin for LM35 input.
2	Initialize ADC for LM35	`ADCON1 = 0x06;`	Configure ADC for LM35 sensor.
3	Start ADC Conversion	`ADCON0bits.GO = 1;`	Start ADC conversion for temperature reading.
4	Wait for ADC Result	`while(ADCON0bits.GO_nDONE);`	Wait until ADC conversion is complete.
5	Read ADC Value	`` `temperature = (ADRESH << 8) ``	`` ADRESL;` ``
6	DS18B20 Start Conversion	`OneWire_Init();`	Initialize the 1-Wire bus for DS18B20.
7	DS18B20 Read Temperature	`temp = DS18B20_ReadTemperature();`	Read temperature from DS18B20.

Syntax Explanation
1. Set LM35 Analog Pin
For the LM35, you need to set the pin connected to the analog output of the sensor as an input. This is done by configuring the appropriate TRIS register bit.

Syntax:
```
TRISA0 = 1;  // Set RA0 pin as input for LM35 analog
signal
```

Example:
```
TRISA0 = 1;   // Set pin RA0 as input for analog signal
```

Explanation:
This line of code configures the pin RA0 as an input to read the analog voltage from the LM35 sensor.

2. Initialize ADC for LM35

Before reading the temperature, you must configure the ADC settings in the microcontroller. This configuration sets the input pin for analog reading, the reference voltage, and other necessary parameters for proper ADC operation.

Syntax:
```
ADCON1 = 0x06;   // Configure ADC with VDD as reference voltage and right justify the result
```

Example:
```
ADCON1 = 0x06;   // ADC configuration for LM35
```

Explanation:
This code configures the ADC to read an analog signal from the LM35 sensor, using VDD as the reference voltage and right-justifying the result.

3. Start ADC Conversion

To start an ADC conversion, set the GO bit in the ADCON0 register. This initiates the conversion process.

Syntax:
```
ADCON0bits.GO = 1;   // Start ADC conversion
```
Example:
```
ADCON0bits.GO = 1;   // Start ADC conversion for temperature reading
```
Explanation:
This command starts the ADC conversion process for the temperature reading. The microcontroller will sample the voltage and convert it to a digital value.

4. Wait for ADC Result

Once the ADC conversion is started, you need to wait for it to complete. This can be done by checking the GO_nDONE bit in the ADCON0 register.

Syntax:
```
while(ADCON0bits.GO_nDONE);  // Wait for ADC conversion to finish
```

Example:
```
while(ADCON0bits.GO_nDONE);  // Wait for the ADC conversion to complete
```

Explanation:
 This loop will keep the program waiting until the ADC conversion is finished. Once the conversion is done, the result will be available in the ADC result registers.

5. Read ADC Value

After the conversion is complete, you can read the result from the ADC data registers (ADRESH and ADRESL). The result is combined to form a 10-bit value.

Syntax:
```
temperature = (ADRESH << 8) | ADRESL;  // Combine ADC result (high byte and low byte)
```

Example:
```
temperature = (ADRESH << 8) | ADRESL;  // Get the 10-bit ADC result for temperature
```

Explanation:
 The ADRESH contains the high byte of the result, and ADRESL contains the low byte. By shifting ADRESH left and combining with ADRESL, you get the 10-bit value representing the temperature.

6. DS18B20 Start Conversion

For the DS18B20, you need to initialize the 1-Wire bus before starting the temperature conversion.
Syntax:
```
OneWire_Init();  // Initialize the 1-Wire bus for
DS18B20
```

Example:
```
OneWire_Init();  // Initialize 1-Wire communication
```

Explanation:
 This code initializes the 1-Wire bus, which is necessary for communication with the DS18B20 sensor.

7. DS18B20 Read Temperature

Once the conversion is complete, you can read the temperature value from the DS18B20 sensor using a specific library function designed to interface with the sensor.
Syntax:
```
temp = DS18B20_ReadTemperature();  // Read temperature
from DS18B20 sensor
```

Example:
```
temp = DS18B20_ReadTemperature();  // Get the
temperature from DS18B20
```

Explanation:
 This function reads the temperature value from the DS18B20 sensor and stores it in the temp variable.

Real-life Applications Project: Temperature Monitoring System
In this project, we will interface an LM35 temperature sensor with a PIC microcontroller to create a temperature monitoring system. The system will continuously monitor the temperature and display the value on an LCD screen.

Required Components

Component	Description
PIC Microcontroller	The main controller for the temperature monitoring.
LM35	The temperature sensor to measure temperature.
LCD Display	To display the temperature value.
Resistors	For voltage division and current limiting.
Jumper Wires	For making necessary connections.

Circuit Connection Table

Component	Pin Connection
LM35	VCC to 5V, GND to ground, Output to RA0.
LCD	Connected to microcontroller's data and control pins.

Project Code

```
#include <xc.h>
#define _XTAL_FREQ 4000000  // Define system clock
frequency

void initADC() {
    ADCON

1 = 0x06;  // Configure ADC
    TRISA0 = 1;      // Set RA0 as input for LM35
    ADCON0bits.ADON = 1;   // Enable ADC
}

unsigned int readADC() {
    ADCON0bits.GO = 1;         // Start conversion
    while(ADCON0bits.GO_nDONE); // Wait for completion
    return (ADRESH << 8) | ADRESL;  // Read ADC result
}

void main() {
    initADC();  // Initialize ADC
    unsigned int temp;  // Variable to store
temperature value
    while(1) {
```

```
        temp = readADC();   // Read temperature value
        // Display temp on LCD or use for further
processing
        __delay_ms(1000);   // Delay before next reading
    }
}
```

Real-life Applications

- **Home Automation**: Temperature sensors can be used in home automation systems to control heating, ventilation, and air conditioning (HVAC) systems based on room temperature.
- **Weather Stations**: These sensors are frequently used in weather stations to monitor outdoor temperatures, humidity, and other environmental factors.
- **Industrial Applications**: In industrial settings, temperature sensors help monitor the temperature of machinery and equipment to prevent overheating and ensure proper operation.

Chapter 29: Light and IR Sensors with PIC Microcontrollers

Light and Infrared (IR) sensors are commonly used in embedded systems to detect environmental conditions like light levels or proximity of objects. By interfacing these sensors with PIC microcontrollers, we can create a variety of practical applications such as automated lighting systems, object detection, and motion sensing. This chapter will cover the basics of using light and IR sensors with PIC microcontrollers, how to interface them, and practical projects that you can build.

Key Concepts of Light and IR Sensors

Concept	Description	Example
LDR (Light Dependent Resistor)	A resistor that changes its resistance based on the amount of light it receives.	Used to sense light levels in a room.
Photodiode	A semiconductor device that generates a current when exposed to light.	Used for precise light measurements.
IR Sensors	Sensors that detect infrared radiation emitted by objects or people.	Used for proximity sensing or object detection.
Active IR Sensor	Uses an emitter and receiver to detect obstacles by reflecting infrared light.	Used for proximity detection.
Passive IR Sensor	Detects infrared radiation emitted by objects without any light source.	Used in motion sensors for security systems.

Basic Rules for Using Light and IR Sensors

Rule	Correct Example	Incorrect Example
Use appropriate ADC channels for LDR readings.	ADCON0 = 0x01;	Using digital read on an analog input pin.
Ensure proper wiring and connection of the IR sensors.	Connect emitter and receiver pins properly.	Incorrect pin connections causing malfunctions.

Filter noise in analog readings for accurate results.	Use delay() to stabilize ADC readings.	Ignoring stabilizing the input, leading to fluctuating readings.
Use proper power supply for sensors.	Providing 5V for the IR sensors.	Using incorrect voltage supply causing sensor malfunction.

Syntax Table

SL	Function	Syntax/Example	Description
1	Configure ADC for LDR reading	`ADCON1 = 0x06; TRISA0 = 1;`	Configures ADC and pin for LDR input.
2	Read analog LDR value	`lightLevel = readADC();`	Reads the analog value from the LDR.
3	Turn on relay	`PORTCbits.RC0 = 1;`	Turns on a relay (connected to the light).
4	Turn off relay	`PORTCbits.RC0 = 0;`	Turns off the relay (turns off the light).
5	Read IR sensor (active)	`IR_read = PORTBbits.RB0;`	Reads the digital signal from the IR sensor.

Syntax Explanation

1. Configure ADC for LDR Reading

What does configuring ADC do?

In order to read analog signals from the Light Dependent Resistor (LDR), you need to configure the Analog-to-Digital Converter (ADC) correctly. By setting the **ADCON1** register, you prepare the PIC microcontroller to read the analog signals coming from the LDR.

Syntax:

```
ADCON1 = 0x06;  // Set ADC to right justification and
configure pins as analog.
TRISA0 = 1;     // Set RA0 as input for LDR.
```

Example Explanation: Here, `ADCON1 = 0x06;` configures the ADC for right justification, and `TRISA0 = 1;` sets the RA0 pin as input to receive the LDR signal.

2. Read Analog LDR Value

What does reading the LDR value do?
This function retrieves the value from the ADC that corresponds to the LDR light intensity. The value can then be used to decide if the light needs to be turned on or off based on a preset threshold.
Syntax:
```
unsigned int lightLevel = readADC();
```

Example Explanation: This command reads the current value from the LDR and stores it in the variable lightLevel. This value will range from 0 (dark) to 1023 (bright).

3. Turn On Relay

What does turning on the relay do?
The relay is activated when the light level falls below the threshold, turning on a connected device, such as a lamp.
Syntax:
```
PORTCbits.RC0 = 1;
```

Example Explanation: Here, setting the pin RC0 to 1 activates the relay, which powers on the light or connected device.

4. Turn Off Relay

What does turning off the relay do?
The relay is deactivated when the light level rises above the threshold, turning off the connected device.
Syntax:
```
PORTCbits.RC0 = 0;
```

Example Explanation: This sets pin RC0 to 0, which deactivates the relay and turns off the light.

5. Read IR Sensor (Active)

What does reading the IR sensor do?
For active IR sensors, this command reads the digital signal output from the IR sensor. If an object is detected, it will output a high signal.

Syntax:
```
unsigned int IR_read = PORTBbits.RB0;
```

Example Explanation: This reads the signal from the IR sensor connected to pin RB0. If an object is detected, IR_read will be high (1); otherwise, it will be low (0).

Real-life Applications Project: Automated Light Control System
In this project, we will interface an LDR (Light Dependent Resistor) with a PIC microcontroller to create an automated light control system. The system will automatically turn on a light when it detects low ambient light levels and turn it off when it gets brighter.

Required Components

Component	Description
PIC Microcontroller	Controls the entire system logic.
LDR (Light Dependent Resistor)	Senses the ambient light level.
Relay	Controls the power to the connected light.
LED	Indicates the light status (on/off).
Resistors	Used to limit current in the circuit.
Power Supply	Powers the PIC and other components.

Circuit Connection Table

Component	Pin Connection
LDR	RA0 (ADC input pin)
Relay	RC0 (Digital output pin)
LED	RB0 (Digital output pin)
PIC Microcontroller	As specified for the components

Project Code: Automated Light Control System

```
// Define necessary constants and pins
#define LDR_PIN   0    // RA0 for LDR (Light Dependent
Resistor)
#define RELAY_PIN 0    // RC0 for Relay
#define LED_PIN   0    // RB0 for LED

// Define light threshold for control (adjust as
necessary)
#define LIGHT_THRESHOLD 512

// Initialize ADC and Digital I/O pins
void initADC() {
    ADCON1 = 0x06;    // Configure ADC for right
justification
    TRISA0 = 1;       // Set RA0 as input for LDR
    TRISC0 = 0;       // Set RC0 as output for Relay
    TRISB0 = 0;       // Set RB0 as output for LED
}

// Start ADC conversion
unsigned int readADC() {
    ADCON0bits.GO = 1;      // Start conversion
    while (ADCON0bits.GO_nDONE);  // Wait for
conversion to finish
    return (ADRESH << 8) | ADRESL; // Combine high and
low byte
}

// Main program to control light based on LDR readings
void main() {
    unsigned int lightLevel;

    // Initialize system
    initADC();

    // Main loop
```

```
while(1) {
    // Read the LDR value through ADC
    lightLevel = readADC();

    // Check if light level is below the threshold
(night or low light)
    if (lightLevel < LIGHT_THRESHOLD) {
        // Turn on the relay and LED (light on)
        PORTCbits.RC0 = 1;   // Relay ON
        PORTBbits.RB0 = 1;   // LED ON
    }
    else {
        // Turn off the relay and LED (light off)
        PORTCbits.RC0 = 0;   // Relay OFF
        PORTBbits.RB0 = 0;   // LED OFF
    }

    // Small delay before the next loop iteration
    __delay_ms(100);
}
}
```

Expected Results
- **At Night or Low Light**: The LDR will register a low value, which will trigger the relay to turn on the connected light, and the LED will also turn on to indicate the light's state.
- **During Daylight**: The LDR will register a high value, causing the system to turn off the light and LED.

Real-life Applications
- **Smart Home Lighting Systems**: Automatically turning on lights when it gets dark, such as in hallways or gardens.
- **Greenhouse Lighting**: Controlling artificial lights to optimize plant growth based on available sunlight.
- **Security Systems**: Activating lights based on the time of day or when motion is detected in dark environments.

Chapter 30: Motion Sensors with PIC Microcontrollers

Motion sensors are commonly used in various applications, from security systems to interactive devices. By detecting movement, these sensors can trigger specific actions, such as turning on lights or sending an alert. In this chapter, we will explore how to interface motion sensors with PIC microcontrollers, covering the basic principles, working with specific sensors like Passive Infrared (PIR) sensors, and practical applications.

Key Concepts of Motion Sensors

Motion sensors detect physical movement or changes in the environment, typically using infrared, ultrasonic, or microwave technology. The most commonly used type in embedded systems is the Passive Infrared (PIR) sensor, which detects changes in infrared radiation levels caused by the motion of warm objects like humans or animals.

Concept	Description	Example
PIR Sensor	Passive Infrared sensor that detects motion by sensing changes in infrared radiation.	Commonly used in security systems for detecting human presence.
Digital Output	The PIR sensor provides a high or low signal depending on whether it detects motion.	Output is either HIGH (motion detected) or LOW (no motion).
Relay	An electronic switch that allows the microcontroller to control higher voltage systems using the signal from a motion sensor.	Can be used to turn on lights when motion is detected.

Basic Rules for Using Motion Sensors

Rule	Correct Example	Incorrect Example
Use a PIR sensor with proper power supply.	Connect the VCC pin of the PIR to the 5V power rail.	Providing voltage higher than the sensor's rated voltage can damage it.
Connect the signal pin to an	Connect the signal pin to an interrupt-	Connecting to a non-interrupt-capable pin may

| I/O pin of the microcontroller. | enabled pin (e.g., RB0 for PIC). | lead to missed events. |
| Ensure the PIR sensor is within its detection range. | Test the sensor in a controlled environment to find its optimal range. | Placing the sensor in a highly reflective or obstructed area may reduce performance. |

Syntax Table

SL	Function	Syntax/Example	Description
1	Read PIR sensor output	motionDetected = PORTBbits.RB0;	Reads the digital output of the PIR sensor connected to RB0.
2	Control relay output	LATAbits.LATA0 = 1;	Turns on a relay connected to pin A0 when motion is detected.
3	Wait for motion	while(PORTBbit s.RB0 == 0);	Loops until the sensor detects motion.
4	Turn off relay	LATAbits.LATA0 = 0;	Turns off the relay after the motion event.

Syntax Explanation

1. Read PIR Sensor Output

What does reading PIR sensor output do?
The PIR sensor outputs a high or low signal depending on whether it detects motion. This can be read using a digital input pin of the microcontroller.
Syntax:
motionDetected = PORTBbits.RB0;

Example:
motionDetected = PORTBbits.RB0; // Read the motion
detected status from PIR sensor on RB0
Example Explanation:
In this example, the program reads the value from pin RB0, which is connected to the PIR sensor. If motion is detected, the sensor will output a high signal (1); otherwise, it will be low (0).

2. Control Relay Output

What does controlling the relay output do?
Using a relay with the motion sensor allows the PIC to control external devices such as lights, alarms, or motors when motion is detected.
Syntax:
```
LATAbits.LATA0 = 1;  // Turns on the relay to power the connected device
```

Example:
```
if (motionDetected == 1) {
    LATAbits.LATA0 = 1;  // Turn on relay to trigger connected light or alarm
}
```
Example Explanation:
When motion is detected, the code sets the output on pin A0 to high, which can control a relay or any other high-power device connected to the microcontroller.

3. Wait for Motion

What does waiting for motion do?
The program can continuously check if the PIR sensor detects motion and wait for the signal to change. This allows the system to respond only when an event occurs.
Syntax:
```
while(PORTBbits.RB0 == 0);  // Wait until motion is detected
```
Example:
```
while(PORTBbits.RB0 == 0);  // Wait until PIR sensor detects motion
LATAbits.LATA0 = 1;  // Turn on light if motion is detected
```
Example Explanation:
This loop continuously checks the PIR sensor's output, and once it detects motion (a high signal), the relay is triggered to turn on the connected device, like a light.

4. Turn off Relay

What does turning off the relay do?
After motion is detected and the action has been performed (e.g., turning on a light), you may want to turn off the relay after a set period or when the motion stops.

Syntax:
```
LATAbits.LATA0 = 0;  // Turns off the relay
```

Example:
```
if (motionDetected == 0) {
    LATAbits.LATA0 = 0;  // Turn off relay after motion
stops
}
```

Example Explanation:
After the motion stops, the relay is turned off, which will disconnect the connected device (such as turning off a light) once the motion is no longer detected.

Real-life Applications Project: PIR Sensor Based Security System
In this project, we will build a simple security system that activates an alarm when motion is detected by a PIR sensor.

Required Components

Component	Description
PIR Sensor	Detects motion and provides a signal.
PIC Microcontroller	Controls the relay and processes the sensor's data.
Relay	Controls high-voltage devices like alarms or lights.
Buzzer	The output device triggered when motion is detected.

Circuit Connection Table

Component	Pin Connection
PIR Sensor	Signal -> RB0, VCC -> 5V, GND -> Ground
PIC Microcontroller	RB0 -> PIR Signal Input, Relay Pin -> RA0
Buzzer	RA0 -> Relay Control Pin

Project Code

```c
#include <xc.h>

#define _XTAL_FREQ 4000000  // Define crystal frequency

void main() {
    TRISBbits.TRISB0 = 1;   // Set RB0 as input for PIR sensor
    TRISAbits.TRISA0 = 0;   // Set RA0 as output for relay

    while(1) {
        if (PORTBbits.RB0 == 1) {  // Check if motion is detected
            LATAbits.LATA0 = 1;   // Turn on the alarm
            __delay_ms(5000);     // Keep the alarm on for 5 seconds
            LATAbits.LATA0 = 0;   // Turn off the alarm
        }
    }
}
```

Expected Results

Once the code is uploaded to the PIC microcontroller, the system will continuously monitor the PIR sensor. When the sensor detects motion, it will trigger the alarm (via the relay). The alarm will sound for 5 seconds and then turn off automatically.

Chapter 31: Ultrasonic Sensors with PIC Microcontrollers

Ultrasonic sensors are widely used in applications requiring distance measurement, obstacle detection, and object positioning. These sensors operate by emitting high-frequency sound waves and measuring the time taken for the echo to return after bouncing off an object. In this chapter, we will explore how to interface ultrasonic sensors with PIC microcontrollers, covering fundamental concepts, working principles, interfacing techniques, and practical applications.

Key Concepts of Ultrasonic Sensors

Ultrasonic sensors use sound waves beyond the range of human hearing to measure distances. The most commonly used type in embedded systems is the HC-SR04 sensor, which provides precise distance measurements by calculating the time delay between transmitted and received sound waves.

Concept	Description	Example
Ultrasonic Sensor	A device that emits ultrasonic waves and measures the reflected signal.	Used in robotic obstacle avoidance systems.
Echo Time	The time interval between the transmission and reception of the ultrasonic pulse.	Measured in microseconds to calculate distance.
Distance Calculation	Distance is computed using the speed of sound and echo time.	Distance = (Speed of Sound × Echo Time) / 2.

Basic Rules for Using Ultrasonic Sensors

Rule	Correct Example	Incorrect Example
Ensure correct power supply.	Connect VCC to 5V and GND to ground.	Connecting to incorrect voltage can damage the sensor.
Use proper trigger and echo connections.	Trigger pin to output, Echo pin to input.	Miswiring can lead to incorrect readings.

Maintain a clear path for sound waves.	Place the sensor in an unobstructed area.	Blocking the sensor may result in inaccurate measurements.

Syntax Table

SL	Function	Syntax/Example	Description
1	**Trigger Ultrasonic Pulse**	LATBbits.LATB0 = 1; __delay_us(10); LATBbits.LATB0 = 0;	Sends a 10-microsecond pulse to initiate measurement.
2	**Read Echo Pulse Width**	echoTime = pulseIn(PORTBbits.RB1, HIGH);	Measures the time taken for the echo to return.
3	**Calculate Distance**	distance = (echoTime * 0.0343) / 2;	Converts echo time into distance using the speed of sound.
4	**Display Distance**	printf("Distance: %d cm", distance);	Outputs the calculated distance value.

Syntax Explanation

1. Trigger Ultrasonic Pulse

What does triggering an ultrasonic pulse do? The ultrasonic sensor needs to be triggered with a short pulse to start the measurement process.

Syntax:

```
LATBbits.LATB0 = 1;
__delay_us(10);
LATBbits.LATB0 = 0;
```

Example:

```
LATBbits.LATB0 = 1;   // Set trigger pin high
__delay_us(10);       // Maintain high for 10 microseconds
LATBbits.LATB0 = 0;   // Set trigger pin low
```

Example Explanation: This example sends a 10-microsecond pulse to the trigger pin, which initiates the ultrasonic wave emission. The sensor transmits an ultrasonic pulse that travels through the air. When the pulse encounters an obstacle, it reflects back to the sensor, and the echo pin generates a response signal. This pulse duration is later used to calculate the distance.

2. Read Echo Pulse Width

What does reading the echo pulse width do? The time taken for the echo to return is measured using a digital input.

Syntax:

```
echoTime = pulseIn(PORTBbits.RB1, HIGH);
```

Example:

```
echoTime = pulseIn(PORTBbits.RB1, HIGH);   // Measure
pulse duration on RB1
```

Example Explanation: This code waits for the echo pin to go high, starts counting the time, and then waits for it to go low again. The recorded time represents how long the pulse took to travel to the obstacle and back. This measurement is essential for determining the object's distance accurately.

3. Calculate Distance

What does calculating distance do? Using the measured echo time, the distance to the object is calculated.

Syntax:

```
distance = (echoTime * 0.0343) / 2;
```

Example:

```
distance = (echoTime * 0.0343) / 2;   // Convert time to
distance in cm
```

Example Explanation: The speed of sound in air is approximately 343 m/s or 0.0343 cm/µs. The time recorded by the echo pin represents the round-trip duration, meaning the pulse travels to the obstacle and then back to the sensor. To determine the actual distance to the obstacle, we divide the total time by 2.

4. Display Distance

What does displaying distance do? The calculated distance can be displayed on an LCD or serial monitor.

Syntax:

```
printf("Distance: %d cm", distance);
```

Example:

```
printf("Distance: %d cm", distance);   // Print distance
on LCD/Serial Monitor
```

Example Explanation: This command outputs the measured distance in centimeters on a display or serial terminal. By continuously printing the values, users can monitor how the distance changes as objects move closer or farther away from the sensor.

Real-life Applications Project: Ultrasonic Distance Measurement System

In this project, we will build a simple system that measures and displays the distance of an object using an ultrasonic sensor and a PIC microcontroller.

Required Components

Component	Description
Ultrasonic Sensor	HC-SR04 to measure distance.
PIC Microcontroller	Processes the sensor data.
LCD Display	Displays the measured distance.
Resistors	Used for circuit stability.

Project Code

```c
#include <xc.h>
#include <stdio.h>

#define _XTAL_FREQ 4000000  // Define crystal frequency

void main() {
    TRISBbits.TRISB0 = 0;  // Set RB0 as output for trigger
    TRISBbits.TRISB1 = 1;  // Set RB1 as input for echo
    unsigned int echoTime;
    float distance;

    while(1) {
        LATBbits.LATB0 = 1;
        __delay_us(10);
        LATBbits.LATB0 = 0;

        while(!PORTBbits.RB1);  // Wait for echo to go high
        TMR1 = 0;                      // Reset Timer
```

```
        while(PORTBbits.RB1);    // Wait for echo to go
low
        echoTime = TMR1;         // Store timer value

        distance = (echoTime * 0.0343) / 2;  //
Calculate distance
        printf("Distance: %d cm", (int)distance);  //
Print result

        __delay_ms(500);  // Delay before next
measurement
    }
}
```

Expected Results

Once the code is uploaded to the PIC microcontroller, the system will continuously measure and display the distance of an object. When an object comes closer or moves away, the displayed distance will change accordingly. This system can be used for applications like obstacle detection in robots, parking assistance systems, and smart measurement tools.

Chapter 32: Humidity Sensors with PIC Microcontrollers

Humidity sensors are used in various applications such as weather monitoring, industrial control, and environmental sensing. These sensors measure the amount of water vapor present in the air and provide either analog or digital output. In this chapter, we will explore how to interface humidity sensors with PIC microcontrollers, covering the working principles, sensor types, interfacing techniques, and practical applications.

Key Concepts of Humidity Sensors

Humidity sensors detect moisture levels in the air and convert this information into an electrical signal. The most commonly used sensors in embedded systems are the DHT11 and DHT22, which provide digital data via a one-wire communication protocol.

Concept	Description	Example
Humidity Sensor	A device that detects and measures the humidity in the surrounding environment.	Used in climate control systems and greenhouses.
Relative Humidity (RH)	The amount of water vapor in the air compared to the maximum it can hold at a given temperature.	Expressed in percentage (%).
DHT11/DHT22 Sensor	Common digital humidity sensors that use a single-wire communication protocol.	Used in weather stations and HVAC systems.

Basic Rules for Using Humidity Sensors

Rule	Correct Example	Incorrect Example
Ensure correct power supply.	Connect VCC to 5V and GND to ground.	Providing incorrect voltage may damage the sensor.
Use a pull-up resistor.	Use a 4.7kΩ resistor on the data pin for stable communication.	Omitting the resistor may cause unstable readings.
Allow adequate measurement intervals.	Read the sensor every 2 seconds for accuracy.	Reading the sensor too frequently may return incorrect values.

Syntax Table

SL	Function	Syntax/Example	Description
1	Initialize Sensor	initDHT();	Prepares the microcontroller for sensor communication.
2	Read Humidity	humidity = readHumidity();	Retrieves the humidity value from the sensor.
3	Read Temperature	temperature = readTemperature();	Retrieves the temperature value from the sensor.
4	Display Data	printf("Humidity: %d%%", humidity);	Outputs the humidity reading.

Syntax Explanation

1. Initialize Sensor

What does initializing the sensor do? The sensor needs to be properly initialized before communication begins.

Syntax:

```
initDHT();
```

Example:

```
initDHT();  // Initialize the DHT11/DHT22 sensor
```

Example Explanation: This function sets up the microcontroller to communicate with the humidity sensor by configuring the data pin as input/output and ensuring proper timing for data retrieval.

2. Read Humidity

What does reading humidity do? It retrieves the relative humidity value from the sensor and converts it into a readable percentage.

Syntax:

```
humidity = readHumidity();
```

Example:

```
humidity = readHumidity();  // Read the humidity value
from the sensor
```

Example Explanation: This function sends a request to the sensor and waits for its response, capturing the data packet and extracting the humidity value.

3. Read Temperature

What does reading temperature do? It retrieves the current ambient temperature, which can be useful for compensating humidity readings.

Syntax:
```
temperature = readTemperature();
```

Example:
```
temperature = readTemperature();  // Read temperature
value from the sensor
```

Example Explanation: The function retrieves the temperature data from the sensor, typically measured in degrees Celsius, which can be displayed alongside humidity readings.

4. Display Data

What does displaying data do? The measured humidity and temperature values can be displayed on an LCD or sent to a serial monitor.

Syntax:
```
printf("Humidity: %d%%", humidity);
```

Example:
```
printf("Humidity: %d%%  Temperature: %d°C", humidity,
temperature);
```
Example Explanation: This line prints the humidity and temperature readings to an output device, allowing real-time monitoring.

Real-life Applications Project: Humidity Monitoring System

In this project, we will build a simple humidity and temperature monitoring system using a PIC microcontroller and a DHT11 sensor.

Required Components

Component	Description
DHT11 Sensor	Measures humidity and temperature.
PIC Microcontroller	Processes the sensor data.
LCD Display	Displays the measured values.
4.7kΩ Resistor	Used as a pull-up resistor for stable data communication.

Circuit Connection Table

Component	Pin Connection
DHT11 Sensor	Data -> RB0, VCC -> 5V, GND -> Ground
PIC Microcontroller	RB0 -> Data Pin, LCD -> PORTD
LCD Display	Connected to PORTD for output

Project Code

```c
#include <xc.h>
#include <stdio.h>

#define _XTAL_FREQ 4000000  // Define crystal frequency

void initDHT();
int readHumidity();
int readTemperature();

void main() {
    int humidity, temperature;
    initDHT();  // Initialize sensor
    while(1) {
        humidity = readHumidity();  // Get humidity reading
        temperature = readTemperature();  // Get temperature reading

        printf("Humidity: %d%%  Temperature: %d°C", humidity, temperature);
        __delay_ms(2000);  // Wait before next reading
    }
}
```

Expected Results

Once the code is uploaded to the PIC microcontroller, the system will continuously measure and display the humidity and temperature. These readings will update every 2 seconds, providing real-time environmental monitoring.

This system can be used in weather monitoring, HVAC control, and agricultural applications where humidity regulation is essential.

Chapter 33: Pressure Sensors with PIC Microcontrollers

Pressure sensors are widely used in industrial automation, weather monitoring, medical devices, and fluid control systems. These sensors measure the force exerted by gases or liquids and convert it into an electrical signal. In this chapter, we will explore how to interface pressure sensors with PIC microcontrollers, covering the working principles, sensor types, interfacing techniques, and practical applications.

Key Concepts of Pressure Sensors

Pressure sensors detect changes in pressure and convert this information into an electrical output. The most commonly used types in embedded systems are piezoresistive and capacitive pressure sensors, which provide either analog or digital output.

Concept	Description	Example
Pressure Sensor	A device that measures pressure and converts it into an electrical signal.	Used in industrial automation and medical devices.
Absolute Pressure	Measures pressure relative to a perfect vacuum.	Used in barometers and altimeters.
Gauge Pressure	Measures pressure relative to atmospheric pressure.	Used in tire pressure monitoring systems.
Differential Pressure	Measures the difference between two pressure points.	Used in airflow and filtration monitoring.

Basic Rules for Using Pressure Sensors

Rule	Correct Example	Incorrect Example
Ensure correct power supply.	Connect VCC to 5V and GND to ground.	Providing incorrect voltage may damage the sensor.
Use an ADC pin for analog sensors.	Connect analog output to an ADC pin for conversion.	Connecting to a digital pin will not read analog values.
Use I2C/SPI communication for digital sensors.	Connect SDA and SCL for I2C sensors.	Miswiring the communication lines may cause incorrect readings.

Calibrate the sensor before use.	Read initial values and apply correction factors.	Using an uncalibrated sensor may lead to inaccurate measurements.

Syntax Table

S L	Function	Syntax/Example	Description
1	Initialize Sensor	initPressureSensor();	Prepares the microcontroller for sensor communication.
2	Read Pressure (Analog)	pressure = readADC(0);	Reads an analog pressure value from channel 0.
3	Read Pressure (Digital)	pressure = readI2C();	Retrieves pressure data from an I2C sensor.
4	Display Data	printf("Pressure: %d Pa", pressure);	Outputs the pressure reading.

Syntax Explanation

1. Initialize Sensor

What does initializing the sensor do? It sets up the microcontroller to communicate with the pressure sensor, configuring ADC or I2C settings as needed.

Syntax:
```
initPressureSensor();
```

Example:
```
initPressureSensor();  // Initialize the pressure
sensor
```

Example Explanation: This function configures the microcontroller's ADC or I2C module based on the sensor type, ensuring proper data acquisition.

2. Read Pressure (Analog)

What does reading an analog pressure value do? It converts the sensor's voltage output into a digital value using the ADC module.

Syntax:
```
pressure = readADC(0);
```

Example:
```
pressure = readADC(0);  // Read analog pressure sensor
on ADC channel 0
```

Example Explanation: This function reads the voltage from an analog pressure sensor, converts it to a digital value, and maps it to a pressure range.

3. Read Pressure (Digital)

What does reading a digital pressure value do? It retrieves sensor data using I2C or SPI communication protocols.

Syntax:
```
pressure = readI2C();
```

Example:
```
pressure = readI2C();  // Read digital pressure value
from I2C sensor
```

Example Explanation: This function sends a request to the pressure sensor via the I2C protocol and retrieves the pressure data in digital form.

4. Display Data

What does displaying pressure data do? It prints the measured pressure value to an LCD or serial monitor.

Syntax:
```
printf("Pressure: %d Pa", pressure);
```

Example:
```
printf("Pressure: %d Pa", pressure);  // Print pressure
reading
```

Example Explanation: This line displays the measured pressure in Pascals (Pa), which is useful for real-time monitoring.

Real-life Applications Project: Digital Pressure Monitoring System

In this project, we will build a pressure monitoring system using a PIC microcontroller and an I2C-based pressure sensor.

Required Components

Component	Description
Pressure Sensor	Measures air or liquid pressure.
PIC Microcontroller	Processes the sensor data.
LCD Display	Displays the measured values.
Resistors	Used for I2C pull-up connections.

Circuit Connection Table

Component	Pin Connection
Pressure Sensor	VCC -> 5V, GND -> Ground, SDA -> RC4, SCL -> RC3
PIC Microcontroller	RC4 -> SDA, RC3 -> SCL, LCD -> PORTD
LCD Display	Connected to PORTD for output

Project Code

```c
#include <xc.h>
#include <stdio.h>

#define _XTAL_FREQ 4000000  // Define crystal frequency

void initPressureSensor();
int readI2C();

void main() {
    int pressure;
    initPressureSensor();  // Initialize sensor
    while(1) {
        pressure = readI2C();  // Get pressure reading
        printf("Pressure: %d Pa", pressure);  //
Display pressure
        __delay_ms(1000);  // Wait before next reading
    }
}
```

Expected Results

Once the code is uploaded to the PIC microcontroller, the system will continuously measure and display the pressure. The readings will update every second, making it useful for real-time pressure monitoring in industrial, medical, and environmental applications.

Chapter 34: Sound Sensors with PIC Microcontrollers

Sound sensors are used in various applications such as voice recognition, noise level monitoring, and security systems. These sensors detect sound waves and convert them into electrical signals, which can then be processed by a microcontroller. In this chapter, we will explore how to interface sound sensors with PIC microcontrollers, covering their working principles, sensor types, interfacing techniques, and practical applications.

Key Concepts of Sound Sensors

Sound sensors detect audio signals and convert them into electrical outputs, either analog or digital. The most commonly used sound sensors in embedded systems include electret microphones and MEMS microphones, which provide signal variations based on sound intensity.

Concept	Description	Example
Sound Sensor	A device that captures sound waves and converts them into electrical signals.	Used in speech recognition systems.
Analog Sound Sensor	Provides a continuous voltage output corresponding to sound intensity.	Used in noise monitoring applications.
Digital Sound Sensor	Outputs HIGH when sound exceeds a threshold.	Used in clapping-controlled devices.
Electret Microphone	A type of microphone that generates an analog signal.	Used in voice amplification circuits.

Basic Rules for Using Sound Sensors

Rule	Correct Example	Incorrect Example
Ensure correct power supply.	Connect VCC to 5V and GND to ground.	Using incorrect voltage may damage the sensor.

Use an ADC pin for analog sensors.	Connect the sensor output to an ADC pin for accurate readings.	Connecting to a digital pin will not read analog values.
Use a comparator for digital sensors.	Set a reference voltage to trigger at a specific sound level.	Without a threshold, random noise may trigger signals.
Filter noise for precise readings.	Use a capacitor to smooth out unwanted fluctuations.	Unfiltered signals may cause unstable readings.

Syntax Table

SL	Function	Syntax/Example	Description
1	Initialize Sensor	initSoundSensor();	Prepares the microcontroller for sensor input.
2	Read Sound Level (Analog)	soundLevel = readADC(0);	Reads an analog value from the sound sensor.
3	Detect Sound (Digital)	if(PORTBbits.RB1 == 1)	Checks if a digital sound sensor detects noise.
4	Display Data	printf("Sound Level: %d", soundLevel);	Outputs the sound level reading.

Syntax Explanation

1. Initialize Sensor

What does initializing the sensor do? It sets up the microcontroller to communicate with the sound sensor, configuring ADC or digital input settings as required.

Syntax:

```
initSoundSensor();
```

Example:

```
initSoundSensor();  // Initialize the sound sensor
```

Example Explanation: This function configures the microcontroller's input pins, ADC, or digital comparator based on the type of sound sensor being used.

2. Read Sound Level (Analog)

What does reading an analog sound level do? It converts the sensor's voltage output into a digital value using the ADC module.

Syntax:
```
soundLevel = readADC(0);
```

Example:
```
soundLevel = readADC(0);   // Read analog sound sensor
on ADC channel 0
```

Example Explanation: This function reads the voltage from an analog sound sensor, converts it to a digital value, and maps it to a sound intensity range.

3. Detect Sound (Digital)

What does detecting a digital sound signal do? It monitors whether the sound level exceeds a predefined threshold.

Syntax:
```
if(PORTBbits.RB1 == 1)
```

Example:
```
if(PORTBbits.RB1 == 1) {
    printf("Sound detected!");
}
```

Example Explanation: This conditional statement checks if the sound sensor's digital output goes HIGH when noise surpasses the threshold, triggering an action.

4. Display Data

What does displaying sound level data do? It prints the measured sound intensity or detection status to an LCD or serial monitor.

Syntax:
```
printf("Sound Level: %d", soundLevel);
```

Example:
```
printf("Sound Level: %d", soundLevel);   // Print sound
intensity value
```

Example Explanation: This command displays the detected sound level, which is useful for real-time monitoring.

Real-life Applications Project: Sound-Activated Alarm System

In this project, we will build a sound-activated alarm system using a PIC microcontroller and a digital sound sensor.

Required Components

Component	Description
Sound Sensor	Detects sound levels and provides output.
PIC Microcontroller	Processes the sensor data.
Buzzer	Produces an alarm sound when triggered.
Resistors	Used for circuit stabilization.

Circuit Connection Table

Component	Pin Connection
Sound Sensor	VCC -> 5V, GND -> Ground, OUT -> RB1
PIC Microcontroller	RB1 -> Sensor OUT, RA0 -> Buzzer
Buzzer	Connected to RA0 for sound output

Project Code

```c
#include <xc.h>
#include <stdio.h>


#define _XTAL_FREQ 4000000  // Define crystal frequency

void initSoundSensor();
void triggerAlarm();

void main() {
    TRISBbits.TRISB1 = 1;  // Set RB1 as input for the
sound sensor
    TRISAbits.TRISA0 = 0;  // Set RA0 as output for the
buzzer

    while(1) {
        if (PORTBbits.RB1 == 1) {  // Check if sound is
detected
            triggerAlarm();  // Activate buzzer
        }
    }
}
```

```
void triggerAlarm() {
    LATAbits.LATA0 = 1;   // Turn on buzzer
    __delay_ms(1000);     // Keep alarm on for 1 second
    LATAbits.LATA0 = 0;   // Turn off buzzer
}
```

Expected Results

Once the code is uploaded to the PIC microcontroller, the system
will continuously monitor sound levels. If a loud noise is detected,
the buzzer will activate for one second, simulating an alarm system.
This type of project can be used for security alarms, voice-activated
devices, and sound-based automation.

Chapter 35: Microphones with PIC Microcontrollers

Microphones are widely used in applications such as voice recognition, sound recording, and noise detection. These devices convert sound waves into electrical signals, which can be processed by a microcontroller. In this chapter, we will explore how to interface different types of microphones with PIC microcontrollers, covering working principles, interfacing techniques, and practical applications.

Key Concepts of Microphones

Microphones detect audio signals and convert them into electrical signals that can be either analog or digital. The most commonly used microphones in embedded systems include electret condenser microphones and MEMS (Micro-Electro-Mechanical System) microphones, which provide various signal outputs.

Concept	Description	Example
Microphone	A device that captures sound and converts it into an electrical signal.	Used in voice-controlled devices.
Analog Microphone	Produces a continuous voltage output corresponding to sound intensity.	Used in audio recording applications.
Digital Microphone	Uses I2S or PDM to output digital sound data.	Used in modern voice assistants.
Electret Microphone	A type of condenser microphone that requires bias voltage.	Commonly used in speech applications.
MEMS Microphone	A miniaturized microphone with a digital output.	Used in smartphones and IoT devices.

Basic Rules for Using Microphones

Rule	Correct Example	Incorrect Example
Ensure correct power supply.	Connect VCC to 5V (or 3.3V for MEMS).	Incorrect voltage may damage the microphone.

Use an amplifier for weak signals.	Use an operational amplifier (Op-Amp) to boost signals.	Directly connecting to a microcontroller may produce weak signals.
Use an ADC pin for analog microphones.	Connect the microphone output to an ADC pin for accurate readings.	Connecting to a digital pin will not read analog signals.
Use proper filtering.	Add capacitors to remove unwanted noise.	Unfiltered signals may cause unstable readings.

Syntax Table

SL	Function	Syntax/Example	Description
1	Initialize Microphone	initMicrophone();	Prepares the microcontroller for microphone input.
2	Read Audio Level (Analog)	audioLevel = readADC(0);	Reads an analog value from the microphone.
3	Detect Sound (Digital)	if(PORTBbits.RB1 == 1)	Checks if a digital microphone detects sound.
4	Display Audio Level	printf("Audio Level: %d", audioLevel);	Outputs the sound intensity reading.

Syntax Explanation

1. Initialize Microphone

What does initializing the microphone do? It sets up the microcontroller to communicate with the microphone, configuring ADC or digital input settings as required.

Syntax:

```
initMicrophone();
```

Example:

```
initMicrophone();  // Initialize the microphone
```

Example Explanation: This function configures the microcontroller's input pins, ADC, or digital interfaces depending on the type of microphone used.

2. Read Audio Level (Analog)

What does reading an analog audio level do? It converts the microphone's voltage output into a digital value using the ADC module.

Syntax:
```
audioLevel = readADC(0);
```

Example:
```
audioLevel = readADC(0);   // Read analog microphone
signal on ADC channel 0
```

Example Explanation: This function reads the voltage from an analog microphone, converts it into a digital value, and maps it to a sound intensity range.

3. Detect Sound (Digital)

What does detecting a digital sound signal do? It checks whether the sound level exceeds a predefined threshold.

Syntax:
```
if(PORTBbits.RB1 == 1)
```

Example:
```
if(PORTBbits.RB1 == 1) {
    printf("Sound detected!");
}
```

Example Explanation: This conditional statement verifies if the digital microphone's output goes HIGH when a sound is detected.

4. Display Audio Level

What does displaying audio level data do? It prints the detected sound intensity to an LCD or serial monitor.

Syntax:
```
printf("Audio Level: %d", audioLevel);
```

Example:
```
printf("Audio Level: %d", audioLevel);   // Print sound
intensity value
```

Example Explanation: This command displays the real-time audio intensity from the microphone.

Real-life Applications Project: Voice-Activated System

In this project, we will build a voice-activated system using a PIC microcontroller and an electret microphone with an amplifier.

Required Components

Component	Description
Electret Microphone	Captures sound and converts it into an electrical signal.
Op-Amp (LM358)	Amplifies weak microphone signals.
PIC Microcontroller	Processes the microphone data.
Speaker/Buzzer	Outputs a response based on detected sound.
Resistors and Capacitors	Used for signal conditioning and filtering.

Circuit Connection Table

Component	Pin Connection
Microphone	VCC -> 5V, GND -> Ground, OUT -> Op-Amp Input
Op-Amp Output	Connected to ADC Channel 0 (AN0)
PIC Microcontroller	AN0 -> Op-Amp Output, RA0 -> Speaker Control
Speaker/Buzzer	Connected to RA0 for sound output

Project Code

```c
#include <xc.h>
#include <stdio.h>

#define _XTAL_FREQ 4000000   // Define crystal frequency

void initMicrophone();
int readADC(int channel);
void activateResponse();

void main() {
    int audioLevel;
    initMicrophone();  // Initialize microphone setup

    while(1) {
        audioLevel = readADC(0);  // Read microphone
signal
```

```
        if (audioLevel > 200) {  // Threshold for voice
detection
            activateResponse();  // Perform an action
based on voice input
        }
    }
}

void activateResponse() {
    LATAbits.LATA0 = 1;  // Turn on speaker or buzzer
    __delay_ms(1000);    // Keep it active for 1 second
    LATAbits.LATA0 = 0;  // Turn off output
}
```

Expected Results

Once the code is uploaded to the PIC microcontroller, the system will continuously monitor sound levels. If a loud noise or voice is detected, it will trigger a response, such as activating a buzzer or playing a sound. This system can be used in voice-activated home automation, noise detection alarms, and interactive audio systems.

Chapter 36: Gas Sensors with PIC Microcontrollers

Gas sensors are widely used in industrial, environmental, and safety applications to detect harmful or combustible gases. These sensors measure the concentration of specific gases in the air and provide an electrical signal that can be processed by a microcontroller. In this chapter, we will explore how to interface gas sensors with PIC microcontrollers, covering the working principles, sensor types, interfacing techniques, and practical applications.

Key Concepts of Gas Sensors

Gas sensors detect the presence and concentration of gases and convert this information into an electrical output. The most commonly used types include metal oxide semiconductor (MOS) sensors, electrochemical sensors, and infrared sensors.

Concept	Description	Example
Gas Sensor	A device that detects gas concentration and converts it into an electrical signal.	Used in air quality monitoring systems.
Analog Gas Sensor	Outputs a variable voltage corresponding to gas concentration.	MQ-series sensors like MQ-2, MQ-7.
Digital Gas Sensor	Uses I2C or UART communication to output gas levels.	CCS811 air quality sensor.
Metal Oxide Semiconductor (MOS) Sensor	Detects gases by measuring changes in resistance.	MQ-series sensors.
Electrochemical Sensor	Measures gas concentration based on chemical reactions.	Used for CO and O2 detection.

Basic Rules for Using Gas Sensors

Rule	Correct Example	Incorrect Example
Ensure correct power supply.	Connect VCC to 5V or 3.3V as per sensor requirements.	Incorrect voltage may damage the sensor.
Allow warm-up time.	MQ sensors need preheating before providing stable readings.	Reading immediately after power-up may give inaccurate results.
Use an ADC pin for analog sensors.	Connect the sensor's output to an ADC pin for accurate measurements.	Connecting to a digital pin will not read variable values.
Use proper filtering for accuracy.	Implement moving average filtering for stable readings.	Raw readings may fluctuate significantly.

Syntax Table

SL	Function	Syntax/Example	Description
1	**Initialize Sensor**	initGasSensor();	Prepares the microcontroller for sensor input.
2	**Read Gas Level (Analog)**	gasLevel = readADC(0);	Reads an analog gas concentration value.
3	**Read Gas Level (Digital)**	gasLevel = readI2C();	Retrieves gas concentration data via I2C.
4	**Display Gas Level**	printf("Gas Level: %d", gasLevel);	Outputs the gas concentration.

Syntax Explanation

1. Initialize Sensor

What does initializing the sensor do? It sets up the microcontroller to communicate with the gas sensor, configuring ADC or digital input settings as required.

Syntax:

```
initGasSensor();
```

Example:
```
initGasSensor();  // Initialize the gas sensor
```

Example Explanation: This function configures the microcontroller's input pins, ADC, or communication interfaces based on the sensor type.

2. Read Gas Level (Analog)

What does reading an analog gas level do? It converts the sensor's voltage output into a digital value using the ADC module.

Syntax:
```
gasLevel = readADC(0);
```

Example:
```
gasLevel = readADC(0);  // Read analog gas sensor on
ADC channel 0
```

Example Explanation: This function reads the voltage from an analog gas sensor, converts it into a digital value, and maps it to gas concentration levels.

3. Read Gas Level (Digital)

What does reading a digital gas level do? It retrieves gas concentration data using communication protocols like I2C or UART.

Syntax:
```
gasLevel = readI2C();
```

Example:
```
gasLevel = readI2C();  // Read gas concentration from
an I2C sensor
```

Example Explanation: This function sends a request to the gas sensor via the I2C protocol and retrieves the gas concentration value in parts per million (ppm).

4. Display Gas Level

What does displaying gas level data do? It prints the detected gas concentration to an LCD or serial monitor.

Syntax:
```
printf("Gas Level: %d ppm", gasLevel);
```

Example:
```
printf("Gas Level: %d ppm", gasLevel);   // Print gas
concentration
```

Example Explanation: This command displays the measured gas concentration in ppm, which is useful for real-time monitoring.

Real-life Applications Project: Air Quality Monitoring System
In this project, we will build an air quality monitoring system using a PIC microcontroller and an MQ-2 gas sensor.

Required Components

Component	Description
MQ-2 Gas Sensor	Detects combustible gases and smoke.
PIC Microcontroller	Processes the sensor data.
LCD Display	Displays the measured gas concentration.
Resistors	Used for signal conditioning.

Circuit Connection Table

Component	Pin Connection
MQ-2 Sensor	VCC -> 5V, GND -> Ground, OUT -> RA0
PIC Microcontroller	AN0 -> Sensor OUT, LCD -> PORTD
LCD Display	Connected to PORTD for output

Project Code
```
#include <xc.h>
#include <stdio.h>

#define _XTAL_FREQ 4000000   // Define crystal frequency

void initGasSensor();
int readADC(int channel);

void main() {
    int gasLevel;
    initGasSensor();   // Initialize the gas sensor

    while(1) {
        gasLevel = readADC(0);   // Read gas
concentration from sensor
```

```
        printf("Gas Level: %d ppm", gasLevel);   //
Display gas level
        __delay_ms(1000);   // Update every second
    }
}
```

Expected Results

Once the code is uploaded to the PIC microcontroller, the system
will continuously measure and display gas concentration. If the gas
level exceeds a threshold, the system can trigger an alarm, making
it useful for air quality monitoring, fire detection, and industrial safety
applications.

Chapter 37: Air Quality Monitoring with PIC Microcontrollers

Air quality monitoring is essential for environmental safety, industrial control, and health applications. Sensors used in air quality monitoring detect pollutants, particulate matter, and gases, providing data that can be processed by a microcontroller. In this chapter, we will explore how to interface air quality sensors with PIC microcontrollers, covering working principles, sensor types, interfacing techniques, and practical applications.

Key Concepts of Air Quality Monitoring

Air quality sensors detect various environmental pollutants such as carbon dioxide (CO_2), carbon monoxide (CO), volatile organic compounds (VOCs), and particulate matter (PM). These sensors provide analog or digital output that can be processed for real-time monitoring and control.

Concept	Description	Example
Air Quality Sensor	A device that detects pollutants in the air and converts the data into an electrical signal.	Used in smart city air monitoring systems.
CO_2 Sensor	Measures carbon dioxide levels in the atmosphere.	Used in indoor air quality monitoring.
CO Sensor	Detects carbon monoxide, a toxic gas.	Used in fire and gas leak detection.
VOCs Sensor	Detects volatile organic compounds from chemicals and industrial emissions.	Used in workplace air monitoring.
Particulate Matter (PM) Sensor	Detects dust, smoke, and airborne particles.	Used in environmental pollution monitoring.

Basic Rules for Using Air Quality Sensors

Rule	Correct Example	Incorrect Example
Ensure correct power supply.	Connect VCC to 5V or 3.3V as per sensor requirements.	Incorrect voltage may damage the sensor.
Allow preheating for accurate results.	Some gas sensors require a warm-up period before stable readings.	Immediate readings may not be accurate.
Use an ADC pin for analog sensors.	Connect the sensor's output to an ADC pin for measurement.	Connecting to a digital pin will not read variable values.
Filter noisy data for accuracy.	Use averaging techniques for stable readings.	Direct readings may have fluctuations.

Syntax Table

SL	Function	Syntax/Example	Description
1	**Initialize Sensor**	initAirQualitySensor();	Prepares the microcontroller for sensor input.
2	**Read Air Quality (Analog)**	airQuality = readADC(0);	Reads an analog air quality value.
3	**Read Air Quality (Digital)**	airQuality = readI2C();	Retrieves air quality data via I2C.
4	**Display Air Quality**	printf("Air Quality: %d", airQuality);	Outputs the air quality reading.

Syntax Explanation

1. Initialize Sensor

What does initializing the sensor do? It sets up the microcontroller to communicate with the air quality sensor, configuring ADC or digital input settings as required.

Syntax:

```
initAirQualitySensor();
```

Example:
```
initAirQualitySensor();  // Initialize the air quality
sensor
```

Example Explanation: This function configures the microcontroller's input pins, ADC, or digital communication protocols based on the sensor type.

   2. **Read Air Quality (Analog)**

What does reading an analog air quality value do? It converts the sensor's voltage output into a digital value using the ADC module.

Syntax:
```
airQuality = readADC(0);
```

Example:
```
airQuality = readADC(0);  // Read analog air quality
sensor on ADC channel 0
```

Example Explanation: This function reads the voltage from an analog air quality sensor, converts it into a digital value, and maps it to pollution levels.

   3. **Read Air Quality (Digital)**

What does reading a digital air quality value do? It retrieves air quality data using communication protocols like I2C or UART.

Syntax:
```
airQuality = readI2C();
```

Example:
```
airQuality = readI2C();  // Read air quality data from
an I2C sensor
```

Example Explanation: This function sends a request to the air quality sensor via the I2C protocol and retrieves pollutant concentration values.

   4. **Display Air Quality**

What does displaying air quality data do? It prints the detected air pollution level to an LCD or serial monitor.

Syntax:
```
printf("Air Quality: %d", airQuality);
```

Example:

```
printf("Air Quality: %d", airQuality);   // Print air
pollution level
```

Example Explanation: This command displays the measured air quality index (AQI) or pollutant concentration, useful for real-time monitoring.

Real-life Applications Project: Smart Air Quality Monitoring System

In this project, we will build a smart air quality monitoring system using a PIC microcontroller and an MQ-135 gas sensor.

Required Components

Component	Description
MQ-135 Gas Sensor	Detects CO_2, CO, and VOCs.
PIC Microcontroller	Processes the sensor data.
LCD Display	Displays the air quality readings.
Resistors	Used for signal conditioning.

Circuit Connection Table

Component	Pin Connection
MQ-135 Sensor	VCC -> 5V, GND -> Ground, OUT -> RA0
PIC Microcontroller	AN0 -> Sensor OUT, LCD -> PORTD
LCD Display	Connected to PORTD for output

Project Code

```
#include <xc.h>
#include <stdio.h>

#define _XTAL_FREQ 4000000   // Define crystal frequency

void initAirQualitySensor();
int readADC(int channel);

void main() {
    int airQuality;
    initAirQualitySensor();   // Initialize the air
quality sensor
```

```
    while(1) {
        airQuality = readADC(0);   // Read air quality
sensor data

        printf("Air Quality Index: %d", airQuality);
// Display AQI value
        __delay_ms(1000);   // Update every second
    }
}
```

Expected Results

Once the code is uploaded to the PIC microcontroller, the system
will continuously measure and display air quality levels. If pollution
levels exceed a threshold, the system can trigger an alert, making it
useful for smart homes, industrial safety, and environmental
monitoring applications.

Chapter 38: Force Sensors with PIC Microcontrollers

Force sensors are used to measure physical pressure, weight, or mechanical force in various applications, including robotics, industrial automation, and biomedical devices. These sensors detect force and convert it into an electrical signal that can be processed by a microcontroller. In this chapter, we will explore how to interface force sensors with PIC microcontrollers, covering their working principles, sensor types, interfacing techniques, and practical applications.

Key Concepts of Force Sensors

Force sensors detect applied force and convert it into a measurable electrical output. The most commonly used force sensors in embedded systems include resistive force sensors, strain gauges, and load cells.

Concept	Description	Example
Force Sensor	A device that detects applied force and converts it into an electrical signal.	Used in electronic weighing scales.
Resistive Force Sensor (FSR)	Changes resistance based on the applied force.	Used in touch-sensitive applications.
Strain Gauge	Measures strain by detecting resistance changes in a thin wire.	Used in industrial force measurement systems.
Load Cell	Uses strain gauges to measure force and provide an analog output.	Used in precision weight scales.

Basic Rules for Using Force Sensors

Rule	Correct Example	Incorrect Example
Ensure correct power supply.	Connect VCC to 5V or 3.3V as required by the sensor.	Incorrect voltage may cause inaccurate readings.

Use an ADC pin for analog force sensors.	Connect the sensor output to an ADC pin.	Connecting to a digital pin will not process analog data.
Use a signal amplifier for small signals.	Use an operational amplifier (Op-Amp) to increase signal strength.	Weak signals may not be accurately detected.
Calibrate the sensor for accurate measurements.	Use known weights to establish a force-to-voltage conversion factor.	Uncalibrated sensors may give incorrect readings.

Syntax Table

SL	Function	Syntax/Example	Description
1	Initialize Sensor	initForceSensor();	Prepares the microcontroller for sensor input.
2	Read Force Level (Analog)	forceValue = readADC(0);	Reads an analog force measurement value.
3	Convert ADC Value to Force	force = map(forceValue, 0, 1023, 0, 100);	Converts ADC readings to meaningful force values.
4	Display Force Value	printf("Force: %d N", force);	Outputs the force measurement.

Syntax Explanation

1. Initialize Sensor

What does initializing the sensor do? It sets up the microcontroller to read data from the force sensor, configuring the ADC module.

Syntax:
```
initForceSensor();
```

Example:
```
initForceSensor();  // Initialize the force sensor
```
Example Explanation: This function configures the microcontroller's input pins and ADC settings based on the type of force sensor used.

2. Read Force Level (Analog)

What does reading an analog force level do? It converts the sensor's voltage output into a digital value using the ADC module.

Syntax:

```
forceValue = readADC(0);
```

Example:

```
forceValue = readADC(0);   // Read analog force sensor
on ADC channel 0
```

Example Explanation: This function reads the voltage from an analog force sensor, converts it into a digital value, and maps it to a force range.

3. Convert ADC Value to Force

What does converting an ADC value to force do? It maps the ADC reading to a force value using a predefined scale.

Syntax:

```
force = map(forceValue, 0, 1023, 0, 100);
```

Example:

```
force = map(forceValue, 0, 1023, 0, 100);   // Convert
ADC value to force (in Newtons)
```

Example Explanation: This function takes the ADC reading and scales it to a real-world force value based on calibration data.

4. Display Force Value

What does displaying force data do? It prints the detected force measurement to an LCD or serial monitor.

Syntax:

```
printf("Force: %d N", force);
```

Example:

```
printf("Force: %d N", force);   // Print force value
```

Example Explanation: This command displays the measured force in Newtons, which is useful for real-time monitoring.

Real-life Applications Project: Digital Weighing Scale System

In this project, we will build a digital weighing scale system using a PIC microcontroller and a load cell sensor.

Required Components

Component	Description
Load Cell Sensor	Measures weight based on applied force.
HX711 Amplifier	Converts load cell signal to a readable voltage.
PIC Microcontroller	Processes the sensor data.
LCD Display	Displays the force measurement.
Resistors	Used for signal conditioning.

Circuit Connection Table

Component	Pin Connection
Load Cell Sensor	Connected to HX711 amplifier
HX711 Amplifier	VCC -> 5V, GND -> Ground, DOUT -> RB0, SCK -> RB1
PIC Microcontroller	RB0 -> HX711 DOUT, RB1 -> HX711 SCK, LCD -> PORTD
LCD Display	Connected to PORTD for output

Project Code

```c
#include <xc.h>
#include <stdio.h>
#define _XTAL_FREQ 4000000  // Define crystal frequency
void initForceSensor();
int readADC(int channel);
void main() {
    int forceValue;
    initForceSensor();  // Initialize the force sensor
    while(1) {
        forceValue = readADC(0);
        int force = map(forceValue, 0, 1023, 0, 100);
        printf("Force: %d N", force);
        __delay_ms(1000);  // Update every second
    }
}
```

Expected Results

Once the code is uploaded to the PIC microcontroller, the system will continuously measure and display the force applied to the sensor. This type of system can be used for electronic weighing scales, pressure-sensitive input devices, and industrial force monitoring applications.

Chapter 39: Touch Sensors with PIC Microcontrollers

Touch sensors are widely used in modern electronic devices for touch-based user interfaces, replacing traditional mechanical buttons. These sensors detect physical contact and convert it into an electrical signal, which can be processed by a microcontroller. In this chapter, we will explore how to interface touch sensors with PIC microcontrollers, covering their working principles, types, interfacing techniques, and practical applications.

Key Concepts of Touch Sensors

Touch sensors detect direct or capacitive contact and provide an output signal that can be processed by a microcontroller. The most commonly used types include capacitive touch sensors and resistive touch sensors.

Concept	Description	Example
Touch Sensor	A device that detects physical touch and converts it into an electrical signal.	Used in touchscreens and smart switches.
Capacitive Touch Sensor	Detects touch by measuring changes in capacitance.	Used in modern touchscreens and smartphones.
Resistive Touch Sensor	Uses two conductive layers to detect touch pressure.	Found in older touchscreen devices.
Digital Touch Sensor	Provides a HIGH or LOW signal when touched.	Used in simple on/off applications.
Analog Touch Sensor	Provides variable output based on touch intensity.	Used in multi-touch sensing applications.

Basic Rules for Using Touch Sensors

Rule	Correct Example	Incorrect Example
Ensure correct power supply.	Connect VCC to 5V or 3.3V as per sensor requirements.	Incorrect voltage may cause sensor failure.

Use an ADC pin for analog sensors.	Connect the sensor's output to an ADC pin.	Connecting to a digital pin will not read touch intensity.
Use a pull-down resistor for digital sensors.	Ensures a stable LOW state when not touched.	Floating input may cause false detections.
Keep sensor surfaces clean.	Dirt or moisture may interfere with touch detection.	Contaminated surfaces can lead to inaccurate responses.

Syntax Table

SL	Function	Syntax/Example	Description
1	Initialize Sensor	initTouchSensor();	Prepares the microcontroller for touch input.
2	Read Touch (Digital)	if(PORTBbits.RB1 == 1)	Checks if a digital touch sensor is activated.
3	Read Touch (Analog)	touchValue = readADC(0);	Reads an analog value from the touch sensor.
4	Display Touch Status	printf("Touch Detected");	Outputs a message when touch is detected.

Syntax Explanation

1. Initialize Sensor

What does initializing the sensor do? It configures the microcontroller's input pins and prepares the system to read data from the touch sensor.

Syntax:

```
initTouchSensor();
```

Example:

```
initTouchSensor();  // Initialize the touch sensor
```

Example Explanation: This function sets up the microcontroller to properly interface with the touch sensor by configuring input pins and setting the necessary pull-down resistors.

2. Read Touch (Digital)

What does reading a digital touch sensor do? It checks if the touch sensor is activated by detecting a HIGH or LOW signal.

Syntax:
```
if(PORTBbits.RB1 == 1)
```

Example:
```
if(PORTBbits.RB1 == 1) {
    printf("Touch detected!");
}
```

Example Explanation: This conditional statement checks if the digital touch sensor's output is HIGH, indicating that a touch has been detected.

3. Read Touch (Analog)

What does reading an analog touch sensor do? It converts the sensor's output voltage into a digital value using the ADC module.

Syntax:
```
touchValue = readADC(0);
```

Example:
```
touchValue = readADC(0);  // Read analog touch sensor
on ADC channel 0
```

Example Explanation: This function reads the voltage from an analog touch sensor and maps it to a range representing touch intensity.

4. Display Touch Status

What does displaying touch status do? It prints a message indicating when the sensor detects a touch event.

Syntax:
```
printf("Touch Detected");
```

Example:
```
printf("Touch detected on sensor!");  // Print when
touch is detected
```
Example Explanation: This command outputs a message on an LCD or serial monitor whenever touch input is detected.

Real-life Applications Project: Touch-Activated Light Switch

In this project, we will build a touch-activated light switch using a PIC microcontroller and a capacitive touch sensor.

Required Components

Component	Description
Capacitive Touch Sensor	Detects touch and provides digital output.
PIC Microcontroller	Processes the touch sensor data.
LED	Turns on/off based on touch input.
Resistors	Used for signal conditioning.

Circuit Connection Table

Component	Pin Connection
Touch Sensor	VCC -> 5V, GND -> Ground, OUT -> RB1
PIC Microcontroller	RB1 -> Sensor OUT, RA0 -> LED
LED	Connected to RA0 for touch-based control

Project Code

```c
#include <xc.h>
#include <stdio.h>
#define _XTAL_FREQ 4000000  // Define crystal frequency
void initTouchSensor();
void toggleLight();
void main() {
    TRISBbits.TRISB1 = 1;
    TRISAbits.TRISA0 = 0;
    while(1) {
        if (PORTBbits.RB1 == 1) {
            toggleLight();  // Turn the LED on/off
            __delay_ms(300);  // Debounce delay
        }
    }
}
void toggleLight() {
    LATAbits.LATA0 = !LATAbits.LATA0;  // Toggle LED
state
}
```

Chapter 40: GPS with PIC Microcontrollers

Global Positioning System (GPS) modules are widely used in navigation, tracking, and location-based applications. These modules receive signals from satellites to determine geographical coordinates such as latitude, longitude, altitude, and speed. In this chapter, we will explore how to interface a GPS module with a PIC microcontroller, covering working principles, communication protocols, interfacing techniques, and practical applications.

Key Concepts of GPS Modules

GPS modules communicate with satellites to calculate location data and provide serial output that can be processed by a microcontroller. Common GPS modules include NEO-6M, NEO-7M, and SIM28.

Concept	Description	Example
GPS Module	A device that receives signals from GPS satellites and calculates location data.	Used in vehicle tracking systems.
NMEA Protocol	Standard format used by GPS modules to transmit location data.	Includes sentences like $GPGGA, $GPRMC.
UART Communication	Serial communication protocol used by GPS modules to send data to microcontrollers.	GPS module TX -> PIC RX.
Latitude & Longitude	Geographic coordinates representing a location on Earth.	Latitude: 37.7749° N, Longitude: 122.4194° W.
Baud Rate	Speed of communication between the GPS module and microcontroller.	Commonly 9600 bps.

Basic Rules for Using GPS Modules

Rule	Correct Example	Incorrect Example
Ensure correct power supply.	Connect VCC to 3.3V or 5V (based on module).	Incorrect voltage may damage the module.

Use UART for data reception.	Connect GPS TX to PIC RX and configure UART.	Connecting to a GPIO pin will not process serial data.
Set correct baud rate.	Use 9600 bps for most modules.	Incorrect baud rate will result in unreadable data.
Place the GPS module in an open area.	Ensures clear satellite reception.	Indoors or obstructed locations reduce accuracy.

Syntax Table

SL	Function	Syntax/Example	Description
1	Initialize UART for GPS	initUART(9600);	Sets up UART communication at 9600 bps.
2	Read GPS Data	gpsData = readUART();	Reads raw GPS data from the module.
3	Parse NMEA Sentence	parseGPSData(gpsData);	Extracts latitude and longitude from the received NMEA string.
4	Display Location	printf("Lat: %f, Long: %f", lat, lon);	Outputs the current GPS coordinates.

Syntax Explanation

1. Initialize UART for GPS

What does initializing UART do? It configures the PIC microcontroller's UART module to communicate with the GPS module at the correct baud rate.

Syntax:

```
initUART(9600);
```

Example:

```
initUART(9600);  // Initialize UART for GPS module
```

Example Explanation: This function sets up the UART communication between the GPS module and PIC microcontroller, enabling serial data reception.

2. Read GPS Data

What does reading GPS data do? It retrieves raw GPS data as a serial string from the module.

Syntax:

```
gpsData = readUART();
```

Example:

```
gpsData = readUART();   // Read raw GPS data from module
```

Example Explanation: This function continuously listens to the GPS module and stores incoming NMEA sentences as a string.

3. Parse NMEA Sentence

What does parsing GPS data do? It extracts meaningful location information such as latitude and longitude from the raw NMEA string.

Syntax:

```
parseGPSData(gpsData);
```

Example:

```
parseGPSData(gpsData);   // Extract latitude and
longitude from raw data
```

Example Explanation: This function processes the raw GPS data and converts it into usable values, such as coordinates.

4. Display Location

What does displaying location do? It prints the extracted GPS coordinates to an LCD or serial monitor.

Syntax:

```
printf("Lat: %f, Long: %f", lat, lon);
```

Example:

```
printf("Lat: %f, Long: %f", lat, lon);   // Print
location data
```

Example Explanation: This command displays the current location coordinates in degrees for tracking applications.

Real-life Applications Project: GPS Tracking System

In this project, we will build a GPS-based tracking system using a PIC microcontroller and a NEO-6M GPS module.

Required Components

Component	Description
NEO-6M GPS Module	Receives satellite signals and provides location data.
PIC Microcontroller	Processes the GPS data.
LCD Display	Displays the latitude and longitude.
Resistors	Used for voltage level shifting if needed.

Circuit Connection Table

Component	Pin Connection
GPS Module	VCC -> 3.3V/5V, GND -> Ground, TX -> RX (PIC), RX -> TX (PIC)
PIC Microcontroller	UART RX -> GPS TX, UART TX -> GPS RX, LCD -> PORTD
LCD Display	Connected to PORTD for output

Project Code

```
#include <xc.h>
#include <stdio.h>

#define _XTAL_FREQ 4000000  // Define crystal frequency

void initUART(int baud);
char readUART();
void parseGPSData(char *gpsData);

void main() {
    char gpsData[100];
    float lat, lon;

    initUART(9600);  // Initialize UART for GPS module

    while(1) {
        gpsData = readUART();  // Read GPS data
```

```
        parseGPSData(gpsData);  // Extract location
data
        printf("Lat: %f, Long: %f", lat, lon);  //
Display GPS coordinates
        __delay_ms(1000);  // Update every second
    }
}
```

Expected Results

Once the code is uploaded to the PIC microcontroller, the system will continuously receive GPS data, extract location coordinates, and display them on an LCD. This project is useful for vehicle tracking, outdoor navigation, and smart location-based applications.

Chapter 41: GSM Modules with PIC Microcontrollers

GSM (Global System for Mobile Communications) modules enable microcontrollers to send and receive messages, make calls, and establish internet connections using a cellular network. These modules are widely used in remote monitoring, IoT applications, and security systems. In this chapter, we will explore how to interface GSM modules with PIC microcontrollers, covering working principles, communication protocols, interfacing techniques, and practical applications.

Key Concepts of GSM Modules

GSM modules communicate with cellular networks using AT commands and UART serial communication to perform operations like SMS, calls, and data transmission.

Concept	Description	Example
GSM Module	A device that connects to cellular networks to send/receive messages and calls.	SIM800L, SIM900
AT Commands	Command set used to control GSM modules.	AT+CMGS for sending SMS.
UART Communication	Serial communication between GSM module and microcontroller.	PIC TX -> GSM RX, PIC RX -> GSM TX.
SIM Card	Required for network connectivity.	Inserted into the GSM module.
Baud Rate	Speed of communication between the GSM module and PIC.	Typically 9600 bps.

Basic Rules for Using GSM Modules

Rule	Correct Example	Incorrect Example
Ensure proper power supply.	Use 5V or 3.7V (depending on module requirements).	Using a higher voltage can damage the module.

Use UART for communication.	Connect GSM TX to PIC RX and vice versa.	Using GPIO pins without UART will not work.
Set correct baud rate.	Use 9600 bps for most modules.	Incorrect baud rate leads to unreadable data.
Use an external antenna.	Improves signal reception.	Poor signal may cause communication failures.

Syntax Table

S L	Function	Syntax/Example	Description
1	Initialize UART for GSM	initUART(9600);	Sets up UART communication at 9600 bps.
2	Send AT Command	sendUART("AT\r");	Sends an AT command to the GSM module.
3	Send SMS	sendUART("AT+CMGS= "+1234567890"\r");	Sends an SMS to a specific number.
4	Receive Data	response = readUART();	Reads response from the GSM module.

Syntax Explanation

1. Initialize UART for GSM

What does initializing UART do? It sets up the PIC microcontroller to communicate with the GSM module using serial communication.

Syntax:

```
initUART(9600);
```

Example:

```
initUART(9600);  // Initialize UART for GSM module
```

Example Explanation: This function configures the UART communication at 9600 baud rate, allowing data exchange between the microcontroller and GSM module.

2. Send AT Command

What does sending an AT command do? It instructs the GSM module to perform a specific operation.

Syntax:

```
sendUART("AT\r");
```

Example:

```
sendUART("AT\r");  // Send AT command to check module
status
```

Example Explanation: This command verifies if the GSM module is working correctly by expecting an "OK" response.

3. Send SMS

What does sending an SMS do? It transmits a text message to a specified phone number.

Syntax:

```
sendUART("AT+CMGS=\"+1234567890\"\r");
```

Example:

```
sendUART("AT+CMGS=\"+1234567890\"\r");
__delay_ms(100);
sendUART("Hello, this is a test message!");
sendUART(0x1A);  // End of message command
```

Example Explanation: This command sends an SMS containing "Hello, this is a test message!" to the specified number.

4. Receive Data

What does reading data from GSM do? It captures responses from the module, such as message delivery status or signal strength.

Syntax:

```
response = readUART();
```

Example:

```
response = readUART();  // Read GSM module response
```

Example Explanation: This function stores incoming data from the GSM module for further processing.

Real-life Applications Project: SMS-Based Alert System

In this project, we will build an SMS-based alert system using a PIC microcontroller and a SIM800L GSM module.

Required Components

Component	Description
SIM800L GSM Module	Sends and receives SMS via a cellular network.
PIC Microcontroller	Processes GSM data.
SIM Card	Provides network connectivity.
Resistors	Used for voltage level shifting if needed.

Circuit Connection Table

Component	Pin Connection
GSM Module	VCC -> 3.7V/5V, GND -> Ground, TX -> RX (PIC), RX -> TX (PIC)
PIC Microcontroller	UART RX -> GSM TX, UART TX -> GSM RX

Project Code

```c
#include <xc.h>
#include <stdio.h>

#define _XTAL_FREQ 4000000  // Define crystal frequency

void initUART(int baud);
void sendUART(char *cmd);
char readUART();

void main() {
    initUART(9600);  // Initialize UART for GSM module

    sendUART("AT\r");  // Check GSM module
    __delay_ms(1000);

    sendUART("AT+CMGF=1\r");  // Set SMS text mode
    __delay_ms(1000);

    sendUART("AT+CMGS=\"+1234567890\"\r");  // Enter
recipient number
```

```
    __delay_ms(1000);
    sendUART("Alert: System Triggered!\r");  // Message
content
    __delay_ms(100);
    sendUART(0x1A);  // End message (CTRL+Z ASCII)
    __delay_ms(1000);
}
```

Expected Results

Once the code is uploaded to the PIC microcontroller, the system will send an SMS alert when triggered. This project can be used in security systems, remote monitoring, and emergency notifications.

Chapter 42: Accelerometers with PIC Microcontrollers

Accelerometers are used to measure acceleration forces in various applications, including motion tracking, vibration analysis, tilt sensing, and impact detection. These sensors can provide data in one, two, or three axes and are commonly used in robotics, automotive systems, and consumer electronics. In this chapter, we will explore how to interface accelerometers with PIC microcontrollers, covering working principles, sensor types, interfacing techniques, and practical applications.

Key Concepts of Accelerometers

Accelerometers detect motion by measuring the force exerted due to acceleration. They provide analog or digital output depending on the sensor type. The most commonly used accelerometers in embedded systems are MEMS-based accelerometers.

Concept	Description	Example
Accelerometer	A device that measures acceleration along different axes.	Used in smartphones for screen orientation.
Analog Accelerometer	Provides voltage output proportional to acceleration.	ADXL335
Digital Accelerometer	Uses I2C or SPI to send acceleration data.	MPU6050, ADXL345
G-Force	Measurement of acceleration relative to gravity (g = 9.81 m/s²).	1g represents Earth's gravity.
Tilt Sensing	Detecting the angle of inclination using acceleration data.	Used in balancing robots.

Basic Rules for Using Accelerometers

Rule	Correct Example	Incorrect Example
Ensure correct power supply.	Connect VCC to 3.3V or 5V as per sensor requirements.	Incorrect voltage may damage the sensor.

Use an ADC pin for analog sensors.	Connect X, Y, and Z outputs to ADC channels.	Connecting to a digital pin will not read analog values.
Use I2C/SPI for digital sensors.	Connect SCL and SDA for I2C communication.	Miswiring may cause incorrect readings.
Calibrate sensor for accurate data.	Measure baseline values and apply offsets.	Uncalibrated sensors may give incorrect results.

Syntax Table

SL	Function	Syntax/Example	Description
1	Initialize Sensor	initAccelerometer();	Prepares the microcontroller for accelerometer input.
2	Read Acceleration (Analog)	xValue = readADC(0);	Reads acceleration along the X-axis.
3	Read Acceleration (Digital)	accelData = readI2C();	Retrieves acceleration data from an I2C accelerometer.
4	Display Acceleration Data	printf("X: %d, Y: %d, Z: %d", x, y, z);	Outputs acceleration values for each axis.

Syntax Explanation

1. Initialize Sensor

What does initializing the sensor do? It sets up the microcontroller to communicate with the accelerometer by configuring ADC or I2C/SPI communication.

Syntax:
```
initAccelerometer();
```

Example:
```
initAccelerometer();  // Initialize the accelerometer
```

Example Explanation: This function sets up the ADC or I2C interface for data communication with the accelerometer.

2. Read Acceleration (Analog)

What does reading acceleration data do? It converts the accelerometer's voltage output into a digital value using the ADC module.

Syntax:

```
xValue = readADC(0);
```

Example:

```
xValue = readADC(0);  // Read X-axis acceleration on
ADC channel 0
```

Example Explanation: This function reads the voltage from the X-axis output of an analog accelerometer and converts it into acceleration data.

3. Read Acceleration (Digital)

What does reading a digital accelerometer do? It retrieves acceleration values using I2C or SPI communication protocols.

Syntax:

```
accelData = readI2C();
```

Example:

```
accelData = readI2C();  // Read acceleration data from
an I2C accelerometer
```

Example Explanation: This function requests acceleration data from a digital accelerometer via the I2C communication protocol.

4. Display Acceleration Data

What does displaying acceleration data do? It prints the detected acceleration along each axis to an LCD or serial monitor.

Syntax:

```
printf("X: %d, Y: %d, Z: %d", x, y, z);
```

Example:

```
printf("X: %d, Y: %d, Z: %d", x, y, z);  // Print
acceleration values
```

Example Explanation: This command displays acceleration values along all three axes for real-time motion analysis.

Real-life Applications Project: Motion Detection System

In this project, we will build a motion detection system using a PIC microcontroller and an ADXL345 digital accelerometer.

Required Components

Component	Description
ADXL345 Accelerometer	Measures acceleration in three axes using I2C communication.
PIC Microcontroller	Processes accelerometer data.
LCD Display	Displays acceleration values.
Resistors	Used for I2C pull-up connections.

Circuit Connection Table

Component	Pin Connection
ADXL345 Sensor	VCC -> 3.3V, GND -> Ground, SCL -> RC3, SDA -> RC4
PIC Microcontroller	RC3 -> SCL, RC4 -> SDA, LCD -> PORTD
LCD Display	Connected to PORTD for output

Project Code

```c
#include <xc.h>
#include <stdio.h>
#define _XTAL_FREQ 4000000  // Define crystal frequency
void initAccelerometer();
int readI2C();
void main() {
    int x, y, z;
    initAccelerometer();  // Initialize accelerometer
    while(1) {
        x = readI2C();  // Read X-axis acceleration
        y = readI2C();  // Read Y-axis acceleration
        z = readI2C();  // Read Z-axis acceleration
        printf("X: %d, Y: %d, Z: %d", x, y, z);  // Display acceleration values
        __delay_ms(500);  // Update every 500ms
    }
}
```

Chapter 43: Gyroscopes with PIC Microcontrollers

Gyroscopes are sensors used to measure angular velocity and rotation in various applications such as robotics, navigation systems, drones, and motion control. These sensors detect rotational movement along different axes and provide data in either analog or digital format. In this chapter, we will explore how to interface gyroscopes with PIC microcontrollers, covering working principles, sensor types, interfacing techniques, and practical applications.

Key Concepts of Gyroscopes

Gyroscopes measure angular velocity and rotation rate along different axes. They are commonly used in conjunction with accelerometers to provide more accurate motion tracking.

Concept	Description	Example
Gyroscope Sensor	A device that measures angular velocity in degrees per second (°/s).	Used in drones for stability control.
Analog Gyroscope	Provides voltage output proportional to rotation.	LPR550AL, ADXRS450
Digital Gyroscope	Uses I2C or SPI for data communication.	MPU6050, L3G4200D
Angular Velocity	The rate of rotation along an axis.	Measured in °/s.
IMU (Inertial Measurement Unit)	A combination of a gyroscope and an accelerometer for motion tracking.	MPU6050

Basic Rules for Using Gyroscopes

Rule	Correct Example	Incorrect Example
Ensure correct power supply.	Connect VCC to 3.3V or 5V based on the module requirements.	Incorrect voltage may damage the sensor.
Use an ADC pin for analog sensors.	Connect the sensor's output to an ADC pin.	Connecting to a digital pin will not read analog values.

Use I2C/SPI for digital sensors.	Connect SCL and SDA for I2C communication.	Incorrect wiring may prevent communication.
Calibrate the sensor for accurate data.	Measure baseline values and apply offsets.	Uncalibrated sensors may give incorrect results.

Syntax Table

SL	Function	Syntax/Example	Description
1	Initialize Gyroscope	initGyroscope();	Prepares the microcontroller for gyroscope input.
2	Read Angular Velocity (Analog)	gyroX = readADC(0);	Reads angular velocity along the X-axis.
3	Read Angular Velocity (Digital)	gyroData = readI2C();	Retrieves angular velocity data from an I2C gyroscope.
4	Display Gyro Data	printf("X: %d, Y: %d, Z: %d", x, y, z);	Outputs angular velocity values for each axis.

Syntax Explanation

1. Initialize Gyroscope

What does initializing the gyroscope do? It sets up the microcontroller to communicate with the gyroscope sensor by configuring ADC or I2C/SPI communication.

Syntax:
```
initGyroscope();
```

Example:
```
initGyroscope();  // Initialize the gyroscope sensor
```
Example Explanation: This function sets up the ADC or I2C interface for data communication with the gyroscope.

2. Read Angular Velocity (Analog)

What does reading an analog gyroscope do? It converts the gyroscope's voltage output into a digital value using the ADC module.

Syntax:
```
gyroX = readADC(0);
```

Example:
```
gyroX = readADC(0);   // Read X-axis angular velocity on
ADC channel 0
```

Example Explanation: This function reads the voltage from the X-axis output of an analog gyroscope and converts it into angular velocity data.

3. Read Angular Velocity (Digital)

What does reading a digital gyroscope do? It retrieves angular velocity values using I2C or SPI communication protocols.

Syntax:
```
gyroData = readI2C();
```

Example:
```
gyroData = readI2C();   // Read angular velocity from an
I2C gyroscope
```

Example Explanation: This function requests angular velocity data from a digital gyroscope via the I2C communication protocol.

4. Display Gyro Data

What does displaying gyroscope data do? It prints the detected angular velocity along each axis to an LCD or serial monitor.

Syntax:
```
printf("X: %d, Y: %d, Z: %d", x, y, z);
```

Example:
```
printf("X: %d, Y: %d, Z: %d", x, y, z);   // Print
angular velocity values
```

Example Explanation: This command displays angular velocity values along all three axes for real-time motion analysis.

Real-life Applications Project: Gyro-Based Motion Control System

In this project, we will build a motion control system using a PIC microcontroller and an L3G4200D digital gyroscope.

Required Components

Component	Description
L3G4200D Gyroscope	Measures angular velocity in three axes using I2C communication.
PIC Microcontroller	Processes gyroscope data.
LCD Display	Displays angular velocity values.
Resistors	Used for I2C pull-up connections.

Circuit Connection Table

Component	Pin Connection
L3G4200D Sensor	VCC -> 3.3V, GND -> Ground, SCL -> RC3, SDA -> RC4
PIC Microcontroller	RC3 -> SCL, RC4 -> SDA, LCD -> PORTD
LCD Display	Connected to PORTD for output

Project Code

```c
#include <xc.h>
#include <stdio.h>

#define _XTAL_FREQ 4000000  // Define crystal frequency

void initGyroscope();
int readI2C();

void main() {
    int x, y, z;
    initGyroscope();  // Initialize gyroscope

    while(1) {
        x = readI2C();  // Read X-axis angular velocity
        y = readI2C();  // Read Y-axis angular velocity
        z = readI2C();  // Read Z-axis angular velocity

        printf("X: %d, Y: %d, Z: %d", x, y, z);  //
Display angular velocity values
        __delay_ms(500);  // Update every 500ms
    }
}
```

Chapter 44: Controlling LEDs with PIC Microcontrollers

LEDs (Light Emitting Diodes) are fundamental components in embedded systems, used for indication, signaling, and display applications. Controlling LEDs with a PIC microcontroller is one of the first tasks in learning microcontroller programming. In this chapter, we will explore how to interface and control LEDs using PIC microcontrollers, covering fundamental principles, different LED configurations, and practical applications.

Key Concepts of LED Control

LEDs are semiconductor devices that emit light when an electric current flows through them. They require appropriate voltage and current-limiting resistors to function correctly.

Concept	Description	Example
LED	A light-emitting semiconductor device.	Used in indicator lights and displays.
Current-Limiting Resistor	Prevents excessive current through the LED.	Typically 220Ω to 1kΩ.
Digital Output Control	Microcontroller sets a pin HIGH or LOW to turn an LED on or off.	LATBbits.LATB0 = 1;
PWM (Pulse Width Modulation)	Controls LED brightness by varying the duty cycle.	Used in dimmable LED applications.
LED Matrix	An array of LEDs controlled in a grid pattern.	Used in display boards and signage.

Basic Rules for Controlling LEDs

Rule	Correct Example	Incorrect Example
Use a current-limiting resistor.	Use a 330Ω resistor in series with the LED.	Connecting directly to 5V may burn the LED.
Configure output pin correctly.	Set TRISBbits.TRISB0 = 0 for output mode.	Keeping TRIS as input will not control the LED.

Use PWM for brightness control.	Adjust duty cycle for dimming effects.	Simply turning on/off will not adjust brightness.
Consider LED polarity.	Connect anode to positive, cathode to ground.	Reversing polarity will prevent illumination.

Syntax Table

SL	Function	Syntax/Example	Description
1	Set LED Pin as Output	TRISBbits.TRISB0 = 0;	Configures pin as output.
2	Turn LED On	LATBbits.LATB0 = 1;	Sets output HIGH to light up the LED.
3	Turn LED Off	LATBbits.LATB0 = 0;	Sets output LOW to turn off the LED.
4	Toggle LED State	LATBbits.LATB0 = !LATBbits.LATB0;	Changes LED state from ON to OFF and vice versa.

Syntax Explanation

1. Set LED Pin as Output

What does configuring a pin as an output do? It sets up the microcontroller's pin to send signals to the LED rather than receive input. This is essential because LEDs require an active signal from the microcontroller to operate correctly.

Syntax:
```
TRISBbits.TRISB0 = 0;
```

Example:
```
TRISBbits.TRISB0 = 0;  // Set RB0 as output for LED control
```

Example Explanation: This command sets the TRISB register for pin RB0 to 0, indicating that this pin is configured as an output. In PIC microcontrollers, TRIS registers define whether a pin is an input (1) or an output (0). By setting TRISBbits.TRISB0 = 0, we ensure that RB0 can drive an LED.

2. Turn LED On

What does turning the LED on do? When an LED is turned on, the microcontroller sets its output pin HIGH, allowing current to flow through the LED, which causes it to emit light.

Syntax:

```
LATBbits.LATB0 = 1;
```

Example:

```
LATBbits.LATB0 = 1;  // Turn on LED connected to RB0
```

Example Explanation: This line sets the LATB0 register to 1, which means a HIGH signal is sent to RB0. As a result, the LED receives sufficient voltage to conduct current and emit light. The LAT register is used to control the output state of the pin, ensuring stable signal transmission.

3. Turn LED Off

What does turning the LED off do? Turning off an LED stops the current flow through it by setting the microcontroller output pin to LOW, which results in no light emission.

Syntax:

```
LATBbits.LATB0 = 0;
```

Example:

```
LATBbits.LATB0 = 0;  // Turn off LED connected to RB0
```

Example Explanation: By setting LATBbits.LATB0 = 0;, the microcontroller outputs a LOW signal on RB0, causing the circuit to be incomplete, preventing current from flowing through the LED. This effectively turns the LED off.

4. Toggle LED State

What does toggling the LED state do? Toggling an LED means changing its state from ON to OFF or from OFF to ON with a single command. This is useful for applications such as blinking LEDs.

Syntax:

```
LATBbits.LATB0 = !LATBbits.LATB0;
```

Example:

```
LATBbits.LATB0 = !LATBbits.LATB0;  // Toggle LED state
```

Example Explanation: This command negates the current state of LATB0. If the LED is currently ON (LATB0 = 1), the command changes it to OFF (LATB0 = 0). Conversely, if it is OFF (LATB0 = 0), the command turns it ON (LATB0 = 1). This method is efficient for blinking LEDs without using multiple conditional statements.

Real-life Applications Project: Blinking LED System

In this project, we will build a simple LED blinking system using a PIC microcontroller.

Required Components

Component	Description
LED	Emits light when current flows through it.
Resistor (330Ω)	Limits current to prevent LED damage.
PIC Microcontroller	Controls the LED.
Breadboard & Wires	Used for circuit assembly.

Circuit Connection Table

Component	Pin Connection
LED	Anode -> RB0, Cathode -> GND (via 330Ω resistor)
PIC Microcontroller	RB0 -> LED Anode

Project Code

```
#include <xc.h>
#include <stdio.h>

#define _XTAL_FREQ 4000000  // Define crystal frequency

void main() {
    TRISBbits.TRISB0 = 0;  // Set RB0 as output

    while(1) {
        LATBbits.LATB0 = 1;   // Turn LED on
        __delay_ms(500);      // Wait 500ms
        LATBbits.LATB0 = 0;   // Turn LED off
        __delay_ms(500);      // Wait 500ms
    }
}
```

Chapter 45: Using 7-Segment Displays with PIC Microcontrollers

7-segment displays are widely used in electronic devices for numerical output, such as digital clocks, counters, and measurement devices. These displays consist of seven individual LEDs arranged in a specific pattern to represent digits from 0 to 9. In this chapter, we will explore how to interface and control a 7-segment display with a PIC microcontroller, covering fundamental principles, different types of 7-segment displays, and practical applications.

Key Concepts of 7-Segment Display Control

7-segment displays use multiple LEDs to create numerical representations. Each segment is controlled independently, allowing the display of numbers and some characters.

Concept	Description	Example
Common Cathode Display	All cathodes are connected together, and segments are turned on by sending HIGH signals.	Used in most digital display applications.
Common Anode Display	All anodes are connected together, and segments are turned on by sending LOW signals.	Used in specific embedded systems.
Segment Control	Each segment (A-G) is individually controlled by a microcontroller.	LATBbits.LATB0 = 1; turns on a segment.
Multiplexing	Controls multiple displays by rapidly switching between digits.	Used in multi-digit displays.

Basic Rules for Controlling 7-Segment Displays

Rule	Correct Example	Incorrect Example
Use current-limiting resistors.	Use a 330Ω resistor in series with each segment.	Directly connecting to VCC may burn out LEDs.
Configure output pins correctly.	Set TRISBbits.TRISB0 = 0 for output mode.	Keeping TRIS as input will not control the segments.

Use a lookup table for digit display.	Define a byte array for segment activation.	Manually setting segments increases complexity.
Implement multiplexing for multi-digit displays.	Use fast switching techniques for better performance.	Driving all digits simultaneously causes ghosting.

Syntax Table

SL	Function	Syntax/Example	Description
1	Set Segment Pins as Output	TRISB = 0x00;	Configures all segment control pins as output.
2	Turn On a Segment	LATBbits.LATB0 = 1;	Activates a specific segment.
3	Display a Number	LATB = digitPattern[5];	Outputs a predefined pattern for digit 5.
4	Implement Multiplexing	switchDigit(1);	Activates a specific digit in a multi-digit display.

Syntax Explanation

1. Set Segment Pins as Output

What does configuring segment pins as output do? It allows the microcontroller to control the state of each segment of the 7-segment display by setting the corresponding port pins as outputs.

Syntax:

```
TRISB = 0x00;
```

Example:

```
TRISB = 0x00;   // Configure all segment pins as outputs
```

Example Explanation: Setting TRISB = 0x00; configures all pins on PORTB as output, which means the microcontroller can control each segment of the 7-segment display by setting the respective pin HIGH or LOW.

2. Turn On a Segment

What does turning on a segment do? Each LED segment in the display is controlled by setting its corresponding microcontroller pin HIGH or LOW (depending on whether the display is common anode or common cathode). Turning a segment on allows it to contribute to forming a number or letter.

Syntax:
```
LATBbits.LATB0 = 1;
```

Example:
```
LATBbits.LATB0 = 1;  // Turn on segment A
```

Example Explanation: Setting `LATBbits.LATB0 = 1;` makes RB0 HIGH, which turns on the corresponding segment of the 7-segment display. This is crucial in forming numbers like 1, 2, 3, etc.

3. Display a Number

What does displaying a number do? Each digit from 0 to 9 is formed by turning on the required combination of segments. Using a predefined lookup table simplifies the process.

Syntax:
```
LATB = digitPattern[5];
```

Example:
```
LATB = 0b01101101;  // Display the number 5 on the 7-
segment display
```

Example Explanation: The binary pattern `0b01101101` represents the combination of segments required to form the number 5. This pattern is stored in a lookup table (array) and is used to simplify number display.

4. Implement Multiplexing

What does multiplexing do? Multiplexing allows multiple digits to be displayed on a single 7-segment display module by quickly switching between digits, making it appear as if all digits are shown simultaneously.

Syntax:
```
switchDigit(1);
```

Example:
```
switchDigit(1);  // Activate the first digit in a
multi-digit display
```

Example Explanation: By calling `switchDigit(1);`, the function enables a particular digit in a multi-digit 7-segment display while ensuring others remain off. This creates the illusion of a continuously displayed number.

Real-life Applications Project: Digital Counter

In this project, we will build a simple digital counter using a PIC microcontroller and a 7-segment display.

Required Components

Component	Description
7-Segment Display	Displays numbers using 7 individual LEDs.
PIC Microcontroller	Controls the display and counter logic.
Resistors (330Ω)	Limits current for each segment.
Push Button	Increments the counter when pressed.

Circuit Connection Table

Component	Pin Connection
7-Segment Display	Segments -> PORTB (RB0-RB6)
PIC Microcontroller	PORTB -> 7-Segment Display, Button -> RB7
Push Button	Connected to RB7 with pull-down resistor

Project Code

```c
#include <xc.h>
#include <stdio.h>
#define _XTAL_FREQ 4000000  // Define crystal frequency
char digitPattern[10] = {0b00111111, 0b00000110,
0b01011011, 0b01001111,
                         0b01100110, 0b01101101,
0b01111101, 0b00000111,
                         0b01111111, 0b01101111};
void main() {
    TRISB = 0x00;  // Configure PORTB as output
    TRISBbits.TRISB7 = 1;  // Set RB7 as input for
button
    int counter = 0;
    while(1) {
        if (PORTBbits.RB7 == 1) {  // Check if button
is pressed
            __delay_ms(200);  // Debounce delay
            counter = (counter + 1) % 10;
            LATB = digitPattern[counter];
        }
    }
}
```

Chapter 46: Interfacing LCD Displays with PIC Microcontrollers

LCD (Liquid Crystal Display) modules are widely used in embedded systems for displaying text, numbers, and graphics. These displays offer a simple and effective way to provide a user interface for microcontroller-based applications. In this chapter, we will explore how to interface and control LCD displays using PIC microcontrollers, covering working principles, communication methods, and practical applications.

Key Concepts of LCD Display Control

LCD displays operate by manipulating liquid crystal molecules to control light passage. They can be interfaced with a microcontroller using parallel (e.g., HD44780) or serial (I2C/SPI) communication.

Concept	Description	Example
Character LCD	Displays alphanumeric characters using a predefined character set.	16x2, 20x4 LCDs.
Graphical LCD	Displays custom graphics and images.	128x64 GLCD.
Parallel Interface	Uses multiple data lines for communication.	HD44780 16x2 LCD (4-bit/8-bit mode).
I2C/SPI Interface	Reduces wiring by using serial communication.	I2C-based LCD modules.
Backlight Control	Adjusts brightness using PWM or direct control.	Used in low-power applications.

Basic Rules for Interfacing LCDs

Rule	Correct Example	Incorrect Example
Use appropriate power supply.	Provide 5V for standard LCDs.	Supplying 3.3V may cause dim display.
Initialize LCD before use.	Use proper initialization sequence.	Writing data before initialization causes gibberish.
Use correct communication method.	Match microcontroller pins to LCD mode (4-bit, 8-bit, I2C).	Incorrect wiring leads to display errors.

Enable display before writing.	Send command to turn on display.	Data may not appear without enabling.

Syntax Table

SL	Function	Syntax/Example	Description
1	Initialize LCD	lcd_init();	Prepares the LCD for operation.
2	Clear Display	lcd_clear();	Clears all text on the screen.
3	Print Text	lcd_print("Hello");	Displays text on the LCD.
4	Move Cursor	lcd_set_cursor(1, 0);	Positions cursor at row 1, column 0.

Syntax Explanation

1. Initialize LCD

What does initializing the LCD do? It sets up the LCD by configuring control signals, communication mode, and display parameters. The initialization process includes setting the LCD mode (4-bit or 8-bit), turning on the display, configuring cursor settings, and preparing the LCD for data writing.

Syntax:
```
lcd_init();
```

Example:
```
lcd_init();   // Initialize LCD for use
```

Example Explanation: This function ensures that the LCD is properly set up for communication with the microcontroller. Without calling lcd_init(), the display will not function correctly, and any attempts to write text will not be successful.

2. Clear Display

What does clearing the display do? It removes all text from the screen and resets the cursor to the home position (row 0, column 0). This is useful when refreshing displayed content.

Syntax:
```
lcd_clear();
```

Example:
```
lcd_clear();  // Clear the LCD screen
```

Example Explanation: Executing `lcd_clear();` sends a command to the LCD module to erase all displayed characters and move the cursor to the top-left corner. This function is often used in dynamic applications where the screen needs to be updated frequently.

3. Print Text

What does printing text do? It writes a string of characters on the LCD starting from the current cursor position. The LCD interprets each character in the string and displays it accordingly.

Syntax:
```
lcd_print("Hello");
```

Example:
```
lcd_print("Hello, World!");  // Display text on LCD
```

Example Explanation: This function sends each character of the string "Hello, World!" to the LCD, displaying the message on the screen. If the text exceeds the display width, it will overflow or wrap to the next line (if supported by the display).

4. Move Cursor

What does moving the cursor do? It positions the cursor at a specified row and column, allowing precise control over where the next text will appear on the display.

Syntax:
```
lcd_set_cursor(1,0);
```

Example:
```
lcd_set_cursor(1,5);  // Move cursor to row 1, column 5
```

Example Explanation: Most LCDs are organized as rows and columns (e.g., 16x2 has 16 columns and 2 rows). Calling `lcd_set_cursor(1,5);` moves the cursor to the second row (index 1) and the sixth column (index 5), allowing text to be written at that specific position without affecting the rest of the display.

Real-life Applications Project: Digital Clock Display

In this project, we will build a digital clock display using a PIC microcontroller and a 16x2 LCD.

Required Components

Component	Description
16x2 LCD Module	Displays time and messages.
PIC Microcontroller	Controls the LCD display and clock logic.
Resistors (1kΩ, 10kΩ)	Used for contrast control and pull-ups.
RTC Module (DS1307)	Provides real-time clock data.

Circuit Connection Table

Component	Pin Connection
LCD	Data -> PORTB (RB0-RB7), Control -> PORTD
PIC Microcontroller	PORTB, PORTD -> LCD, I2C -> RTC
RTC (DS1307)	SDA, SCL -> PIC I2C pins

Project Code

```c
#include <xc.h>
#include <stdio.h>

#define _XTAL_FREQ 4000000   // Define crystal frequency

void lcd_init();
void lcd_clear();
void lcd_print(char *text);
void lcd_set_cursor(int row, int col);

void main() {
    lcd_init();   // Initialize LCD
    lcd_clear();   // Clear display

    while(1) {
        lcd_set_cursor(0,0);
        lcd_print("Time: 12:30 PM");   // Display time
        __delay_ms(1000);   // Update every second
    }
}
```

Chapter 47: Working with OLED Displays with PIC Microcontrollers

OLED (Organic Light-Emitting Diode) displays offer high contrast, low power consumption, and better visibility compared to LCDs. These displays are commonly used in embedded systems for graphical user interfaces, text output, and dynamic visual elements. In this chapter, we will explore how to interface and control OLED displays with PIC microcontrollers, covering working principles, communication methods, and practical applications.

Key Concepts of OLED Display Control

OLED displays use organic compounds that emit light when an electric current passes through them. They can be interfaced with a microcontroller using I2C or SPI communication protocols.

Concept	Description	Example
OLED Display	Self-emitting display that does not require a backlight.	SSD1306, SH1106
I2C Communication	Uses two wires (SDA, SCL) for serial data transmission.	Common with SSD1306 OLEDs.
SPI Communication	Uses four wires (MOSI, MISO, SCLK, CS) for high-speed communication.	Used for faster display updates.
Contrast Control	Adjusts brightness using software commands.	Reduces power consumption.
Graphics Support	Can display text, images, and animations.	Used in smart devices.

Basic Rules for Interfacing OLEDs

Rule	Correct Example	Incorrect Example
Use the correct power supply.	Provide 3.3V or 5V based on OLED specifications.	Incorrect voltage may damage the display.
Initialize the OLED before writing data.	Send proper initialization commands.	Writing data before initialization may result in errors.
Use correct I2C/SPI wiring.	Match OLED pins to PIC microcontroller I2C/SPI ports.	Incorrect wiring will prevent communication.

Use software libraries for graphics.	Utilize prebuilt libraries for text and image rendering.	Manually controlling pixels is complex.

Syntax Table

SL	Function	Syntax/Example	Description
1	Initialize OLED	oled_init();	Prepares the OLED for operation.
2	Clear Display	oled_clear();	Clears the screen.
3	Print Text	oled_print("Hello");	Displays text on the OLED.
4	Draw Pixel	oled_draw_pixel(10,10);	Lights up a specific pixel.

Syntax Explanation

1. Initialize OLED

What does initializing the OLED do? It sets up the display by configuring communication settings, contrast settings, and rendering parameters. The initialization process ensures that the display is ready to receive data and interpret commands correctly.

Syntax:
```
oled_init();
```

Example:
```
oled_init();  // Initialize OLED for display operations
```

Example Explanation: Calling oled_init(); initializes the OLED by configuring I2C or SPI communication settings, setting display properties such as contrast, and clearing any previous data in the display buffer. Without initialization, any commands sent to the display may not be processed correctly.

2. Clear Display

What does clearing the display do? It removes all graphics and text from the screen and resets the display buffer. This ensures that new content does not overlap with previous frames.

Syntax:
```
oled_clear();
```

Example:

```
oled_clear();  // Clear the OLED screen
```

Example Explanation: Executing `oled_clear();` sends a command to the OLED to reset the display memory. This is particularly useful when updating dynamic content to prevent ghosting effects where previous frames are still partially visible.

3. Print Text

What does printing text do? It writes a string of characters to the display starting from the current cursor position. The text is formatted using a predefined font stored in the OLED driver library.

Syntax:

```
oled_print("Hello");
```

Example:

```
oled_print("Hello, PIC!");  // Display text on OLED
```

Example Explanation: The `oled_print("Hello, PIC!");` function sends each character of the string to the OLED, which then maps each character to the corresponding pixel arrangement on the screen. The text will remain displayed until new data is written or the screen is cleared.

4. Draw Pixel

What does drawing a pixel do? It turns on a single pixel at a specified X and Y coordinate on the OLED screen. This function is useful for creating custom graphics, icons, or patterns.

Syntax:

```
oled_draw_pixel(10,10);
```

Example:

```
oled_draw_pixel(20,15);  // Light up the pixel at
(20,15)
```

Example Explanation: Calling `oled_draw_pixel(20,15);` activates the pixel at coordinate (20,15). Since OLEDs allow pixel-based control, this function can be used to draw lines, shapes, and animations by activating multiple pixels in a pattern.

Real-life Applications Project: OLED-Based Digital Dashboard

In this project, we will build a simple digital dashboard using a PIC microcontroller and an SSD1306 OLED display.

Required Components

Component	Description
SSD1306 OLED Display	Displays graphical content.
PIC Microcontroller	Controls the OLED and processes data.
Resistors (4.7kΩ)	Used as pull-ups for I2C lines.
Sensors (Temperature, Voltage, etc.)	Provides real-time data for display.

Circuit Connection Table

Component	Pin Connection
OLED Display	SDA, SCL -> PIC I2C pins
PIC Microcontroller	I2C -> OLED, Sensor Inputs -> ADC
Resistors (4.7kΩ)	Pull-ups on SDA, SCL lines

Project Code

```
#include <xc.h>
#include <stdio.h>

#define _XTAL_FREQ 4000000  // Define crystal frequency

void oled_init();
void oled_clear();
void oled_print(char *text);
void oled_draw_pixel(int x, int y);

void main() {
    oled_init();  // Initialize OLED
    oled_clear();  // Clear display

    while(1) {
        oled_print("Temp: 25C");  // Display
temperature reading
        oled_draw_pixel(10,10);  // Example pixel
```

```
drawing
        __delay_ms(1000);   // Update every second
    }
}
```

Expected Results

Once the code is uploaded to the PIC microcontroller, the OLED will
display "Temp: 25C" while also rendering individual pixels. This
project can be extended to include real-time sensor data and
graphical elements for a more advanced dashboard.

Chapter 49: Buzzer Integration with PIC Microcontrollers

Buzzers are commonly used in embedded systems for audio feedback, alarms, notifications, and sound-based alerts. These devices can be either passive (requiring external frequency control) or active (self-contained with internal oscillators). In this chapter, we will explore how to interface and control buzzers with PIC microcontrollers, covering working principles, types of buzzers, interfacing techniques, and practical applications.

Key Concepts of Buzzer Control

Buzzers convert electrical signals into sound waves. They can be interfaced with a microcontroller using a digital signal or a PWM (Pulse Width Modulation) signal for frequency control.

Concept	Description	Example
Active Buzzer	Generates sound when powered, requiring only an ON/OFF signal.	Used in alarms and notifications.
Passive Buzzer	Requires an external PWM signal to generate sound.	Used in musical tone generation.
PWM Control	Allows frequency variation to generate different tones.	Used for melodies and alerts.
Digital ON/OFF	A simple HIGH/LOW signal activates or deactivates the buzzer.	Used in basic beeping systems.

Basic Rules for Interfacing Buzzers

Rule	Correct Example	Incorrect Example
Use the correct voltage rating.	Provide 5V for most buzzers.	Supplying incorrect voltage may damage the buzzer.
Use a transistor for high-power buzzers.	Connect the buzzer via a transistor switch.	Directly connecting a high-current buzzer may damage the microcontroller.
Use PWM for passive buzzers.	Generate different tones using PWM.	Sending a direct HIGH signal to a passive buzzer produces no sound.

| Control active buzzers with digital signals. | Turn ON/OFF using a GPIO pin. | Using PWM with an active buzzer is unnecessary. |

Syntax Table

S L	Function	Syntax/Example	Description
1	Set Buzzer Pin as Output	TRISBbits.TRISB0 = 0;	Configures a pin as output.
2	Turn Buzzer On	LATBbits.LATB0 = 1;	Activates an active buzzer.
3	Turn Buzzer Off	LATBbits.LATB0 = 0;	Deactivates the buzzer.
4	Generate PWM Sound	PWM_Set_Freque ncy(1000);	Produces a 1kHz tone on a passive buzzer.

Syntax Explanation

1. Set Buzzer Pin as Output

What does configuring a pin as an output do? It allows the microcontroller to control the buzzer by sending a HIGH or LOW signal.

Syntax:

```
TRISBbits.TRISB0 = 0;
```

Example:

```
TRISBbits.TRISB0 = 0;  // Configure RB0 as output for
the buzzer
```

Example Explanation: Setting TRISBbits.TRISB0 = 0; ensures that the RB0 pin is configured as an output, enabling it to send control signals to the buzzer.

2. Turn Buzzer On

What does turning the buzzer on do? It sends a HIGH signal to the active buzzer, causing it to emit a continuous sound.

Syntax:

```
LATBbits.LATB0 = 1;
```

Example:
```
LATBbits.LATB0 = 1;  // Activate the buzzer
```

Example Explanation: This command sets the RB0 pin to HIGH, which allows current to flow through the active buzzer, producing a sound.

3. Turn Buzzer Off

What does turning the buzzer off do? It sends a LOW signal to the active buzzer, stopping the sound.

Syntax:
```
LATBbits.LATB0 = 0;
```

Example:
```
LATBbits.LATB0 = 0;  // Deactivate the buzzer
```

Example Explanation: This command sets RB0 to LOW, stopping the current flow and silencing the buzzer.

4. Generate PWM Sound

What does generating a PWM sound do? It allows frequency control of a passive buzzer, producing different tones.

Syntax:
```
PWM_Set_Frequency(1000);
```

Example:
```
PWM_Set_Frequency(1000);  // Generate 1kHz tone on
passive buzzer
```

Example Explanation: This function generates a 1kHz PWM signal, causing the passive buzzer to produce a sound of that frequency.

Real-life Applications Project: Alarm System with Buzzer

In this project, we will build a simple alarm system using a PIC microcontroller and a buzzer.

Required Components

Component	Description
Active Buzzer	Emits sound when powered.
PIC Microcontroller	Controls the buzzer logic.
Resistor (1kΩ)	Limits current flow if necessary.
Push Button	Triggers the alarm system.

Circuit Connection Table

Component	Pin Connection
Buzzer	Anode -> RB0, Cathode -> GND
PIC Microcontroller	RB0 -> Buzzer, RB1 -> Button Input
Push Button	Connected to RB1 with pull-down resistor

Project Code

```c
#include <xc.h>
#include <stdio.h>

#define _XTAL_FREQ 4000000   // Define crystal frequency

void main() {
    TRISBbits.TRISB0 = 0;   // Set RB0 as output for
buzzer
    TRISBbits.TRISB1 = 1;   // Set RB1 as input for
button

    while(1) {
        if (PORTBbits.RB1 == 1) {   // Check if button
is pressed
            LATBbits.LATB0 = 1;   // Turn on buzzer
            __delay_ms(500);   // Sound duration
            LATBbits.LATB0 = 0;   // Turn off buzzer
        }
    }
}
```

Expected Results

Once the code is uploaded to the PIC microcontroller, pressing the button will trigger the buzzer, producing a short alarm sound. This project can be expanded to include motion sensors, timers, or security systems.

Chapter 50: Speaker Integration with PIC Microcontrollers

Speakers are widely used in embedded systems to generate sounds, tones, melodies, and voice outputs. Unlike buzzers, speakers require an external driving signal, often using Pulse Width Modulation (PWM) or a Digital-to-Analog Converter (DAC). In this chapter, we will explore how to interface and control speakers with PIC microcontrollers, covering working principles, signal generation techniques, interfacing methods, and practical applications.

Key Concepts of Speaker Control

Speakers convert electrical signals into sound waves. They can be driven by a microcontroller using PWM, DAC, or external amplifiers for louder output.

Concept	Description	Example
Analog Speaker	Converts electrical signals into sound waves.	Used in music playback systems.
PWM Sound Generation	Uses pulse width modulation to create audio signals.	Used for tone and melody generation.
DAC Signal Generation	Converts digital signals to analog sound.	Used in voice and complex audio playback.
Amplifier Circuit	Increases speaker output power.	Used for high-volume applications.

Basic Rules for Interfacing Speakers

Rule	Correct Example	Incorrect Example
Use the correct voltage rating.	Provide 5V or 3.3V as per speaker specifications.	Supplying incorrect voltage may cause distortion.
Use an amplifier for loud output.	Connect the speaker to an amplifier circuit.	Directly connecting a high-power speaker may damage the microcontroller.
Use PWM for tone generation.	Generate different tones using PWM.	Directly applying DC voltage will not produce sound.

Use DAC for voice playback.	Convert digital signals to smooth analog sound.	Using PWM alone may cause low-quality output.

Syntax Table

S L	Function	Syntax/Example	Description
1	Set Speaker Pin as Output	TRISBbits.TRISB0 = 0;	Configures a pin as output.
2	Generate PWM Tone	PWM_Set_Frequency(1000);	Produces a 1kHz sound signal.
3	Stop Sound	PWM_Stop();	Turns off the speaker output.
4	Play Melody	playMelody();	Generates a sequence of musical notes.

Syntax Explanation

1. Set Speaker Pin as Output

What does configuring a pin as an output do? It allows the microcontroller to send signals to the speaker by toggling the pin at different frequencies. This is essential for controlling the speaker, whether it is generating simple tones or complex audio.

Syntax:
```
TRISBbits.TRISB0 = 0;
```

Example:
```
TRISBbits.TRISB0 = 0;  // Configure RB0 as output for speaker control
```

Example Explanation: By setting TRISBbits.TRISB0 = 0;, the microcontroller configures the RB0 pin as an output. This allows the PIC to send signals to the speaker, controlling its operation and producing sound.

2. Generate PWM Tone

What does generating a PWM tone do? It creates an oscillating signal that drives the speaker at a specific frequency. The frequency determines the pitch of the sound.

Syntax:
```
PWM_Set_Frequency(1000);
```

Example:
```
PWM_Set_Frequency(2000);   // Generate a 2kHz tone on
the speaker
```

Example Explanation: This command generates a 2kHz PWM signal, making the speaker emit a tone at that pitch. By varying the frequency, different musical notes or alert sounds can be produced.

3. Stop Sound

What does stopping the sound do? It disables the PWM signal, cutting off the electrical signal to the speaker and stopping sound production.

Syntax:
```
PWM_Stop();
```

Example:
```
PWM_Stop();  // Turn off speaker output
```

Example Explanation: Executing PWM_Stop(); stops the PWM signal, which immediately silences the speaker. This function is useful in alarms, alerts, and interactive audio feedback systems.

4. Play Melody

What does playing a melody do? It sequences multiple frequencies with time delays, creating a simple tune. Each frequency represents a musical note.

Syntax:
```
playMelody();
```

Example:
```
void playMelody() {
    PWM_Set_Frequency(262);   // Play C note
    __delay_ms(500);
    PWM_Set_Frequency(294);   // Play D note
    __delay_ms(500);
    PWM_Set_Frequency(330);   // Play E note
    __delay_ms(500);
    PWM_Stop();
}
```

Example Explanation: This function generates three musical notes (C, D, and E), each lasting 500 milliseconds. When played sequentially, this creates a recognizable melody. By extending this function with more frequencies, entire musical compositions can be played.

Real-life Applications Project: Speaker-Based Alarm System

In this project, we will build a speaker-based alarm system using a PIC microcontroller.

Required Components

Component	Description
Speaker	Converts electrical signals into sound waves.
PIC Microcontroller	Generates the sound signal.
Resistor (1kΩ)	Limits current flow if necessary.
Push Button	Triggers the alarm system.
Amplifier Circuit (optional)	Boosts speaker volume.

Circuit Connection Table

Component	Pin Connection
Speaker	One terminal -> RB0, Other terminal -> GND
PIC Microcontroller	RB0 -> Speaker, RB1 -> Button Input
Push Button	Connected to RB1 with pull-down resistor

Project Code

```c
#include <xc.h>
#include <stdio.h>

#define _XTAL_FREQ 4000000  // Define crystal frequency

void playAlarm();

void main() {
    TRISBbits.TRISB0 = 0;  // Set RB0 as output for
speaker
    TRISBbits.TRISB1 = 1;  // Set RB1 as input for
button
```

```
    while(1) {
        if (PORTBbits.RB1 == 1) {  // Check if button
is pressed
            playAlarm();  // Activate alarm sound
        }
    }
}

void playAlarm() {
    PWM_Set_Frequency(1000);  // Generate alarm tone
    __delay_ms(1000);
    PWM_Stop();
    __delay_ms(500);
}
```

Expected Results

Once the code is uploaded to the PIC microcontroller, pressing the button will trigger an alarm sound for one second. This project can be expanded to include sensors, volume control, and advanced sound effects.

Chapter 51: Generating Sounds with PWM with PIC Microcontrollers

Pulse Width Modulation (PWM) is an essential technique for generating sound in embedded systems. By varying the duty cycle and frequency of a PWM signal, different tones, alarms, and melodies can be produced using a speaker or buzzer. In this chapter, we will explore how to generate different sounds using PWM with PIC microcontrollers, covering fundamental principles, frequency control, duty cycle manipulation, and practical applications.

Key Concepts of PWM Sound Generation

PWM allows microcontrollers to create sound by modulating the signal at different frequencies. The frequency of the PWM signal determines the pitch of the sound, while the duty cycle affects volume and tone quality.

Concept	Description	Example
PWM Signal	A square wave with a controlled duty cycle and frequency.	Used for audio tone generation.
Frequency Control	Defines the pitch of the generated sound.	Higher frequencies produce higher-pitched sounds.
Duty Cycle Control	Adjusts the waveform's ON/OFF ratio, influencing volume.	Used in amplitude modulation.
Speaker or Buzzer	Converts PWM signals into audible sound.	Used in alarms and musical applications.

Basic Rules for Using PWM for Sound

Rule	Correct Example	Incorrect Example
Choose the correct frequency range.	Use 500Hz–5kHz for common tones.	Using very low frequencies may be inaudible.
Ensure proper duty cycle.	Use a 50% duty cycle for clear tones.	Extreme duty cycles may cause distorted sounds.

Use an amplifier for loud sounds.	Drive high-power speakers using an amplifier.	Directly connecting large speakers may damage the microcontroller.
Use timers for accurate frequency control.	Generate PWM using Timer2.	Using software loops for PWM may be unstable.

Syntax Table

SL	Function	Syntax/Example	Description
1	**Set PWM Mode**	setup_PWM();	Configures PWM on the PIC microcontroller.
2	**Generate PWM Tone**	PWM_Set_Freque ncy(1000);	Produces a 1kHz sound signal.
3	**Adjust Duty Cycle**	PWM_Set_DutyCyc le(50);	Sets duty cycle to 50%.
4	**Stop PWM Sound**	PWM_Stop();	Turns off the sound.

Syntax Explanation

1. Set PWM Mode

What does setting PWM mode do? It configures the microcontroller to generate a PWM signal on a specific pin, enabling sound generation. This function ensures that the microcontroller is ready to produce sound waves with controlled frequency and duty cycle.
Syntax:
setup_PWM();

Example:
setup_PWM(); // Initialize PWM mode on the microcontroller

Example Explanation: Calling setup_PWM(); initializes the hardware PWM module, allowing the microcontroller to generate signals that can drive a speaker or buzzer. This setup is necessary before producing any sound.

2. Generate PWM Tone

What does generating a PWM tone do? It produces an oscillating signal at a specified frequency, which creates a corresponding audio tone. The frequency determines the pitch of the sound produced.

Syntax:

```
PWM_Set_Frequency(1000);
```

Example:

```
PWM_Set_Frequency(2000);   // Generate a 2kHz sound
```

Example Explanation: This command generates a PWM signal at 2kHz, making the speaker produce a high-pitched sound. Changing the frequency value will change the pitch of the sound, allowing different notes to be played.

3. Adjust Duty Cycle

What does adjusting the duty cycle do? It changes the ON/OFF ratio of the PWM signal, affecting sound quality and volume. A higher duty cycle increases the energy delivered to the speaker, making the sound louder.

Syntax:

```
PWM_Set_DutyCycle(50);
```

Example:

```
PWM_Set_DutyCycle(70);   // Set duty cycle to 70%
```

Example Explanation: Increasing the duty cycle makes the sound more pronounced, while lowering it can reduce volume and distortion. Typically, a 50% duty cycle is used for clean, balanced tones.

4. Stop PWM Sound

What does stopping PWM sound do? It disables the PWM signal, stopping the sound output from the speaker. This is useful when implementing pauses in sound sequences or turning off an alarm.

Syntax:

```
PWM_Stop();
```

Example:

```
PWM_Stop();  // Turn off sound generation
```

Example Explanation: Executing PWM_Stop(); disables the PWM module, which immediately stops sound production. This function is often used in alarm or melody systems where sound needs to be controlled dynamically.

Real-life Applications Project: PWM-Based Musical Note Generator

In this project, we will build a musical note generator using a PIC microcontroller and a speaker.

Required Components

Component	Description
Speaker	Converts PWM signals into sound.
PIC Microcontroller	Generates the PWM sound signals.
Resistor (1kΩ)	Limits current flow if necessary.
Push Button	Plays a note when pressed.
Amplifier (Optional)	Boosts speaker output volume.

Circuit Connection Table

Component	Pin Connection
Speaker	One terminal -> RB0, Other terminal -> GND
PIC Microcontroller	RB0 -> Speaker, RB1 -> Button Input
Push Button	Connected to RB1 with pull-down resistor

Project Code

```
#include <xc.h>
#include <stdio.h>

#define _XTAL_FREQ 4000000  // Define crystal frequency

void playNote(int frequency);

void main() {
    TRISBbits.TRISB0 = 0;  // Set RB0 as output for
speaker
    TRISBbits.TRISB1 = 1;  // Set RB1 as input for
button

    while(1) {
        if (PORTBbits.RB1 == 1) {  // Check if button
```

```
is pressed
            playNote(262);  // Play C note
      }
   }
}


void playNote(int frequency) {
    PWM_Set_Frequency(frequency);   // Set frequency for
tone
    __delay_ms(500);   // Hold note for 500ms
    PWM_Stop();
}
```

Expected Results

Once the code is uploaded to the PIC microcontroller, pressing the button will generate a musical note at 262Hz (C note). This project can be expanded to play different notes and even create melodies.

Chapter 52: Controlling DC Motors with PIC Microcontrollers

DC motors are widely used in embedded systems for motion control applications. They are commonly found in robotics, automation, and industrial machinery. To control a DC motor with a PIC microcontroller, techniques such as Pulse Width Modulation (PWM) and H-Bridge circuits are used. In this chapter, we will explore how to interface and control DC motors with PIC microcontrollers, covering speed control, direction control, and real-world applications.

Key Concepts of DC Motor Control

DC motors can be controlled using direct ON/OFF signals or advanced techniques like PWM for speed variation. H-Bridge circuits allow bidirectional control, enabling forward and reverse motion.

Concept	Description	Example
PWM Speed Control	Adjusts motor speed by varying duty cycle.	Used in robotic drive systems.
H-Bridge Circuit	Enables motor direction control using transistors.	L298N motor driver.
MOSFET Switching	Controls high-power motors efficiently.	Used in industrial automation.
Braking and Freewheeling	Controls stopping behavior of the motor.	Used in motor safety applications.

Basic Rules for Controlling DC Motors

Rule	Correct Example	Incorrect Example
Use proper voltage levels.	Use 12V for standard DC motors.	Supplying too high a voltage may damage the motor.
Use an H-Bridge for bidirectional control.	Use L298N to drive motors in both directions.	Directly connecting a motor to a microcontroller can cause failure.
Use PWM for speed control.	Generate a PWM signal to control speed.	Using only ON/OFF control limits flexibility.

Include protection diodes.	Use flyback diodes to prevent voltage spikes.	Omitting diodes may damage circuit components.

Syntax Table

SL	Function	Syntax/Example	Description
1	**Set Motor Control Pins as Output**	TRISB = 0x00;	Configures motor control pins as outputs.
2	**Turn Motor ON**	LATBbits.LATB0 = 1;	Starts motor rotation.
3	**Turn Motor OFF**	LATBbits.LATB0 = 0;	Stops motor rotation.
4	**Set Motor Speed with PWM**	PWM_Set_Duty Cycle(75);	Runs motor at 75% speed.

Syntax Explanation

1. Set Motor Control Pins as Output

What does configuring motor control pins as output do? It ensures that the microcontroller can send ON/OFF signals to control the motor driver, determining the motor's movement.

Syntax:
```
TRISB = 0x00;
```

Example:
```
TRISBbits.TRISB0 = 0;  // Set RB0 as output for motor control
```

Example Explanation: This line configures pin RB0 as an output. Without setting the pin as an output, the microcontroller will not be able to control the motor driver, preventing motor operation.

2. Turn Motor ON

What does turning the motor ON do? It sends a HIGH signal to the motor driver, allowing current to flow through the motor and causing it to rotate.

Syntax:
```
LATBbits.LATB0 = 1;
```

Example:
```
LATBbits.LATB0 = 1;  // Turn on motor
```

Example Explanation: This command sets pin RB0 to HIGH, activating the motor driver, which in turn powers the motor. If the motor driver is connected correctly, the motor will begin rotating.

3. Turn Motor OFF

What does turning the motor OFF do? It sets the motor control pin LOW, cutting off power and stopping motor rotation.

Syntax:
```
LATBbits.LATB0 = 0;
```

Example:
```
LATBbits.LATB0 = 0;  // Stop the motor
```

Example Explanation: Setting RB0 to LOW disables the motor driver, stopping power delivery to the motor, effectively halting movement. This is essential for controlled stopping in automation.

4. Set Motor Speed with PWM

What does setting motor speed with PWM do? It controls how much power the motor receives by adjusting the duty cycle of the PWM signal, allowing speed variations.

Syntax:
```
PWM_Set_DutyCycle(75);
```

Example:
```
PWM_Set_DutyCycle(50);  // Run motor at 50% speed
```

Example Explanation: This function adjusts the motor speed by controlling how long the motor receives power in each cycle. A 50% duty cycle means the motor gets power half of the time, running at half speed. A 100% duty cycle results in full speed operation.

Real-life Applications Project: DC Motor Speed and Direction Control

In this project, we will build a motor control system using a PIC microcontroller and an H-Bridge circuit.

Required Components

Component	Description
DC Motor	Converts electrical energy into motion.
PIC Microcontroller	Controls the motor operation.
L298N Motor Driver	Allows bidirectional motor control.
Resistors (10kΩ)	Pull-down resistors for safety.
Push Buttons	Used to control motor direction.

Circuit Connection Table

Component	Pin Connection
Motor Driver (L298N)	IN1 -> RB0, IN2 -> RB1, PWM -> RB2
PIC Microcontroller	RB0, RB1 -> Motor Direction, RB2 -> PWM Speed Control
Push Buttons	Connected to RB3, RB4 for control

Project Code

```
#include <xc.h>
#include <stdio.h>

#define _XTAL_FREQ 4000000  // Define crystal frequency

void setMotorSpeed(int dutyCycle);
void setMotorDirection(int direction);

void main() {
    TRISB = 0x00;  // Set PORTB as output for motor
control

    while(1) {
        if (PORTBbits.RB3 == 1) {  // Check if Forward
button is pressed
            setMotorDirection(1);  // Set forward
direction
            setMotorSpeed(75);  // Run at 75% speed
        }
        if (PORTBbits.RB4 == 1) {  // Check if Reverse
button is pressed
            setMotorDirection(0);  // Set reverse
```

```
direction
            setMotorSpeed(50);   // Run at 50% speed
        }
    }
}


void setMotorSpeed(int dutyCycle) {
    PWM_Set_DutyCycle(dutyCycle);   // Set PWM duty
cycle for speed control
}


void setMotorDirection(int direction) {
    if (direction == 1) {
        LATBbits.LATB0 = 1;   // Forward direction
        LATBbits.LATB1 = 0;
    } else {
        LATBbits.LATB0 = 0;   // Reverse direction
        LATBbits.LATB1 = 1;
    }
}
```

Expected Results

Once the code is uploaded to the PIC microcontroller, pressing the forward button will move the motor forward at 75% speed, while pressing the reverse button will run the motor in the opposite direction at 50% speed. This project can be extended with sensors for autonomous motion control.

Chapter 53: Servo Motor Control with PIC Microcontrollers

Servo motors are widely used in embedded systems for precise angular position control. They are commonly found in robotics, automation, and remote control applications. Unlike DC motors, servo motors do not require H-Bridge circuits; instead, they are controlled using Pulse Width Modulation (PWM). In this chapter, we will explore how to interface and control servo motors with PIC microcontrollers, covering PWM signal generation, angle control, and practical applications.

Key Concepts of Servo Motor Control

Servo motors operate by receiving a PWM signal with a specific duty cycle, which determines the motor's angular position. The typical PWM frequency for servo control is 50Hz, with pulse widths ranging from 1ms (0°) to 2ms (180°).

Concept	Description	Example
PWM Control	Controls the angle of the servo motor.	Used in robotic arms.
Pulse Width	Determines the exact servo position.	1ms (0°), 1.5ms (90°), 2ms (180°).
Position Holding	Servo holds its position after receiving a command.	Used in actuators.
5V Power Supply	Most servos operate on 5V.	Directly powered by microcontroller or external source.

Basic Rules for Controlling Servo Motors

Rule	Correct Example	Incorrect Example
Use the correct PWM frequency.	50Hz (20ms period).	Using a higher frequency may cause jitter.
Use the correct pulse width range.	1ms (0°) to 2ms (180°).	Exceeding limits may damage the servo.

Use an external power supply for large servos.	Use a dedicated 5V source.	Drawing too much current from the PIC may cause resets.
Wait before updating the position.	Provide at least 20ms between commands.	Rapid updates may cause erratic movement.

Syntax Table

SL	Function	Syntax/Example	Description
1	Set PWM Mode	setup_PWM();	Configures PWM on the PIC microcontroller.
2	Set Servo Angle	setServoAngle(90);	Moves the servo to 90°.
3	Set PWM Duty Cycle for Angle	PWM_Set_Duty Cycle(7.5);	Sets duty cycle to 7.5% for 90°.
4	Stop Servo Movement	PWM_Stop();	Stops sending PWM signal.

Syntax Explanation

1. Set PWM Mode

What does setting PWM mode do? It configures the microcontroller to generate a PWM signal, which is required for controlling the servo motor. The PWM module ensures accurate timing and frequency generation, essential for stable servo operation.

Syntax:

```
setup_PWM();
```

Example:

```
setup_PWM();  // Initialize PWM mode on the
microcontroller
```

Example Explanation: Calling setup_PWM(); configures the PWM module to generate signals at the required frequency (50Hz) and prepares the microcontroller for servo control. Without this initialization, the servo motor will not receive proper signals.

2. Set Servo Angle

What does setting the servo angle do? It sends a specific PWM pulse width to move the servo motor to the desired angle. The microcontroller calculates the correct pulse width based on the angle input.

Syntax:

```
setServoAngle(90);
```

Example:

```
setServoAngle(45);   // Move the servo to 45 degrees
```

Example Explanation: This function converts the angle into a corresponding PWM duty cycle, ensuring the servo positions itself accurately. If the angle is outside the valid range (0-180°), the function should prevent invalid values to avoid damaging the servo.

3. Set PWM Duty Cycle for Angle

What does setting the PWM duty cycle do? It determines the position of the servo by adjusting the length of the HIGH pulse within a 20ms period. The servo motor reads this pulse width and moves to the corresponding position.

Syntax:

```
PWM_Set_DutyCycle(7.5);
```

Example:

```
PWM_Set_DutyCycle(5);   // Move servo to 0 degrees
```

Example Explanation: A duty cycle of 5% corresponds to a 1ms pulse (0°), while a 7.5% duty cycle corresponds to 1.5ms (90°), and 10% corresponds to 2ms (180°). Adjusting the duty cycle changes the servo position. This method allows precise control over angular positioning, making it ideal for robotics applications.

4. Stop Servo Movement

What does stopping the servo do? It disables the PWM signal, preventing further position updates. The servo will hold its last known position unless mechanical resistance forces it to move.

Syntax:

```
PWM_Stop();
```

Example:
```
PWM_Stop();  // Stop sending PWM signal
```

Example Explanation: When `PWM_Stop();` is called, the PWM signal is disabled, causing the servo to remain at its last position without further movement. This is useful for applications where the servo needs to hold its position without consuming unnecessary power.

Real-life Applications Project: Servo-Based Robotic Arm

In this project, we will build a simple robotic arm using a PIC microcontroller and a servo motor.

Required Components

Component	Description
Servo Motor	Converts PWM signals into precise angular motion.
PIC Microcontroller	Generates PWM signals to control the servo.
Resistor (1kΩ)	Used for signal conditioning.
Push Buttons	Used to move the servo to preset positions.

Circuit Connection Table

Component	Pin Connection
Servo Motor	Signal -> RB0, VCC -> 5V, GND -> Ground
PIC Microcontroller	RB0 -> Servo Signal, RB1/RB2 -> Button Inputs
Push Buttons	Connected to RB1 (Move Left), RB2 (Move Right)

Project Code

```
#include <xc.h>
#include <stdio.h>

#define _XTAL_FREQ 4000000  // Define crystal frequency

void setServoAngle(int angle);

void main() {
    TRISBbits.TRISB0 = 0;  // Set RB0 as output for
servo signal
    TRISBbits.TRISB1 = 1;  // Set RB1 as input for
button 1
```

```
    TRISBbits.TRISB2 = 1;   // Set RB2 as input for
button 2

    while(1) {
        if (PORTBbits.RB1 == 1) {  // Check if button 1
is pressed
            setServoAngle(0);   // Move servo to 0°
        }
        if (PORTBbits.RB2 == 1) {  // Check if button 2
is pressed
            setServoAngle(180);   // Move servo to 180°
        }
    }
}
```

Expected Results

Once the code is uploaded to the PIC microcontroller, pressing Button 1 will move the servo to 0°, while pressing Button 2 will move it to 180°. This project can be expanded for precise servo positioning in robotic applications.

Chapter 54: Using Stepper Motors with PIC Microcontrollers

Stepper motors are widely used in applications requiring precise position control, such as CNC machines, robotics, and 3D printers. Unlike DC motors, stepper motors move in discrete steps, making them ideal for applications requiring precise rotation without feedback mechanisms. Stepper motors are controlled using pulse signals sent in a specific sequence to the motor windings. In this chapter, we will explore how to interface and control stepper motors with PIC microcontrollers, covering step sequencing, speed control, and real-world applications.

Key Concepts of Stepper Motor Control

Stepper motors operate by energizing coils in a sequence to move the motor shaft in small steps. The stepping sequence and timing determine the motor's speed and direction.

Concept	Description	Example
Full-Step Mode	Each step moves the motor by a fixed angle.	Common in basic control applications.
Half-Step Mode	Increases resolution by energizing coils halfway between steps.	Used for finer position control.
Microstepping	Smoothens motion by varying current levels.	Used in CNC and 3D printers.
Stepper Driver	Controls stepper motor efficiently using PWM or step signals.	A4988, ULN2003.

Basic Rules for Controlling Stepper Motors

Rule	Correct Example	Incorrect Example
Use a driver circuit.	Use an A4988 or ULN2003 driver.	Directly connecting to PIC I/O pins may damage them.
Control stepping sequence properly.	Follow full-step, half-step, or microstep sequences.	Incorrect sequencing may cause jitter.

Use PWM for speed control.	Adjust pulse frequency to change speed.	Using constant delay limits flexibility.
Provide adequate power.	Use an external power source (12V) for high-power motors.	Powering from the PIC may cause resets.

Syntax Table

SL	Function	Syntax/Example	Description
1	Set Stepper Pins as Output	TRISB = 0x00;	Configures motor control pins as outputs.
2	Step Forward	stepMotor (1);	Moves motor one step forward.
3	Step Backward	stepMotor (-1);	Moves motor one step backward.
4	Control Speed	delay_ms(10);	Adjusts delay between steps to control speed.

Syntax Explanation

1. Set Stepper Pins as Output

What does configuring stepper motor pins as output do? It enables the microcontroller to send step sequences to the motor driver, controlling movement. Setting specific pins as output ensures they can drive the stepper motor correctly.

Syntax:
```
TRISB = 0x00;
```

Example:
```
TRISBbits.TRISB0 = 0;  // Set RB0 as output for step
signal
```

Example Explanation: This line ensures that the microcontroller can control the motor driver by sending appropriate HIGH and LOW signals to the stepper motor windings. If the pin is not set as output, the stepper motor will not receive the necessary signals to operate.

2. Step Forward

What does stepping forward do? It sends a sequence of HIGH and LOW signals to the motor coils to rotate the shaft in one direction. This function ensures precise stepwise movement.

Syntax:

```
stepMotor(1);
```

Example:

```
stepMotor(1);  // Move motor one step forward
```

Example Explanation: This function advances the stepper motor one step in the forward direction by following the correct stepping sequence. Each call moves the motor by a small fixed angle, making it useful for applications requiring accurate control.

3. Step Backward

What does stepping backward do? It reverses the step sequence to rotate the stepper motor in the opposite direction, allowing bidirectional motion control.

Syntax:

```
stepMotor(-1);
```

Example:

```
stepMotor(-1);  // Move motor one step backward
```

Example Explanation: This function sends control signals in the reverse stepping sequence, causing the motor shaft to rotate in the opposite direction. This is useful in automation systems where precise movement in both directions is needed.

4. Control Speed

What does controlling speed do? It adjusts the time delay between steps to change the motor speed. Reducing the delay increases speed, while increasing it slows the motor down.

Syntax:

```
delay_ms(10);
```

Example:

```
delay_ms(5);  // Increase speed by reducing delay
```

Example Explanation: Reducing the delay between steps increases the motor speed, while increasing the delay slows it down. This allows for smooth acceleration and deceleration, preventing sudden jerks in motor movement.

Real-life Applications Project: Stepper Motor Positioning System

In this project, we will build a simple stepper motor positioning system using a PIC microcontroller.

Required Components

Component	Description
Stepper Motor (28BYJ-48)	Moves in steps for precise control.
PIC Microcontroller	Generates step signals for the motor driver.
ULN2003 Motor Driver	Controls stepper motor operation.
Resistors (10kΩ)	Used for pull-down configurations.
Push Buttons	Used to control stepper movement.

Circuit Connection Table

Component	Pin Connection
Stepper Driver (ULN2003)	IN1 -> RB0, IN2 -> RB1, IN3 -> RB2, IN4 -> RB3
PIC Microcontroller	RB0-RB3 -> Stepper Motor Driver
Push Buttons	Connected to RB4 (Forward), RB5 (Backward)

Project Code

```
#include <xc.h>
#include <stdio.h>

#define _XTAL_FREQ 4000000  // Define crystal frequency

void stepMotor(int direction);

void main() {
    TRISB = 0x00;  // Set PORTB as output for motor
control

    while(1) {
        if (PORTBbits.RB4 == 1) {  // Check if Forward
button is pressed
```

```
            stepMotor(1);  // Move one step forward
        }
        if (PORTBbits.RB5 == 1) {  // Check if Backward
button is pressed
            stepMotor(-1);  // Move one step backward
        }
    }
}

void stepMotor(int direction) {
    if (direction == 1) {
        LATBbits.LATB0 = 1;
        __delay_ms(10);
        LATBbits.LATB0 = 0;
    } else {
        LATBbits.LATB3 = 1;
        __delay_ms(10);
        LATBbits.LATB3 = 0;
    }
}
```

Expected Results

Once the code is uploaded to the PIC microcontroller, pressing
Button 1 will move the stepper motor forward one step, while
pressing Button 2 will move it backward. This project can be
expanded for precise positioning and automated control.

Chapter 55: Implementing Relays in Projects with PIC Microcontrollers

Relays are electromechanical switches that allow a low-power microcontroller to control high-power devices, such as lights, motors, and appliances. They are widely used in automation, security systems, and industrial applications. In this chapter, we will explore how to interface and control relays with PIC microcontrollers, covering relay operation, driving circuits, and real-world applications.

Key Concepts of Relay Control

Relays use an electromagnetic coil to mechanically switch a high-power circuit on or off. Since PIC microcontrollers cannot directly drive relays, a transistor is used as an intermediary switch.

Concept	Description	Example
Electromechanical Relay	Uses a coil and mechanical contacts to switch circuits.	SPDT, DPDT relays.
Solid-State Relay (SSR)	Uses semiconductor components to switch circuits.	Faster switching, no moving parts.
Relay Driver Circuit	Uses a transistor to switch the relay coil.	Common in microcontroller applications.
Flyback Diode	Protects against voltage spikes from the relay coil.	1N4007, 1N4148 diodes.

Basic Rules for Controlling Relays

Rule	Correct Example	Incorrect Example
Use a transistor to drive the relay.	Use a BC547 or 2N2222 NPN transistor.	Directly connecting the relay to a PIC pin may damage it.
Use a flyback diode for protection.	Place a diode in parallel with the relay coil.	Omitting the diode may cause voltage spikes.

Choose the correct relay voltage.	Use a 5V or 12V relay based on your application.	Using a higher voltage relay may not activate properly.
Provide enough current for activation.	Ensure the transistor can handle the relay coil current.	Choosing a weak transistor may cause failure.

Syntax Table

SL	Function	Syntax/Example	Description
1	**Set Relay Pin as Output**	TRISBbits.TRISB0 = 0;	Configures the relay control pin as an output.
2	**Turn Relay ON**	LATBbits.LATB0 = 1;	Activates the relay by setting the transistor ON.
3	**Turn Relay OFF**	LATBbits.LATB0 = 0;	Deactivates the relay by turning the transistor OFF.
4	**Toggle Relay State**	LATBbits.LATB0 ^= 1;	Switches the relay between ON and OFF states.

Syntax Explanation

1. Set Relay Pin as Output

What does configuring a relay pin as output do? It allows the microcontroller to control the relay circuit by setting the transistor ON or OFF.

Syntax:
```
TRISBbits.TRISB0 = 0;
```

Example:
```
TRISBbits.TRISB0 = 0;   // Configure RB0 as output for relay control
```

Example Explanation: This command sets RB0 as an output pin, allowing the microcontroller to control the transistor that switches the relay.

2. Turn Relay ON

What does turning the relay ON do? It energizes the relay coil, closing the switch and activating the connected high-power device.

Syntax:

```
LATBbits.LATB0 = 1;
```

Example:

```
LATBbits.LATB0 = 1;  // Activate the relay
```

Example Explanation: Setting RB0 to HIGH turns on the transistor, allowing current to flow through the relay coil, activating the switch.

3. Turn Relay OFF

What does turning the relay OFF do? It de-energizes the relay coil, opening the switch and turning off the connected device.

Syntax:

```
LATBbits.LATB0 = 0;
```

Example:

```
LATBbits.LATB0 = 0;  // Deactivate the relay
```

Example Explanation: Setting RB0 to LOW turns off the transistor, cutting off current to the relay coil, opening the switch and disconnecting the high-power device.

4. Toggle Relay State

What does toggling the relay state do? It switches the relay between ON and OFF states using a single command.

Syntax:

```
LATBbits.LATB0 ^= 1;
```

Example:

```
LATBbits.LATB0 ^= 1;  // Toggle relay state
```

Example Explanation: This command inverts the current state of RB0. If the relay is ON, it turns OFF, and if it is OFF, it turns ON.

Real-life Applications Project: Automatic Relay-Controlled Light System

In this project, we will build a simple automatic light control system using a relay and a PIC microcontroller.

Required Components

Component	Description
5V Relay Module	Switches high-power devices using a low-power control signal.
PIC Microcontroller	Controls the relay switching operation.
NPN Transistor (BC547)	Acts as a switch to control the relay.
Flyback Diode (1N4007)	Protects the circuit from voltage spikes.
Resistor (1kΩ)	Limits base current to the transistor.
Push Button	Used to toggle the relay state.

Circuit Connection Table

Component	Pin Connection
Relay Module	IN -> Transistor Collector, VCC -> 5V, GND -> Ground
Transistor (BC547)	Base -> RB0 (via 1kΩ resistor), Emitter -> Ground, Collector -> Relay IN
PIC Microcontroller	RB0 -> Transistor Base, RB1 -> Button Input
Push Button	One side -> RB1, Other side -> Ground

Project Code

```c
#include <xc.h>
#include <stdio.h>
#define _XTAL_FREQ 4000000  // Define crystal frequency
void main() {
    TRISBbits.TRISB0 = 0;  // Set RB0 as output for relay control
    TRISBbits.TRISB1 = 1;  // Set RB1 as input for push button
    while(1) {
        if (PORTBbits.RB1 == 1) {  // Check if button is pressed
            LATBbits.LATB0 ^= 1;  // Toggle relay state
            __delay_ms(500);  // Debounce delay
        }
    }
}
```

Chapter 56: Bluetooth Modules with PIC Microcontrollers

Bluetooth modules allow wireless communication between microcontrollers and other devices such as smartphones, computers, and embedded systems. These modules enable remote control, data exchange, and IoT applications. In this chapter, we will explore how to interface and communicate with Bluetooth modules using PIC microcontrollers, covering serial communication (UART), pairing, and practical applications.

Key Concepts of Bluetooth Communication

Bluetooth modules operate using UART (Universal Asynchronous Receiver-Transmitter) communication, which allows data to be sent and received wirelessly. Most common modules include the HC-05 and HC-06, which support serial communication with microcontrollers.

Concept	Description	Example
Bluetooth UART Communication	Uses TX and RX pins for wireless serial data transmission.	HC-05, HC-06 modules.
AT Commands	Commands used to configure the Bluetooth module.	AT+NAME=DeviceName
Master/Slave Mode	Defines whether the module initiates or responds to connections.	HC-05 supports master/slave mode.
Pairing Process	Bluetooth devices must pair before communication.	Default pin: 1234 or 0000.

Basic Rules for Using Bluetooth Modules

Rule	Correct Example	Incorrect Example
Use correct baud rate.	9600 bps for HC-05 and HC-06.	Using an incorrect baud rate will result in communication failure.
Connect TX to RX and RX to TX.	TX of PIC -> RX of HC-05, RX of PIC -> TX of HC-05.	Connecting TX to TX and RX to RX will prevent data transmission.

Use 3.3V logic level for RX pin.	Use a voltage divider for HC-05 RX pin.	Directly connecting a 5V signal may damage the module.
Use AT commands to configure the module.	Send "AT+NAME=MyDevice" to change the module's name.	Skipping configuration may cause pairing issues.

Syntax Table

SL	Function	Syntax/Example	Description
1	Initialize UART	UART_Init(9600);	Configures UART communication at 9600 bps.
2	Send Data via Bluetooth	UART_Write("Hello");	Sends a string over Bluetooth.
3	Receive Data	receivedData = UART_Read();	Reads incoming Bluetooth data.
4	Send AT Command	UART_Write("AT+NAME=MyDevice\r\n");	Configures Bluetooth module settings.

Syntax Explanation

1. Initialize UART

What does initializing UART do? It sets up serial communication between the PIC microcontroller and the Bluetooth module, allowing data to be transmitted and received.

Syntax:
UART_Init(9600);

Example:
UART_Init(9600); // Initialize UART at 9600 bps for Bluetooth communication

Example Explanation: Calling UART_Init(9600); configures the UART peripheral of the PIC microcontroller to communicate at a baud rate of 9600 bps. This is essential for reliable communication with Bluetooth modules like HC-05 and HC-06, which use this baud rate by default.

2. Send Data via Bluetooth

What does sending data via Bluetooth do? It transmits a message from the microcontroller to a paired Bluetooth device, such as a smartphone or another embedded system.

Syntax:

```
UART_Write("Hello");
```

Example:

```
UART_Write("LED ON");   // Send command to turn on LED
```

Example Explanation: When `UART_Write("LED ON");` is executed, the microcontroller sends the text "LED ON" wirelessly via Bluetooth. A receiving device (like a smartphone running a Bluetooth terminal app) will display this message. This function is crucial for command-based communication in IoT and automation projects.

3. Receive Data

What does receiving data via Bluetooth do? It listens for incoming data from the paired Bluetooth device and stores it in a variable for further processing.

Syntax:

```
receivedData = UART_Read();
```

Example:

```
char data;
data = UART_Read();   // Read incoming Bluetooth data
```

Example Explanation: This function waits for incoming data and assigns it to the `data` variable. If a smartphone sends a command such as '1', the microcontroller can interpret it and execute an action, such as turning on an LED.

4. Send AT Command

What does sending an AT command do? It allows configuration of the Bluetooth module by modifying settings such as device name, PIN, and connection mode.

Syntax:

```
UART_Write("AT+NAME=MyDevice\r\n");
```

Example:

```
UART_Write("AT+PIN1234\r\n");   // Change Bluetooth PIN
to 1234
```

Example Explanation: Sending the command AT+PIN1234 updates the Bluetooth module's PIN to 1234. AT commands are used to configure the module before deployment, ensuring compatibility with different devices and applications.

Real-life Applications Project: Bluetooth-Based Home Automation

In this project, we will build a simple home automation system using a PIC microcontroller and a Bluetooth module to control appliances remotely.

Required Components

Component	Description
HC-05 Bluetooth Module	Enables wireless communication.
PIC Microcontroller	Controls appliances based on received Bluetooth commands.
Relay Module	Switches electrical devices ON/OFF.
Resistors (1kΩ, 2kΩ)	Used for voltage level shifting.
Smartphone App (Bluetooth Terminal)	Sends commands to the microcontroller.

Circuit Connection Table

Component	Pin Connection
HC-05 Bluetooth Module	TX -> RC7 (RX of PIC), RX -> RC6 (TX of PIC) via voltage divider
PIC Microcontroller	RC6 -> TX, RC7 -> RX
Relay Module	Control pin -> RB0
Smartphone	Connects via Bluetooth

Project Code

```c
#include <xc.h>
#include <stdio.h>

#define _XTAL_FREQ 4000000   // Define crystal frequency

void UART_Init(unsigned long baudrate);
```

```c
void UART_Write(char data);
char UART_Read();

void main() {
    TRISBbits.TRISB0 = 0;   // Set RB0 as output for
relay control
    UART_Init(9600);   // Initialize Bluetooth
communication

    while(1) {
        char receivedData = UART_Read();   // Read
Bluetooth input

        if (receivedData == '1') {
            LATBbits.LATB0 = 1;   // Turn on relay
(appliance ON)
        }
        else if (receivedData == '0') {
            LATBbits.LATB0 = 0;   // Turn off relay
(appliance OFF)
        }
    }
}
```

Expected Results

Once the code is uploaded to the PIC microcontroller and paired with a smartphone via Bluetooth, sending '1' will turn ON the connected appliance, while sending '0' will turn it OFF. This project can be expanded with voice control, sensor inputs, or multi-device communication.

Chapter 57: Wi-Fi and ESP8266 with PIC Microcontrollers

Wi-Fi connectivity enables microcontrollers to communicate wirelessly with networks, cloud servers, and IoT platforms. The ESP8266 Wi-Fi module is a popular choice for adding Wi-Fi capabilities to PIC microcontrollers. In this chapter, we will explore how to interface and communicate with the ESP8266 Wi-Fi module using PIC microcontrollers, covering serial communication (UART), sending HTTP requests, and real-world applications.

Key Concepts of Wi-Fi Communication

The ESP8266 module operates using AT commands via UART communication, allowing the PIC microcontroller to connect to Wi-Fi networks, send data to web servers, and receive responses.

Concept	Description	Example
Wi-Fi Connectivity	Connects microcontrollers to a network.	ESP8266 module.
AT Commands	Commands used to configure and control ESP8266.	AT+CWJAP="SSID","PASSWORD"
HTTP Requests	Sends and retrieves data over the internet.	AT+CIPSTART, AT+CIPSEND
TCP/IP Communication	Enables internet-based data exchange.	Used in IoT applications.

Basic Rules for Using ESP8266 with PIC

Rule	Correct Example	Incorrect Example
Use correct baud rate.	115200 or 9600 bps (depending on firmware).	Using an incorrect baud rate prevents communication.
Use level shifter for 3.3V logic.	Use a voltage divider for TX pin of the PIC.	Connecting directly from a 5V PIC may damage the ESP8266.
Check Wi-Fi connection before sending data.	Use AT+CWJAP? to verify connection.	Sending data without a connection may cause errors.

Use AT+CWMODE to set the correct mode.	AT+CWMODE=1 for station mode.	Incorrect mode settings may prevent communication.

Syntax Table

SL	Function	Syntax/Example	Description
1	Initialize UART	UART_Init(115200);	Configures UART communication at 115200 bps.
2	Connect to Wi-Fi	UART_Write("AT+CWJAP="SSID","PASSWORD"\r\n");	Connects the ESP8266 to a Wi-Fi network.
3	Start TCP Connection	UART_Write("AT+CIPSTART="TCP","server.com",80\r\n");	Establishes a TCP connection to a server.
4	Send Data to Server	UART_Write("AT+CIPSEND=length\r\n");	Sends an HTTP request to a web server.

Syntax Explanation

1. Initialize UART

What does initializing UART do? It configures the PIC microcontroller to communicate with the ESP8266 module via serial communication. UART is essential for sending commands and receiving responses between the microcontroller and the Wi-Fi module.

Syntax:
UART_Init(115200);

Example:
UART_Init(115200); // Initialize UART at 115200 bps for ESP8266 communication

Example Explanation: Calling UART_Init(115200); sets up the UART interface at 115200 bps, which is the default baud rate for ESP8266. If the ESP8266 does not respond correctly, its baud rate might need to be changed using AT commands or set to 9600 in firmware.

2. Connect to Wi-Fi

What does connecting to Wi-Fi do? It allows the ESP8266 to join a Wi-Fi network, enabling internet access and data exchange with online servers.

Syntax:

```
UART_Write("AT+CWJAP=\"SSID\",\"PASSWORD\"\r\n");
```

Example:

```
UART_Write("AT+CWJAP=\"MyWiFi\",\"12345678\"\r\n");  //
Connect to Wi-Fi network
```

Example Explanation: This command instructs the ESP8266 to connect to the Wi-Fi network with the SSID "MyWiFi" and password "12345678". If the connection is successful, the ESP8266 will receive an IP address from the router, allowing it to communicate over the internet.

3. Start TCP Connection

What does starting a TCP connection do? It establishes a communication link between the ESP8266 and a remote web server, enabling data transmission over the internet.

Syntax:

```
UART_Write("AT+CIPSTART=\"TCP\",\"server.com\",80\r\n")
;
```

Example:

```
UART_Write("AT+CIPSTART=\"TCP\",\"example.com\",80\r\n"
);  // Open a connection to example.com
```

Example Explanation: This command tells the ESP8266 to start a TCP connection with "example.com" on port 80. This is commonly used for sending HTTP GET and POST requests to online servers, such as cloud platforms or IoT dashboards.

4. Send Data to Server

What does sending data to the server do? It transmits an HTTP request from the ESP8266 to a remote server, allowing the PIC microcontroller to send data over the internet.

Syntax:

```
UART_Write("AT+CIPSEND=length\r\n");
```

Example:

```
UART_Write("AT+CIPSEND=20\r\n");   // Send 20 bytes of
data
```

Example Explanation: This command informs the ESP8266 that the microcontroller is about to send 20 bytes of data. After the module acknowledges, the HTTP request can be transmitted, such as sending sensor data to a cloud server.

Real-life Applications Project: Wi-Fi-Based IoT Data Logger

In this project, we will build an IoT data logger that sends sensor readings to a web server using a PIC microcontroller and an ESP8266 Wi-Fi module.

Required Components

Component	Description
ESP8266 Wi-Fi Module	Enables internet communication.
PIC Microcontroller	Collects and sends sensor data.
Temperature Sensor (LM35)	Measures temperature readings.
Resistors (1kΩ, 2kΩ)	Used for voltage level shifting.
Web Server (Thingspeak, Firebase, etc.)	Stores and displays sensor data.

Project Code

```c
#include <xc.h>
#include <stdio.h>

#define _XTAL_FREQ 4000000  // Define crystal frequency

void UART_Init(unsigned long baudrate);
void UART_Write(char *data);
char UART_Read();

void main() {
    UART_Init(115200);  // Initialize Wi-Fi
communication
    UART_Write("AT+CWJAP=\"MyWiFi\",\"12345678\"
");  // Connect to Wi-Fi
    __delay_ms(5000);  // Wait for connection
```

```
        while(1) {

UART_Write("AT+CIPSTART=\"TCP\",\"api.thingspeak.com\",
80
");   // Open TCP connection
            __delay_ms(2000);

            UART_Write("AT+CIPSEND=45
");   // Indicate length of data
            __delay_ms(1000);

            UART_Write("GET
/update?api_key=YOUR_API_KEY&field1=25.5
");   // Send sensor data
            __delay_ms(5000);
        }
}
void UART_Init(unsigned long baudrate) {
    // Configuration code for UART
}
void UART_Write(char *data) {
    while(*data) {
        // Transmit each character
        *data++;
    }
}
char UART_Read() {
    // Function to read data from UART
    return '0';
}
```

Expected Results

Once the code is uploaded, the PIC microcontroller will connect to Wi-Fi and send temperature sensor data to a web server, enabling remote monitoring. This project can be expanded for IoT applications, remote automation, and real-time data analytics.

Chapter 58: LoRa Communication with PIC Microcontrollers

LoRa (Long Range) is a wireless communication technology designed for long-distance, low-power applications. It is widely used in IoT networks, remote sensing, and industrial automation. LoRa modules, such as the SX1278, enable PIC microcontrollers to communicate over long distances using low-bandwidth signals. In this chapter, we will explore how to interface LoRa modules with PIC microcontrollers, configure communication settings, and build real-world applications.

Key Concepts of LoRa Communication

LoRa operates on sub-GHz frequency bands (e.g., 433MHz, 868MHz, 915MHz) and uses Chirp Spread Spectrum (CSS) modulation to achieve long-range transmission with minimal power consumption.

Concept	Description	Example
LoRa Modulation	Uses Chirp Spread Spectrum (CSS) for data transmission.	SX1278, RFM95 modules.
LoRaWAN	Network protocol built on LoRa for IoT applications.	Used in smart cities.
Spreading Factor	Determines data rate and range.	SF7 to SF12 configurations.
Bandwidth & Coding Rate	Adjusts transmission reliability and speed.	125kHz, 250kHz, 4/5, 4/8.

Basic Rules for Using LoRa with PIC

Rule	Correct Example	Incorrect Example
Use correct SPI configuration.	Configure SPI for SX1278 communication.	Incorrect SPI settings will prevent transmission.
Select proper frequency.	Use 433MHz for Europe, 915MHz for the USA.	Using an unlicensed frequency may violate regulations.
Set appropriate Spreading Factor	SF7 for fast data, SF12 for long range.	Using SF12 for short distances wastes power.

		(SF).	
Use correct antenna.	Use a matched 50Ω antenna for better range.	Poor antenna selection reduces performance.

Syntax Table

SL	Function	Syntax/Example	Description
1	Initialize SPI	SPI_Init();	Configures SPI for LoRa module communication.
2	Set LoRa Mode	LoRa_SetMode(0x81);	Configures LoRa in standby mode.
3	Send Data	LoRa_Send("Hello");	Transmits data using LoRa.
4	Receive Data	receivedData = LoRa_Receive();	Reads received LoRa messages.

Syntax Explanation

1. Initialize SPI

What does initializing SPI do? It sets up the SPI interface between the PIC microcontroller and the LoRa module, allowing the microcontroller to send commands and exchange data with the module.

Syntax:
SPI_Init();

Example:
SPI_Init(); // Initialize SPI for LoRa communication

Example Explanation: Calling SPI_Init(); configures the SPI bus, enabling the PIC microcontroller to communicate with the SX1278 LoRa module. Without this setup, the microcontroller will not be able to send or receive LoRa signals.

2. Set LoRa Mode

What does setting the LoRa mode do? It puts the LoRa module into a specific mode, such as standby, transmission, or reception, to control its behavior.

Syntax:
```
LoRa_SetMode(0x81);
```

Example:
```
LoRa_SetMode(0x81);   // Set LoRa module to standby mode
```

Example Explanation: This command sets the LoRa module into standby mode, meaning it is powered on and ready to transmit or receive data. Standby mode is useful to reduce power consumption when the module is not actively transmitting or receiving.

3. Send Data

What does sending data do? It transmits a message or data packet over the LoRa network to a receiving device or gateway.

Syntax:
```
LoRa_Send("Hello");
```

Example:
```
LoRa_Send("Sensor Data");   // Transmit sensor readings
via LoRa
```

Example Explanation: When LoRa_Send("Sensor Data"); is called, the LoRa module modulates and transmits the text "Sensor Data" wirelessly. Any receiving LoRa module in range will pick up the signal and decode it. This function is crucial for sending sensor readings and other IoT data.

4. Receive Data

What does receiving data do? It listens for incoming LoRa messages and stores the received data in a variable for processing.

Syntax:
```
receivedData = LoRa_Receive();
```

Example:
```
char receivedData[50];
receivedData = LoRa_Receive();   // Get incoming LoRa
message
```

Example Explanation: The function LoRa_Receive(); retrieves incoming messages sent over the LoRa network. The received data is stored in a character array so it can be processed or displayed later.

Real-life Applications Project: LoRa-Based Weather Monitoring System

In this project, we will build a LoRa-based wireless weather station that transmits temperature and humidity data to a remote receiver.

Required Components

Component	Description
SX1278 LoRa Module	Enables long-range communication.
PIC Microcontroller	Collects sensor data and transmits it.
DHT11 Temperature Sensor	Measures temperature and humidity.
Antenna (433MHz/915MHz)	Improves range and signal quality.
LoRa Gateway (Optional)	For cloud-based IoT integration.

Expected Results

Once the code is uploaded, the PIC microcontroller will continuously send temperature data over LoRa every 5 seconds. A LoRa receiver or gateway can be used to collect and analyze the transmitted data remotely. This project can be expanded for smart agriculture, environmental monitoring, or industrial IoT applications.

Chapter 59: GSM and GPRS with PIC Microcontrollers

GSM (Global System for Mobile Communications) and GPRS (General Packet Radio Service) modules allow microcontrollers to send messages, make calls, and access the internet using mobile networks. These modules, such as SIM800L and SIM900, communicate with PIC microcontrollers via UART and AT commands. In this chapter, we will explore how to interface GSM/GPRS modules with PIC microcontrollers, send SMS messages, make calls, and establish internet connections.

Key Concepts of GSM and GPRS Communication

GSM modules use cellular networks to send and receive messages, voice calls, and internet data via AT commands.

Concept	Description	Example
GSM Communication	Enables sending SMS and making calls via cellular networks.	SIM800L, SIM900 modules.
GPRS Data	Allows internet access via mobile networks.	HTTP requests over GPRS.
AT Commands	Used to configure and control GSM modules.	AT+CMGS for SMS, AT+HTTP for internet.
Network Registration	The module must register on the network before use.	AT+CREG? checks status.

Basic Rules for Using GSM/GPRS with PIC

Rule	Correct Example	Incorrect Example
Use correct baud rate.	9600 bps for SIM800L and SIM900.	Using an incorrect baud rate prevents communication.
Use appropriate power supply.	Provide a 4V power source with 2A current.	Using a low-current supply may cause module resets.
Check network registration.	Use AT+CREG? to verify network status.	Trying to send SMS before registration will fail.

Use AT commands to configure module.	AT+CMGF=1 to set text mode for SMS.	Skipping configuration may cause errors.

Syntax Table

SL	Function	Syntax/Example	Description
1	Initialize UART	UART_Init(9600);	Configures UART communication at 9600 bps.
2	Check Network Status	UART_Write("AT+CREG ?\r\n");	Checks if the module is registered on the network.
3	Send SMS	UART_Write("AT+CMG S="+1234567890"\r\n");	Sends an SMS to the specified number.
4	Establish GPRS Connection	UART_Write("AT+SAPB R=1,1\r\n");	Opens a GPRS session for internet access.

Syntax Explanation

1. Initialize UART

What does initializing UART do? It configures the PIC microcontroller to communicate with the GSM module via serial communication.

Syntax:
UART_Init(9600);

Example:
UART_Init(9600); // Initialize UART at 9600 bps for GSM module communication

Example Explanation: Calling UART_Init(9600); sets up the UART interface at 9600 bps, which is the default baud rate for most GSM modules like SIM800L and SIM900. Without this initialization, the microcontroller cannot send commands to the module.

2. Check Network Status

What does checking network status do? It verifies if the GSM module has successfully connected to a mobile network before performing operations like calling or sending SMS.

Syntax:

```
UART_Write("AT+CREG?\r\n");
```

Example:

```
UART_Write("AT+CREG?\r\n");  // Check GSM network
registration status
```

Example Explanation: This command checks whether the module is registered with a mobile network. A response of +CREG: 0,1 or +CREG: 0,5 indicates successful registration.

3. Send SMS

What does sending an SMS do? It transmits a text message from the PIC microcontroller to a specified phone number.

Syntax:

```
UART_Write("AT+CMGS=\"+1234567890\"\r\n");
```

Example:

```
UART_Write("AT+CMGS=\"+1234567890\"\r\n");  // Send SMS
to phone number
UART_Write("Hello from PIC!\r\n");  // Message content
UART_Write(0x1A);  // End message with Ctrl+Z (ASCII
26)
```

Example Explanation: This sequence sets the recipient's phone number, sends the message "Hello from PIC!", and terminates the SMS with Ctrl+Z. The SMS will be sent through the cellular network.

4. Establish GPRS Connection

What does establishing a GPRS connection do? It enables internet access, allowing the PIC microcontroller to send data to web servers.

Syntax:

```
UART_Write("AT+SAPBR=1,1\r\n");
```

Example:

```
UART_Write("AT+SAPBR=3,1,\"CONTYPE\",\"GPRS\"\r\n");
// Set GPRS mode
UART_Write("AT+SAPBR=1,1\r\n");   // Open GPRS session
```

Example Explanation: This command initializes a GPRS session, which is necessary for sending HTTP requests and communicating with online servers.

Real-life Applications Project: GSM-Based Remote Alert System

In this project, we will build a GSM-based remote alert system that sends an SMS notification when a sensor detects an event.

Required Components

Component	Description
SIM800L GSM Module	Enables GSM communication.
PIC Microcontroller	Detects events and triggers SMS.
PIR Sensor	Detects motion for security alerts.
SIM Card	Required for mobile network access.

Project Code

```
#include <xc.h>
#include <stdio.h>

#define _XTAL_FREQ 4000000   // Define crystal frequency

void UART_Init(unsigned long baudrate);
void UART_Write(char *data);
char UART_Read();

void main() {
    UART_Init(9600);   // Initialize GSM communication
    UART_Write("AT+CREG?\r\n");   // Check network
status
    __delay_ms(2000);   // Wait for response

    while(1) {
        if (PORTBbits.RB0 == 1) {   // Motion detected
            UART_Write("AT+CMGS=\"+1234567890\"\r\n");
```

```
// Set recipient number
            __delay_ms(500);
            UART_Write("Intruder Alert!\r\n");   //
Message content
            UART_Write(0x1A);   // End message with
Ctrl+Z
            __delay_ms(5000);   // Wait before sending
another alert
        }
    }
}
```

Expected Results

Once the code is uploaded and the GSM module registers on the
network, the system will monitor the PIR sensor. If motion is
detected, an SMS alert will be sent to a specified phone number.
This project can be expanded for security, automation, and
emergency response systems.

Chapter 60: RF Modules and Communication with PIC Microcontrollers

RF (Radio Frequency) modules allow wireless communication between microcontrollers over short to medium distances. These modules operate on various frequencies such as 315MHz, 433MHz, and 2.4GHz, making them useful for remote controls, wireless sensor networks, and automation systems. In this chapter, we will explore how to interface RF modules with PIC microcontrollers, covering data transmission, reception, and practical applications.

Key Concepts of RF Communication

RF communication involves a transmitter and a receiver module that send and receive signals over the air. Some modules operate with ASK (Amplitude Shift Keying), FSK (Frequency Shift Keying), or SPI-based digital protocols.

Concept	Description	Example
RF Transmitter	Sends digital data over a radio frequency.	433MHz RF TX module
RF Receiver	Receives transmitted RF signals and converts to data.	433MHz RF RX module
ASK Modulation	Uses amplitude variation to encode data.	Used in simple RF modules
SPI-Based RF	Uses SPI communication for advanced wireless data.	nRF24L01 module

Basic Rules for Using RF Modules with PIC

Rule	Correct Example	Incorrect Example
Use appropriate power supply.	Provide 5V for ASK RF modules.	Using lower voltage may cause failure.
Use proper antenna.	Use a 17cm wire for 433MHz modules.	Omitting the antenna reduces range.
Match transmitter and receiver.	Use same frequency (e.g., 433MHz TX & RX).	Mismatched frequencies won't communicate.
Use Manchester Encoding for reliability.	Implement encoding for better data integrity.	Sending raw signals may cause errors.

Syntax Table

S L	Function	Syntax/Example	Description
1	Initialize TX Module	RF_InitTx();	Configures the RF transmitter.
2	Send Data	RF_Send("Hello");	Transmits data via RF.
3	Initialize RX Module	RF_InitRx();	Configures the RF receiver.
4	Receive Data	receivedData = RF_Receive();	Reads incoming RF data.

Syntax Explanation

1. Initialize TX Module

What does initializing the RF transmitter do? It sets up the transmitter module to send digital signals over RF by configuring the necessary control pins and settings.

Syntax:

```
RF_InitTx();
```

Example:

```
RF_InitTx();  // Initialize RF transmitter module
```

Example Explanation: Calling RF_InitTx(); sets up the microcontroller's GPIO pins to control the RF transmitter module. This ensures that the transmitter is ready to send data packets wirelessly.

2. Send Data

What does sending data do? It transmits a string or binary data over the RF link to be received by a matching receiver module.

Syntax:

```
RF_Send("Hello");
```

Example:

```
RF_Send("Temperature: 25C");  // Send temperature data
via RF
```

Example Explanation: This function transmits the text "Temperature: 25C" over the RF module. The receiver must be tuned to the same frequency and protocol to properly decode and process the received data.

3. Initialize RX Module

What does initializing the RF receiver do? It configures the receiver module to listen for incoming RF signals and prepares it to process received data.

Syntax:

```
RF_InitRx();
```

Example:

```
RF_InitRx();   // Initialize RF receiver module
```

Example Explanation: The function `RF_InitRx();` configures the PIC microcontroller's GPIO pins to interface with the RF receiver. Once initialized, the receiver can continuously monitor the airwaves for incoming transmissions.

4. Receive Data

What does receiving data do? It captures incoming RF transmissions, converts them into digital data, and stores the received message in a variable.

Syntax:

```
receivedData = RF_Receive();
```

Example:

```
char receivedData[50];
receivedData = RF_Receive();   // Get incoming RF
message
```

Example Explanation: The function `RF_Receive();` listens for RF signals, processes the received data, and stores it in `receivedData`. The receiver must be configured properly to decode the signal accurately.

Real-life Applications Project: RF-Based Wireless Sensor System

In this project, we will build a wireless sensor system that transmits temperature readings from one PIC microcontroller to another using RF modules.

Required Components

Component	Description
433MHz RF TX Module	Transmits sensor data wirelessly.
433MHz RF RX Module	Receives transmitted data.
PIC Microcontroller (TX)	Collects sensor data.
PIC Microcontroller (RX)	Receives and processes data.
Temperature Sensor (LM35)	Measures temperature readings.

Project Code

Transmitter Code (PIC TX):

```c
#include <xc.h>
#include <stdio.h>

#define _XTAL_FREQ 4000000  // Define crystal frequency

void RF_InitTx();
void RF_Send(char *data);

void main() {
    RF_InitTx();  // Initialize RF Transmitter
    while(1) {
        RF_Send("Temperature: 25C");  // Send
temperature data
        __delay_ms(5000);  // Send data every 5 seconds
    }
}
```

Receiver Code (PIC RX):

```c
#include <xc.h>
#include <stdio.h>
```

```c
#define _XTAL_FREQ 4000000   // Define crystal frequency

void RF_InitRx();
char RF_Receive();

void main() {
    RF_InitRx();   // Initialize RF Receiver
    char receivedData[50];
    while(1) {
        receivedData = RF_Receive();   // Get incoming
RF message
        // Process received data
    }
}
```

Expected Results

Once the code is uploaded, the transmitter PIC will continuously send temperature data over RF every 5 seconds. The receiver PIC will capture the data and process it accordingly. This project can be expanded for home automation, remote controls, and security systems.

Chapter 61: Gesture Recognition with PIC Microcontrollers

Gesture recognition allows microcontrollers to interpret human hand or body movements and convert them into commands. This technology is widely used in human-machine interfaces, smart devices, and assistive technologies. Gesture recognition sensors, such as the APDS-9960 and accelerometer-based modules, can be interfaced with PIC microcontrollers to detect and process gestures. In this chapter, we will explore how to interface gesture recognition sensors with PIC microcontrollers, process data, and build real-world applications.

Key Concepts of Gesture Recognition

Gesture recognition works by detecting motion using optical, infrared, or inertial sensors. These sensors process hand movements, directional swipes, and predefined motion patterns.

Concept	Description	Example
Optical Gesture Sensors	Detects motion using infrared light reflection.	APDS-9960, TMG3993
Accelerometer-Based Gestures	Uses motion and orientation data to detect gestures.	MPU6050, ADXL345
Predefined Gesture Recognition	Recognizes specific movements like swipes, taps, and rotations.	Swiping left to change pages
Machine Learning-Based Gesture Recognition	Uses AI models for advanced pattern detection.	Embedded TensorFlow

Basic Rules for Using Gesture Sensors with PIC

Rule	Correct Example	Incorrect Example
Use correct I2C or SPI configuration.	Configure I2C for APDS-9960 sensor.	Using incorrect communication settings will prevent detection.
Provide the correct power supply.	Use 3.3V for most optical sensors.	Powering a 3.3V sensor with 5V can damage it.

Calibrate the sensor before use.	Use calibration functions for accuracy.	Skipping calibration leads to incorrect gestures.
Use filters to remove noise.	Implement moving average or Kalman filter.	Unfiltered data can cause misdetection.

Syntax Table

SL	Function	Syntax/Example	Description
1	Initialize Gesture Sensor	Gesture_Init();	Configures the sensor for gesture detection.
2	Read Gesture Data	gesture = Gesture_Read();	Reads raw gesture data from the sensor.
3	Process Gesture	Gesture_Process (gesture);	Converts raw data into meaningful gestures.
4	Perform Action	Perform_Action(gesture);	Triggers an action based on detected gestures.

Syntax Explanation

1. Initialize Gesture Sensor

What does initializing the gesture sensor do? It sets up the gesture recognition module for communication and detection, configuring necessary registers and communication protocols.

Syntax:

```
Gesture_Init();
```

Example:

```
Gesture_Init();  // Initialize APDS-9960 for gesture
detection
```

Example Explanation: Calling `Gesture_Init();` configures the I2C communication, initializes sensor parameters such as sensitivity, gain, and detection range, and prepares it for detecting gestures. If the sensor is not initialized correctly, it will not be able to detect gestures.

2. Read Gesture Data

What does reading gesture data do? It retrieves raw motion-related data from the gesture sensor, representing different types of hand movements.

Syntax:
```
gesture = Gesture_Read();
```

Example:
```
char gesture;
gesture = Gesture_Read();   // Read detected gesture
```

Example Explanation: This function fetches gesture input from the sensor and stores it in a variable for further processing. The raw data might indicate directional movement, proximity, or rotational motion.

3. Process Gesture

What does processing the gesture do? It interprets the raw sensor data and determines which predefined gesture (e.g., left swipe, right swipe, up swipe) has been performed.

Syntax:
```
Gesture_Process(gesture);
```

Example:
```
Gesture_Process(gesture);   // Convert raw data into a
recognized gesture
```

Example Explanation: This function analyzes the movement pattern from the raw data and categorizes it as a specific gesture. It applies filtering techniques to eliminate false detections and ensures accuracy in gesture classification.

4. Perform Action

What does performing an action do? It executes a predefined action, such as turning on an LED or controlling a device, based on the recognized gesture.

Syntax:
```
Perform_Action(gesture);
```

Example:

```
if (gesture == 'L') {
    LED_Toggle();  // Toggle an LED when left swipe is
detected
}
```

Example Explanation: When a left swipe ('L') is detected, the microcontroller toggles an LED as a response. Similarly, other gestures can be mapped to different actions, such as controlling a servo motor or sending a command to another device.

Real-life Applications Project: Gesture-Controlled Home Automation

In this project, we will build a home automation system where appliances are controlled using hand gestures detected by an APDS-9960 sensor.

Required Components

Component	Description
APDS-9960 Gesture Sensor	Detects hand gestures.
PIC Microcontroller	Processes gestures and controls devices.
Relay Module	Controls electrical appliances.
LCD Display (Optional)	Displays recognized gestures.

Project Code

```
#include <xc.h>
#include <stdio.h>

#define _XTAL_FREQ 4000000  // Define crystal frequency

void Gesture_Init();
char Gesture_Read();
void Gesture_Process(char gesture);
void Perform_Action(char gesture);

void main() {
    Gesture_Init();  // Initialize Gesture Sensor
    char gesture;
    while(1) {
        gesture = Gesture_Read();  // Read gesture data
```

```
        Gesture_Process(gesture);   // Process the
detected gesture
        Perform_Action(gesture);    // Perform the
action
    }
}

void Perform_Action(char gesture) {
    if (gesture == 'L') {
        LATBbits.LATB0 = !LATBbits.LATB0;  // Toggle
LED on Left Swipe
    } else if (gesture == 'R') {
        LATBbits.LATB1 = !LATBbits.LATB1;  // Toggle
LED on Right Swipe
    }
}
```

Expected Results

Once the code is uploaded, swiping left will toggle one LED, while swiping right will toggle another. This project can be expanded for smart home applications, gesture-controlled robots, and accessibility solutions.

Chapter 62: Speech Processing with PIC Microcontrollers

Speech processing allows microcontrollers to recognize and process voice commands, enabling voice-controlled systems in embedded applications. This is commonly used in voice assistants, automation systems, and assistive technologies. By integrating PIC microcontrollers with speech recognition modules such as the HM2007, EasyVR, or AI-based solutions, we can achieve real-time speech recognition. In this chapter, we will explore how to interface speech processing modules with PIC microcontrollers, process voice commands, and implement real-world applications.

Key Concepts of Speech Processing

Speech processing involves analyzing voice signals, converting them into digital data, and recognizing predefined words or phrases.

Concept	Description	Example
Speech Recognition	Detects predefined voice commands.	HM2007, EasyVR modules.
Analog-to-Digital Conversion (ADC)	Converts audio signals into digital form.	PIC ADC module.
Keyword Spotting	Detects specific words from speech input.	"Turn on light" command.
Machine Learning-Based Speech Recognition	Uses AI models for improved voice command detection.	TensorFlow Lite, Edge Impulse.

Basic Rules for Using Speech Processing with PIC

Rule	Correct Example	Incorrect Example
Use correct communication protocol.	Use UART or SPI for EasyVR module.	Incorrect wiring may cause data loss.
Provide stable power supply.	Use regulated 5V or 3.3V for modules.	Unstable power can cause recognition failures.
Use noise filtering techniques.	Implement FFT or moving average for clear audio.	Noisy input may lead to incorrect recognition.

Pre-train and calibrate recognition.	Train the module with different voice samples.	Untrained modules may fail to recognize commands.

Syntax Table

S L	Function	Syntax/Example	Description
1	Initialize Speech Module	Speech_Init();	Configures the speech module for voice recognition.
2	Read Voice Command	command = Speech_Read();	Reads recognized voice command.
3	Process Voice Command	Speech_Process(command);	Converts raw speech data into recognizable commands.
4	Execute Action	Execute_Comma nd(command);	Performs an action based on the recognized voice command.

Syntax Explanation

1. Initialize Speech Module

What does initializing the speech module do? It configures the speech recognition module, sets up communication protocols, and prepares it for detecting voice commands. This step is essential for ensuring stable recognition performance.

Syntax:
```
Speech_Init();
```

Example:
```
Speech_Init();  // Initialize EasyVR speech recognition module
```

Example Explanation: Calling Speech_Init(); sets up UART or SPI communication, initializes recognition parameters such as sensitivity, noise filtering, and gain settings, and enables voice command detection. Without this initialization, the module will not function properly.

2. Read Voice Command

What does reading a voice command do? It captures audio input, processes it, and outputs a recognized command as digital data. This function retrieves processed speech data from the speech recognition module.

Syntax:

```
command = Speech_Read();
```

Example:

```
char command;
command = Speech_Read();   // Read the detected voice command
```

Example Explanation: This function fetches a recognized command from the speech module and stores it in a variable for further processing. The received command is compared against predefined voice commands in the system.

3. Process Voice Command

What does processing the voice command do? It interprets the recognized command and determines the associated action. It checks the stored command against predefined instructions and maps it to a specific function.

Syntax:

```
Speech_Process(command);
```

Example:

```
Speech_Process(command);   // Convert voice command into a system action
```

Example Explanation: The function analyzes the speech recognition output, checks for valid commands, and prepares the system to execute a corresponding action. If the command does not match a predefined action, the system can prompt the user to repeat the command.

4. Execute Action

What does executing an action do? It triggers a function or hardware action based on the recognized voice command. The microcontroller processes the command and performs the associated action, such as turning on an LED, activating a motor, or controlling a display.

Syntax:

```
Execute_Command(command);
```

Example:

```
if (command == 'L') {
    LED_Toggle();  // Toggle LED on "Light On" command
}
```

Example Explanation: When the "Light On" command is detected, the LED toggles as a response. Different commands can be mapped to various actions such as controlling a fan, motor, or display. The system can also include a feedback mechanism, such as an LCD display, to confirm command execution.

Real-life Applications Project: Voice-Controlled Home Automation

In this project, we will build a home automation system where appliances are controlled using voice commands detected by a speech recognition module.

Required Components

Component	Description
EasyVR Speech Module	Detects and recognizes voice commands.
PIC Microcontroller	Processes voice commands and controls devices.
Relay Module	Controls electrical appliances.
Microphone	Captures user speech.

Project Code

```
#include <xc.h>
#include <stdio.h>


#define _XTAL_FREQ 4000000  // Define crystal frequency
```

```c
void Speech_Init();
char Speech_Read();
void Speech_Process(char command);
void Execute_Command(char command);

void main() {
    Speech_Init();  // Initialize Speech Recognition
Module
    char command;
    while(1) {
        command = Speech_Read();  // Read voice command
        Speech_Process(command);  // Process the
recognized command
        Execute_Command(command); // Perform the action
    }
}

void Execute_Command(char command) {
    if (command == 'L') {
        LATBbits.LATB0 = !LATBbits.LATB0;  // Toggle
LED on "Light On" command
    } else if (command == 'F') {
        LATBbits.LATB1 = !LATBbits.LATB1;  // Toggle
Fan on "Fan On" command
    }
}
```

Expected Results

Once the code is uploaded, saying "Light On" will toggle an LED, while saying "Fan On" will toggle a fan. This project can be expanded for smart home applications, hands-free control, and assistive voice-controlled technologies.

Chapter 63: Image Processing with PIC Microcontrollers

Image processing involves analyzing and manipulating images to extract useful information. PIC microcontrollers, despite their limited processing power, can be interfaced with external image sensors and processing units such as the OV7670 camera module or FPGA-based accelerators to perform basic image processing tasks like edge detection, object tracking, and motion detection. This chapter explores how to interface image sensors with PIC microcontrollers and implement real-world applications.

Key Concepts of Image Processing

Image processing in embedded systems involves capturing, processing, and analyzing images in real time or offline.

Concept	Description	Example
Image Sensor	Captures images and sends pixel data to the microcontroller.	OV7670 camera module.
Grayscale Conversion	Converts color images to black and white for simplicity.	Edge detection algorithms.
Edge Detection	Identifies boundaries of objects in an image.	Sobel, Canny filters.
Object Detection	Recognizes objects based on shape, color, or size.	Face detection, QR code scanning.

Basic Rules for Using Image Processing with PIC

Rule	Correct Example	Incorrect Example
Use an external image processing unit if needed.	Use an FPGA or DSP for complex tasks.	Running complex algorithms on a low-end PIC will be too slow.
Use correct communication protocol.	Use I2C or SPI for camera modules.	Incorrect wiring will prevent image data reception.
Optimize memory usage.	Use external RAM or SD cards for image storage.	Storing large images in internal memory can cause overflows.

Process only necessary data.	Use region-of-interest (ROI) techniques.	Processing entire images wastes resources.

Syntax Table

SL	Function	Syntax/Example	Description
1	Initialize Camera Module	Camera_Init();	Configures the camera module for image capture.
2	Capture Image Data	image_data = Camera_Capture();	Captures and stores an image frame.
3	Process Image Data	Process_Image(image_data);	Applies image processing algorithms.
4	Extract Object Features	Extract_Features(image_data);	Identifies objects or patterns in the image.

Syntax Explanation

1. Initialize Camera Module

What does initializing the camera module do? It configures the camera sensor, sets resolution, and prepares the module for capturing images.

Syntax:

```
Camera_Init();
```

Example:

```
Camera_Init();  // Initialize OV7670 camera module
```

Example Explanation: Calling `Camera_Init();` sets up I2C/SPI communication, configures camera parameters such as resolution and frame rate, and prepares it for image capture.

2. Capture Image Data

What does capturing image data do? It retrieves pixel data from the camera module and stores it in a buffer for processing.

Syntax:

```
image_data = Camera_Capture();
```

Example:

```
char image_data[640*480];
image_data = Camera_Capture();  // Capture an image
frame
```

Example Explanation: This function fetches image data from the camera and stores it in an array. The resolution and color format of the captured image depend on the camera's configuration.

3. Process Image Data

What does processing image data do? It applies image processing algorithms like filtering, edge detection, or thresholding.

Syntax:

```
Process_Image(image_data);
```

Example:

```
Process_Image(image_data);  // Apply grayscale
conversion and edge detection
```

Example Explanation: The function analyzes the pixel data, modifies it based on the selected algorithm (e.g., converting color images to grayscale), and prepares the image for further analysis.

4. Extract Object Features

What does extracting object features do? It identifies specific patterns, shapes, or objects in the image data.

Syntax:

```
Extract_Features(image_data);
```

Example:

```
Extract_Features(image_data);  // Detect edges and
recognize objects
```

Example Explanation: This function detects predefined objects, edges, or patterns in the image. It can be used in applications such as motion detection, barcode scanning, and object tracking.

Real-life Applications Project: Motion Detection Using PIC

In this project, we will build a motion detection system where a PIC microcontroller processes image frames and detects movement.

Required Components

Component	Description
OV7670 Camera Module	Captures images for processing.
PIC Microcontroller	Analyzes image frames.
SD Card Module	Stores captured images.
LCD Display (Optional)	Displays detected objects.

Project Code

```c
#include <xc.h>
#include <stdio.h>

#define _XTAL_FREQ 4000000  // Define crystal frequency

void Camera_Init();
char Camera_Capture();
void Process_Image(char image_data[]);
void Detect_Motion(char image_data[]);

void main() {
    Camera_Init();  // Initialize Camera Module
    char image_data[640*480];
    while(1) {
        image_data = Camera_Capture();
        Process_Image(image_data);
        Detect_Motion(image_data);
    }
}

void Detect_Motion(char image_data[]) {
difference
}
```

Expected Results

Once the code is uploaded, the system will continuously capture image frames, process them for motion detection, and trigger an event (such as an alarm) when movement is detected. This project can be expanded for surveillance systems, industrial automation, and smart security solutions.

Chapter 64: Smart Wearables with PIC Microcontrollers

Smart wearables are compact, wearable electronic devices equipped with sensors, communication modules, and processing units to monitor health, track activity, and provide notifications. PIC microcontrollers can be integrated into smart wearable devices to process sensor data, communicate wirelessly, and display information. This chapter explores how to develop smart wearable applications using PIC microcontrollers.

Key Concepts of Smart Wearables

Wearables use sensors, displays, and communication modules to collect and process user data in real-time.

Concept	Description	Example
Heart Rate Monitoring	Uses a pulse sensor to detect heartbeats.	MAX30102, Pulse Sensor
Step Counting	Uses an accelerometer to detect steps.	ADXL345, MPU6050
Wireless Communication	Sends and receives data via Bluetooth or Wi-Fi.	HC-05, ESP8266
Display Integration	Displays real-time information on a wearable screen.	OLED, LCD

Basic Rules for Using Smart Wearables with PIC

Rule	Correct Example	Incorrect Example
Use low-power components.	Use low-power sensors like MAX30102.	Using high-power modules reduces battery life.
Optimize power management.	Use sleep modes to save power.	Running components continuously drains battery quickly.
Ensure comfortable design.	Use compact PCB designs for wearables.	Bulky components make wearables impractical.
Use energy-efficient displays.	Use OLED or e-paper screens.	High-power LCDs drain battery faster.

Syntax Table

SL	Function	Syntax/Example	Description
1	Initialize Sensors	Sensor_Init();	Configures sensors for data acquisition.
2	Read Sensor Data	sensor_value = Sensor_Read();	Reads data from the wearable sensor.
3	Process Data	Process_Data(senso r_value);	Converts raw sensor data into useful information.
4	Display Data	Display_Update(sen sor_value);	Shows processed data on the screen.

Syntax Explanation

1. Initialize Sensors

What does initializing the sensors do? It sets up the sensors used in the wearable device, such as heart rate, accelerometer, or temperature sensors, ensuring proper communication and stable data acquisition.

Syntax:
```
Sensor_Init();
```

Example:
```
Sensor_Init();  // Initialize heart rate and step
counter sensors
```

Example Explanation: Calling `Sensor_Init();` configures the necessary GPIO pins and communication protocols (I2C, SPI, or UART) for different sensors used in the wearable device. Without initialization, the sensors will not be able to collect data.

2. Read Sensor Data

What does reading sensor data do? It retrieves real-time measurements from the sensor and stores them in a variable for further processing.

Syntax:
```
sensor_value = Sensor_Read();
```

Example:
```
int heart_rate;
heart_rate = Sensor_Read();   // Read heart rate data
```

Example Explanation: This function collects raw sensor values, such as heart rate or acceleration data, and stores them in a variable. The raw sensor data may need filtering to remove noise and ensure accuracy before further processing.

3. **Process Data**

What does processing the data do? It converts raw sensor readings into meaningful information, such as beats per minute (BPM) for heart rate or step count for an accelerometer.

Syntax:
```
Process_Data(sensor_value);
```

Example:
```
Process_Data(heart_rate);   // Convert heart rate sensor
data into BPM
```

Example Explanation: This function processes the raw data by applying filters, noise reduction techniques, and calculations to derive meaningful insights. For example, the heart rate sensor might return an analog value, which needs conversion into BPM.

4. **Display Data**

What does displaying data do? It updates the wearable's display with processed sensor values, such as heart rate or step count, providing real-time feedback to the user.

Syntax:
```
Display_Update(sensor_value);
```

Example:
```
Display_Update(heart_rate);   // Show heart rate on an
OLED display
```
Example Explanation: This function sends the processed data to the display module, ensuring that the user can see real-time sensor readings on their wearable device. The display module could be an OLED screen, LCD, or even an LED indicator.

Real-life Applications Project: Heart Rate Monitoring Wearable

In this project, we will build a heart rate monitoring wearable that measures the user's heart rate and displays it on an OLED screen.

Required Components

Component	Description
MAX30102 Pulse Sensor	Detects heartbeats using infrared light.
PIC Microcontroller	Processes sensor data and controls the display.
OLED Display	Shows heart rate in real time.
Battery Module	Provides power to the wearable.

Project Code

```
#include <xc.h>
#include <stdio.h>
#define _XTAL_FREQ 4000000  // Define crystal frequency
void Sensor_Init();
int Sensor_Read();
void Process_Data(int data);
void Display_Update(int data);
void main() {
    Sensor_Init();
    while(1) {
        heart_rate = Sensor_Read();
        Process_Data(heart_rate);
        Display_Update(heart_rate);  // Show heart rate
on OLED
    }
}
```

Expected Results

Once the code is uploaded, the wearable device will continuously monitor the user's heart rate, process the data, and display it on an OLED screen. This project can be expanded for fitness tracking, health monitoring, and medical applications.

Chapter 65: Home Automation with PIC Microcontrollers

Home automation refers to using microcontrollers to control home appliances, security systems, and other electronic devices remotely or automatically. PIC microcontrollers can be interfaced with sensors, relays, and wireless communication modules to build intelligent home automation systems. This chapter explores how to integrate PIC microcontrollers into home automation projects.

Key Concepts of Home Automation

Home automation systems use sensors, actuators, and communication interfaces to control home appliances efficiently.

Concept	Description	Example
Remote Appliance Control	Uses relays to switch appliances on/off remotely.	Controlling lights and fans.
Temperature Monitoring	Monitors room temperature and adjusts AC settings.	DHT11, LM35 sensors.
Security System	Uses motion sensors and cameras for security.	PIR sensors, door locks.
Wireless Connectivity	Allows remote control using Bluetooth, Wi-Fi, or GSM.	HC-05, ESP8266, SIM800L.

Basic Rules for Using Home Automation with PIC

Rule	Correct Example	Incorrect Example
Use appropriate power relays.	Use 5V relays to control AC appliances.	Using high-power relays may damage PIC.
Ensure proper sensor placement.	Place motion sensors near doorways.	Placing sensors in unstable locations reduces accuracy.
Use communication modules for remote control.	Integrate Bluetooth or Wi-Fi for remote access.	Using only manual controls limits functionality.
Incorporate safety features.	Use optocouplers for high-voltage isolation.	Directly connecting high voltage to PIC can be dangerous.

Syntax Table

SL	Function	Syntax/Example	Description
1	Initialize System	Home_Init();	Sets up relays and sensors for automation.
2	Read Sensor Data	sensor_value = Sensor_Read();	Reads data from home automation sensors.
3	Control Appliance	Control_Device(device, state);	Turns home appliances on/off.
4	Send Remote Command	Send_Command(command);	Sends a command over Bluetooth/Wi-Fi.

Syntax Explanation

1. Initialize System

What does initializing the system do? It sets up the sensors, relays, and communication modules used in the home automation project. This ensures that all components are ready to interact and function as expected.

Syntax:

```
Home_Init();
```

Example:

```
Home_Init();  // Initialize sensors, relays, and
communication modules
```

Example Explanation: Calling Home_Init(); configures input and output pins, initializes communication protocols (UART, SPI, I2C), and sets up the automation system. Without initialization, devices may not function correctly, leading to unexpected behavior.

2. Read Sensor Data

What does reading sensor data do? It retrieves environmental data such as temperature, motion, or light levels from the connected sensors. This data can be used to make intelligent automation decisions.

Syntax:

```
sensor_value = Sensor_Read();
```

Example:
```
int temperature;
temperature = Sensor_Read();   // Read room temperature
```

Example Explanation: This function collects sensor values and stores them in a variable for further processing. For example, a temperature sensor like LM35 can provide room temperature data, which can be used to control an air conditioning system based on predefined conditions.

3. Control Appliance

What does controlling an appliance do? It allows the PIC microcontroller to switch an appliance on or off using a relay module. This is essential for automating lights, fans, and other household devices.

Syntax:
```
Control_Device(device, state);
```
Example:
```
Control_Device("Fan", ON);   // Turn on the fan
```
Example Explanation: This function sends a control signal to the relay module, activating or deactivating the connected home appliance. If the relay is properly wired, the device will turn on or off as expected.

4. Send Remote Command

What does sending a remote command do? It transmits control signals wirelessly to the home automation system using Bluetooth, Wi-Fi, or GSM. This allows users to control home devices remotely via a mobile app or web interface.

Syntax:
```
Send_Command(command);
```
Example:
```
Send_Command("Turn on Lights");   // Send a command via
Bluetooth
```
Example Explanation: This function enables remote operation of the home automation system. For example, using a Bluetooth or Wi-Fi module, the microcontroller can receive and execute user commands, making it possible to control appliances from a smartphone or web dashboard.

Real-life Applications Project: Smart Home Automation System

In this project, we will build a smart home automation system where users can control appliances remotely via Bluetooth.

Required Components

Component	Description
HC-05 Bluetooth Module	Enables wireless communication.
PIC Microcontroller	Processes commands and controls appliances.
Relay Module	Controls AC devices like lights and fans.
Temperature Sensor (LM35)	Monitors room temperature.

Project Code

```c
#include <xc.h>
#include <stdio.h>
#define _XTAL_FREQ 4000000   // Define crystal frequency
void Home_Init();
int Sensor_Read();
void Control_Device(char device[], int state);
void Send_Command(char command[]);
void main() {
    Home_Init();
    while(1) {
        temperature = Sensor_Read();
        if (temperature > 25) {
            Control_Device("Fan", ON);
        }
    }
}
```

Expected Results

Once the code is uploaded, the home automation system will automatically control appliances based on sensor data. Users can also send remote commands via Bluetooth to control devices manually. This project can be expanded for IoT-based automation, security systems, and voice-controlled smart homes.

Chapter 66: Weather Monitoring System with PIC Microcontrollers

A weather monitoring system collects and processes environmental data such as temperature, humidity, and air pressure. Using PIC microcontrollers, sensors, and wireless modules, real-time weather monitoring can be implemented for agricultural, industrial, and smart city applications. This chapter explores how to interface weather sensors with PIC microcontrollers and develop a weather monitoring system.

Key Concepts of Weather Monitoring

Weather monitoring involves using sensors to measure and analyze different environmental parameters.

Concept	Description	Example
Temperature Monitoring	Measures environmental temperature.	LM35, DHT11, DS18B20
Humidity Measurement	Detects moisture levels in the air.	DHT11, DHT22
Pressure Sensing	Monitors atmospheric pressure.	BMP180, BMP280
Wireless Connectivity	Sends collected data to cloud or remote systems.	ESP8266, GSM modules

**Basic Rules for Using Weather Monitoring with PIC

Rule	Correct Example	Incorrect Example
Use precise sensors.	Use BMP280 for accurate pressure reading.	Using cheap sensors may reduce accuracy.
Ensure proper calibration.	Calibrate sensors periodically.	Using sensors without calibration may result in incorrect readings.
Use data logging.	Store weather data on an SD card.	Not saving data limits long-term analysis.
Implement wireless transmission.	Send data via Wi-Fi or GSM.	Relying only on local storage reduces remote access.

Syntax Table

S.L	Function	Syntax/Example	Description
1	Initialize Sensors	`Weather_Init();`	Configures temperature, humidity, and pressure sensors.
2	Read Sensor Data	`data = Weather_Read();`	Retrieves environmental data.
3	Store Data	`Log_Data(data);`	Saves weather data in memory.
4	Send Data Wirelessly	`Send_Data(data);`	Transmits weather data via Wi-Fi or GSM.

Syntax Explanation

1. Initialize Sensors

What does it do?
It sets up the sensors used in the system, such as temperature, humidity, and pressure sensors, ensuring proper communication with the PIC microcontroller.

Syntax:
`Weather_Init();`

Example:
`Weather_Init();  // Initialize all weather sensors`

Example Explanation: Calling `Weather_Init();` configures GPIO pins, sets up I2C/SPI/UART communication for different sensors, and ensures proper power management. Without initialization, the sensors will not function properly, leading to incorrect readings.

2. Read Sensor Data

What does it do?
It retrieves temperature, humidity, and pressure readings from the sensors, which are essential for weather monitoring.

Syntax:
```
data = Weather_Read();
```

Example:
```
float temperature;
temperature = Weather_Read();  // Read temperature
sensor data
```

Example Explanation: This function queries the connected sensors for real-time weather data and stores the values in a variable for further processing or display. The function reads digital or analog signals from the sensors and converts them into meaningful units such as °C for temperature, %RH for humidity, and hPa for pressure.

3. Store Data

What does it do?
It saves the collected weather data to an SD card, EEPROM, or cloud storage for later analysis and logging.
Syntax:
```
Log_Data(data);
```

Example:
```
Log_Data(temperature);  // Save temperature reading to
memory
```

Example Explanation: The `Log_Data();` function writes the collected sensor readings to storage, allowing for long-term weather trend analysis. This helps in scientific research, farming, and industrial monitoring where historical weather data is valuable.

4. Send Data Wirelessly

What does it do?
It transmits weather sensor readings to an IoT platform, mobile device, or web server using Wi-Fi, Bluetooth, or GSM communication.
Syntax:

```
Send_Data(data);
```

Example:
```
Send_Data(temperature);  // Transmit data over Wi-Fi
```

Example Explanation: This function allows remote monitoring by sending data via wireless modules like ESP8266 (Wi-Fi), HC-05 (Bluetooth), or SIM800L (GSM). Once transmitted, the data can be displayed on a mobile application or cloud dashboard, making it accessible from anywhere.

Real-life Applications Project: IoT-Based Weather Monitoring System

In this project, we will build an IoT-based weather monitoring system that records environmental data and transmits it via Wi-Fi.

Required Components

Component	Description
DHT11 Temperature & Humidity Sensor	Measures environmental data.
BMP280 Pressure Sensor	Measures atmospheric pressure.
PIC Microcontroller	Processes and transmits sensor data.
ESP8266 Wi-Fi Module	Sends data to an IoT platform.
SD Card Module	Stores weather data.

Circuit Connection Table

Component	PIC Microcontroller Pin	Power Source	Communication Protocol
DHT11 Temperature & Humidity Sensor	GPIO Pin (e.g., RB0)	3.3V or 5V	Digital Data
BMP280 Pressure Sensor	I2C SDA, SCL (e.g., RC3, RC4)	3.3V	I2C
ESP8266 Wi-Fi Module	UART TX/RX (e.g., RC6, RC7)	3.3V	UART
SD Card Module	SPI MOSI, MISO, SCK (e.g., RA0,	3.3V	SPI

	RA1, RA2)		

Project Code

```
include <xc.h>
include <stdio.h>

define _XTAL_FREQ 4000000  // Define crystal frequency

void Weather_Init();
float Weather_Read();
void Log_Data(float data);
void Send_Data(float data);

void main() {
    Weather_Init();  // Initialize weather monitoring
system
    float temperature;
    while(1) {
        temperature = Weather_Read();  // Read
temperature data
        Log_Data(temperature);  // Save temperature to
memory
        Send_Data(temperature);  // Send data via Wi-Fi
    }
}
```

Expected Results

Once the code is uploaded, the weather monitoring system will continuously collect environmental data, log it, and transmit it to a cloud server or mobile application for remote monitoring. This project can be expanded for climate research, agriculture, and industrial applications.

Chapter 67: Smart Agriculture with PIC Microcontrollers

Smart agriculture integrates modern technology into farming practices to improve efficiency, optimize resources, and enhance productivity. PIC microcontrollers play a crucial role in automating irrigation, monitoring soil conditions, and controlling agricultural equipment. This chapter explores how to develop smart agricultural systems using PIC microcontrollers and various sensors.

Key Concepts of Smart Agriculture

Smart agriculture systems utilize various sensors and actuators to collect, analyze, and respond to environmental data.

Concept	Description	Example
Soil Moisture Monitoring	Measures the soil's water content.	YL-69, FC-28
Automated Irrigation	Controls water flow based on soil conditions.	Relay, Solenoid Valves
Weather Monitoring	Detects temperature, humidity, and rainfall.	DHT11, BMP280
Remote Control & Data Logging	Sends and stores agricultural data wirelessly.	ESP8266, GSM Modules

Basic Rules for Using Smart Agriculture with PIC

Rule	Correct Example	Incorrect Example
Use water-resistant sensors.	Choose waterproof soil moisture sensors.	Using non-protected sensors may lead to failure.
Optimize power consumption.	Use solar panels for sustainable operation.	Running on battery alone limits system runtime.
Ensure accurate sensor placement.	Place soil sensors at plant root levels.	Placing sensors too shallow may result in incorrect readings.
Incorporate automation.	Use relays for automatic irrigation control.	Relying only on manual intervention reduces efficiency.

Syntax Table

SL	Function	Syntax/Example	Description
1	Initialize Sensors	`Agri_Init();`	Configures soil moisture, temperature, and other sensors.
2	Read Sensor Data	`data = Agri_Read();`	Retrieves real-time agricultural data.
3	Control Irrigation	`Control_Irri gation(state );`	Turns the irrigation system on/off.
4	Send Data Wirelessly	`Send_Data(da ta);`	Transmits agricultural data via Wi-Fi or GSM.

Syntax Explanation

1. Initialize Sensors

What does it do? It sets up the sensors used in the smart agriculture system, such as soil moisture, temperature, and humidity sensors, ensuring proper communication with the PIC microcontroller.
Syntax:
`Agri_Init();`

Example:
`Agri_Init();  // Initialize all agricultural sensors`

Example Explanation: Calling `Agri_Init();` sets up the input and output pins, configures I2C/SPI/UART communication, and ensures the sensors are correctly initialized for accurate readings. Without initialization, the sensors will not function properly, leading to incorrect or missing data.

2. Read Sensor Data

What does it do? It retrieves real-time soil moisture, temperature, and humidity readings from the sensors and processes the data for decision-making.

Syntax:
```
data = Agri_Read();
```

Example:
```
float moisture;
moisture = Agri_Read();  // Read soil moisture sensor
data
```

Example Explanation: This function communicates with the sensors and retrieves raw values representing soil moisture, temperature, or humidity. These values can then be processed or displayed to the user. The microcontroller converts the raw sensor signal into meaningful environmental parameters.

3. Control Irrigation

What does it do? It turns the irrigation system on or off based on the soil moisture levels detected by the sensor, ensuring optimal water distribution.

Syntax:
```
Control_Irrigation(state);
```

Example:
```
Control_Irrigation(ON);  // Activate irrigation system
```

Example Explanation: This function allows the microcontroller to trigger the irrigation system when predefined conditions are met. For example, if the soil moisture sensor detects dry soil, the system activates the irrigation process, preventing water waste and ensuring plant health.

4. Send Data Wirelessly

What does it do? It transmits collected sensor data to an IoT platform, mobile device, or web server using Wi-Fi, Bluetooth, or GSM, enabling real-time remote monitoring.

Syntax:
```
Send_Data(data);
```

Example:
```
Send_Data(moisture);  // Transmit soil moisture data
over Wi-Fi
```

Example Explanation: This function allows remote access to live data, enabling farmers or agricultural operators to monitor field conditions from a distance. The microcontroller connects to a wireless module (e.g., ESP8266 or GSM) and sends real-time updates to an IoT cloud platform or smartphone application.

Real-life Applications Project: IoT-Based Smart Irrigation System

In this project, we will build an IoT-based smart irrigation system that monitors soil moisture and controls water flow automatically.

Required Components

Component	Description
YL-69 Soil Moisture Sensor	Measures soil moisture.
DHT11 Temperature & Humidity Sensor	Monitors environmental conditions.
PIC Microcontroller	Processes and transmits sensor data.
Relay Module	Controls irrigation system.
ESP8266 Wi-Fi Module	Sends data to an IoT platform.
Solenoid Valve	Controls water flow.

Circuit Connection Table

Component	PIC Microcontroller Pin	Power Source	Communication Protocol
YL-69 Soil Moisture Sensor	Analog Pin (e.g., RA0)	3.3V or 5V	Analog Data
DHT11 Temperature & Humidity Sensor	GPIO Pin (e.g., RB0)	3.3V or 5V	Digital Data
Relay Module	GPIO Pin (e.g., RC1)	5V	Digital Output
ESP8266 Wi-Fi Module	UART TX/RX (e.g., RC6, RC7)	3.3V	UART

Solenoid Valve	Relay-Controlled	External 12V	Relay-Based

Project Code

```c
#include <xc.h>
#include <stdio.h>

#define _XTAL_FREQ 4000000  // Define crystal frequency

void Agri_Init();
float Agri_Read();
void Control_Irrigation(int state);
void Send_Data(float data);

void main() {
    Agri_Init();  // Initialize smart agriculture system
    float moisture;
    while(1) {
        moisture = Agri_Read();  // Read soil moisture data
        if (moisture < 30) {  // If soil is dry
            Control_Irrigation(ON);  // Activate irrigation
        }
        Send_Data(moisture);  // Send data via Wi-Fi
    }
}
```

Expected Results

Once the code is uploaded, the smart agriculture system will continuously monitor soil moisture and control the irrigation system accordingly. The collected data will also be transmitted to an IoT platform, allowing farmers to access real-time information remotely. This project can be expanded to include weather forecasting, pest control automation, and precision farming.

Chapter 68: Common Issues in PIC Development

Developing with PIC microcontrollers can sometimes present challenges, especially for beginners. Common issues include programming errors, hardware misconfigurations, and debugging difficulties. Understanding these issues and how to resolve them can significantly improve the development process. This chapter explores frequent problems encountered in PIC development and provides solutions to address them.

Key Concepts of Troubleshooting PIC Development

PIC development issues can arise from hardware, software, or communication errors.

Concept	Description	Example
Programming Issues	Errors in writing and uploading code.	Incorrect fuses, syntax errors.
Power Supply Problems	Inadequate or unstable voltage to the microcontroller.	Brownouts, unexpected resets.
Clock Configuration	Incorrect oscillator settings causing timing issues.	Misconfigured internal/external clock.
Peripheral Misuse	Incorrect setup of ADC, UART, I2C, etc.	No response from peripherals.
Faulty Connections	Poor wiring or loose connections.	Sensors not working.

Basic Rules for Avoiding Common Issues in PIC Development

Rule	Correct Example	Incorrect Example
Check Power Supply.	Use a stable 5V regulated source.	Using unregulated power may cause resets.
Configure Fuses Correctly.	Set the correct oscillator mode in fuses.	Incorrect fuses may disable clock.
Verify Connections.	Use a multimeter to check wiring.	Loose connections lead to erratic behavior.
Debug Using	Send debug messages	Without debugging, errors

		over UART for errors.	are harder to trace.
LEDs or UART.			
Ensure Proper Reset Circuit.		Use a pull-up resistor on the MCLR pin.	Floating MCLR pin can cause unintended resets.

Syntax Table

SL	Issue	Solution Syntax/Example	Description
1	**Incorrect Clock Setting**	`#pragma config FOSC = HS`	Configures the PIC to use a high-speed external oscillator.
2	**Brownout Reset**	`#pragma config BOREN = ON`	Enables brownout reset to prevent instability.
3	**Faulty GPIO Initialization**	`TRISB = 0x00;`	Ensures that PORTB is configured as an output.
4	**UART Not Responding**	`SPBRG = 25; TXSTA = 0x24;`	Properly configures UART baud rate and transmission.

Syntax Explanation

1. Incorrect Clock Setting

What does it do?
Configures the microcontroller to use an external high-speed oscillator, ensuring stable operation.

Syntax:
`#pragma config FOSC = HS`

Example:
```
#pragma config FOSC = HS  // Set external crystal
oscillator mode
```

Example Explanation: If the incorrect oscillator mode is selected, the PIC may not start or may operate at an incorrect frequency, leading to timing errors in PWM, UART, and other peripherals.

2. Brownout Reset

What does it do?
Enables brownout reset, preventing the microcontroller from operating under low-voltage conditions that could cause erratic behavior.
Syntax:
```
#pragma config BOREN = ON
```

Example:
```
#pragma config BOREN = ON   // Enable brownout reset
```

Example Explanation: If brownout reset is disabled and voltage fluctuates, the PIC may randomly reset or enter an unstable state, making debugging difficult.

3. Faulty GPIO Initialization

What does it do?
Ensures that GPIO pins are properly configured for input or output, preventing unintended behavior.
Syntax:
```
TRISB = 0x00;  // Set PORTB as output
```

Example:
```
TRISB = 0x00;  // Configure all PORTB pins as outputs
```

Example Explanation: If GPIO pins are not set correctly, they may not respond as expected, leading to issues in LED blinking, motor control, or sensor interfacing.

4. UART Not Responding

What does it do?
Configures the UART communication to ensure proper serial data transmission and reception.
Syntax:
```
SPBRG = 25;
TXSTA = 0x24;
```

Example:

```
SPBRG = 25;  // Set baud rate
TXSTA = 0x24;  // Enable UART transmission
```

Example Explanation: Without properly configuring the UART module, data transmission may fail, preventing debugging messages from being sent.

Real-life Applications Project: Debugging and Error Handling in PIC Development

This project demonstrates how to debug a PIC microcontroller system using LEDs and UART.

Required Components

Component	Description
PIC Microcontroller	The main processing unit.
LEDs	Used for debugging.
UART Module (FTDI/USB-UART)	Sends debug messages to a computer.
Oscilloscope (Optional)	Helps diagnose clock issues.

Circuit Connection Table

Component	PIC Microcontroller Pin	Power Source	Purpose
LED	RB0	5V	Debugging Output
UART TX	RC6	3.3V or 5V	Serial Communication
Oscillator	OSC1, OSC2	3.3V or 5V	Provides external clock

Project Code

```
#include <xc.h>
#include <stdio.h>

#define _XTAL_FREQ 4000000  // Define crystal frequency

void Debug_LED();
void Debug_UART(const char *message);
```

```c
void main() {
    TRISB = 0x00;  // Set PORTB as output
    TXSTA = 0x24;  // Enable UART transmission
    SPBRG = 25;   // Set baud rate

    while(1) {
        Debug_LED();  // Blink LED for debugging
        Debug_UART("System Running\n");  // Send debug
message
        __delay_ms(1000);
    }
}

void Debug_LED() {
    LATBbits.LATB0 = 1;  // Turn on LED
    __delay_ms(500);
    LATBbits.LATB0 = 0;  // Turn off LED
}

void Debug_UART(const char *message) {
    while(*message) {
        while(!TXIF);  // Wait until TX buffer is empty
        TXREG = *message++;  // Send character
    }
}
```

Expected Results

After uploading the code, the LED on RB0 will blink, and debug
messages will be sent via UART. This approach helps diagnose
issues in real-time, making debugging PIC projects easier and more
efficient.

Chapter 69: Reducing Power Consumption with PIC Microcontrollers

Reducing power consumption in PIC microcontrollers is essential for battery-operated and energy-efficient applications. Various techniques, such as sleep modes, clock adjustments, and power management peripherals, can be used to extend battery life and reduce overall energy consumption. This chapter explores different methods to optimize power usage in PIC-based systems.

Key Concepts of Power Management in PIC

Concept	Description	Example
Sleep Mode	Puts the PIC into low-power mode to conserve energy.	SLEEP() function
Peripheral Control	Disables unused peripherals to save power.	Disabling ADC, UART when not in use
Clock Frequency Scaling	Reduces the system clock speed to lower power usage.	Adjusting OSCCON register
Low-Power Components	Uses energy-efficient sensors and components.	Using ePaper displays instead of LCDs

Basic Rules for Reducing Power Consumption in PIC

Rule	Correct Example	Incorrect Example
Use Sleep Mode when Idle.	SLEEP();	Keeping PIC active when not required wastes power.
Disable Unused Peripherals.	Disable ADC, UART, and PWM if not needed.	Keeping all peripherals enabled increases power consumption.
Lower the Clock Speed when Possible.	Reduce clock frequency when high speed is unnecessary.	Running PIC at maximum speed always drains power quickly.
Use Low-Power External Components.	Choose energy-efficient sensors and displays.	Using high-power LEDs unnecessarily increases drain.

Syntax Table

S L	Function	Syntax/Example	Description
1	Enable Sleep Mode	`SLEEP();`	Reduces power consumption by putting PIC to sleep.
2	Disable Peripherals	`ADCON0bits.ADON = 0;`	Turns off ADC module when not in use.
3	Reduce Clock Speed	`OSCCON = 0x30;`	Sets internal oscillator to a lower frequency.
4	Turn Off Unused Ports	`TRISB = 0xFF;`	Configures all PORTB pins as input to reduce power.

Syntax Explanation

1. Enable Sleep Mode

What does it do?
Sleep mode turns off the CPU and most peripherals, reducing power consumption significantly. It is useful in battery-powered applications where the microcontroller only wakes up when necessary.

Syntax:
```
SLEEP();
```

Example:
```
SLEEP();  // Put PIC into sleep mode
```

Example Explanation: When `SLEEP();` is called, the microcontroller enters low-power mode and stops execution until an external event (like an interrupt) wakes it up. This helps extend battery life by turning off unnecessary operations.

2. Disable Peripherals

What does it do?
Disabling unused peripherals like ADC, UART, or timers can significantly reduce power usage.

Syntax:
```
ADCON0bits.ADON = 0;
```

Example:

```
ADCON0bits.ADON = 0;   // Turn off ADC module when not
in use
```

Example Explanation: If an application does not require analog-to-digital conversion, turning off the ADC prevents it from drawing unnecessary power.

3. Reduce Clock Speed

What does it do?
Lowering the clock speed reduces power consumption because the microcontroller runs at a slower rate, requiring less energy.
Syntax:
```
OSCCON = 0x30;
```

Example:

```
OSCCON = 0x30;   // Set internal oscillator to a lower
frequency
```

Example Explanation: Reducing the oscillator frequency lowers power usage, but may also slow down system performance. This is ideal for applications that do not require high processing speed.

4. Turn Off Unused Ports

What does it do?
Configuring unused pins as inputs prevents them from consuming power.
Syntax:
```
TRISB = 0xFF;
```

Example:

```
TRISB = 0xFF;   // Set all PORTB pins as inputs to
reduce power usage
```
Example Explanation: If a GPIO pin is set as an output but is not driving a connected load, it can still consume unnecessary power. Setting all unused pins as inputs reduces power wastage.

Real-life Applications Project: Low-Power Sensor Node

In this project, we will create a low-power wireless sensor node that periodically reads temperature data and sends it via a wireless module, minimizing power usage when idle.

Required Components

Component	Description
PIC Microcontroller	Controls the system.
Temperature Sensor (LM35)	Reads temperature data.
ESP8266 Wi-Fi Module	Sends data wirelessly.
Battery Pack	Powers the system.

Circuit Connection Table

Component	PIC Microcontroller Pin	Power Source	Purpose
LM35 Temperature Sensor	Analog Pin (e.g., RA0)	3.3V or 5V	Reads temperature.
ESP8266 Wi-Fi Module	UART TX/RX (e.g., RC6, RC7)	3.3V	Transmits data wirelessly.
Battery Pack	VCC, GND	3.3V or 5V	Powers the system.

Project Code

```c
#include <xc.h>
#include <stdio.h>

#define _XTAL_FREQ 4000000  // Define crystal frequency

void Power_Optimize();
float Read_Temperature();
void Send_Data(float data);

void main() {
    Power_Optimize();  // Enable power-saving features
    float temperature;
    while(1) {
        temperature = Read_Temperature();  // Read
```

```
temperature
        Send_Data(temperature);  // Transmit data
wirelessly
        SLEEP();  // Enter low-power mode until next
cycle
    }
}

void Power_Optimize() {
    OSCCON = 0x30;  // Lower clock speed
    ADCON0bits.ADON = 0;  // Disable ADC when not in
use
    TRISB = 0xFF;  // Set unused ports to inputs
}
```

Expected Results

Once the code is uploaded, the PIC microcontroller will periodically wake up, read the temperature, transmit data, and go back into sleep mode. This approach maximizes battery life while maintaining functionality. The project can be expanded to include solar power integration and advanced scheduling mechanisms.

Chapter 70: Enhancing Code Efficiency with PIC Microcontrollers

Efficient coding in PIC microcontrollers is crucial for optimizing performance, reducing memory usage, and improving execution speed. By using structured programming, interrupt handling, efficient data storage, and code optimization techniques, PIC programs can run faster and consume fewer resources. This chapter explores best practices to enhance code efficiency in PIC microcontrollers.

Key Concepts of Code Efficiency in PIC

Concept	Description	Example
Interrupt-Driven Programming	Uses interrupts to handle real-time events efficiently.	Using `INTCONbits.GIE = 1;` for global interrupts.
Code Optimization	Reduces redundant instructions for better performance.	Using `#pragma optimize` directives.
Efficient Memory Management	Minimizes RAM and Flash usage for optimized execution.	Using `const` for fixed data storage.
Loop Optimization	Improves iteration efficiency to reduce execution time.	Using `for` loops instead of `while` where applicable.

Basic Rules for Writing Efficient PIC Code

Rule	Correct Example	Incorrect Example
Use interrupts for real-time events.	Implement ISR handlers for input changes.	Polling in the main loop increases CPU load.
Optimize loops and conditions.	Minimize unnecessary iterations.	Using multiple nested loops slows down execution.
Use lookup tables where possible.	Store frequently used values in Flash memory.	Recalculating values every time wastes CPU cycles.
Reduce function	Call functions outside	Calling functions inside

| calls inside loops. | loops where possible. | loops increases overhead. |

Syntax Table

S L	Function	Syntax/Example	Description
1	Enable Global Interrupts	`INTCONbits.GIE = 1;`	Allows handling of interrupts efficiently.
2	Optimize Loop Execution	`for(i = 0; i < 10; i++)`	Reduces unnecessary iterations and improves speed.
3	Use Lookup Tables	`const char table[] = {1,2,3};`	Stores fixed values efficiently.
4	Minimize Function Overhead	`inline void FastFunc()`	Reduces function call overhead by using inline functions.

Syntax Explanation

1. Enable Global Interrupts

What does it do?
Enables global interrupts, allowing the PIC to efficiently handle external and internal events without constant polling.
Syntax:
`INTCONbits.GIE = 1;`

Example:
`INTCONbits.GIE = 1;   // Enable global interrupts for efficient event handling`

Example Explanation: Instead of constantly checking for a change in sensor input in the main loop, enabling global interrupts ensures that the PIC responds only when an event occurs, freeing up CPU cycles for other tasks.

2. Optimize Loop Execution

What does it do?
Improves execution speed by using efficient looping techniques.
Syntax:
```
for(i = 0; i < 10; i++) {
    // Perform action
}
```

Example:
```
for(i = 0; i < 10; i++) {
    PORTB = i;   // Assign value to PORTB
}
```

Example Explanation: Using a `for` loop instead of `while` ensures that the loop runs a defined number of times without unnecessary checks, reducing execution time.

3. Use Lookup Tables

What does it do?
Improves execution efficiency by storing precomputed values instead of recalculating them during runtime.
Syntax:
```
const char table[] = {1,2,3};
```

Example:
```
const char sinTable[] = {0, 25, 50, 75, 100};   //
Precomputed sine values
```

Example Explanation: Instead of recalculating sine values every time they are needed, storing them in a lookup table reduces CPU workload and increases execution speed.

4. Minimize Function Overhead

What does it do?
Reduces execution time by using inline functions, which replace function calls with their actual code at compile time.

Syntax:
```
inline void FastFunc() {
    // Perform action
}
```

Example:
```
inline void ToggleLED() {
    PORTBbits.RB0 ^= 1;  // Toggle LED
}
```

Example Explanation: Using `inline` functions eliminates function call overhead, making execution faster, especially for frequently called functions inside loops.

Real-life Applications Project: Optimized LED Blinking Using Interrupts

In this project, we will use an optimized approach to blink an LED using interrupts instead of a delay function.

Required Components

Component	Description
PIC Microcontroller	The main processing unit.
LED	Indicator output.
Push Button	Used to trigger an interrupt.

Circuit Connection Table

Component	PIC Microcontroller Pin	Power Source	Purpose
LED	RB0	5V	Visual indicator
Button	RB1 (External Interrupt)	3.3V or 5V	Triggers an interrupt

Project Code

```
#include <xc.h>
#include <stdio.h>

#define _XTAL_FREQ 4000000  // Define crystal frequency

void __interrupt() ISR();  // Interrupt Service Routine
```

```
void main() {
    TRISBbits.TRISB0 = 0;   // Set RB0 as output for LED
    TRISBbits.TRISB1 = 1;   // Set RB1 as input for
button
    INTCONbits.INT0IF = 0; // Clear interrupt flag
    INTCONbits.INT0IE = 1; // Enable external interrupt
    INTCONbits.GIE = 1;     // Enable global interrupts

    while(1) {
        // Main loop does nothing, LED controlled by
ISR
    }
}

void __interrupt() ISR() {
    if (INTCONbits.INT0IF) {  // If external interrupt
occurred
        PORTBbits.RB0 ^= 1;   // Toggle LED
        INTCONbits.INT0IF = 0;  // Clear interrupt flag
    }
}
```

Expected Results

After uploading the code, pressing the button connected to RB1 will
trigger an interrupt, toggling the LED on RB0 without using a delay
function. This approach improves efficiency by using interrupts
instead of a CPU-blocking delay function, making the system more
responsive and power-efficient.

www.ingramcontent.com/pod-product-compliance
Lightning Source LLC
LaVergne TN
LVHW051429050326
832903LV00030BD/2987